LITERARY ART
AND THE UNCONSCIOUS

LITERARY ART AND THE UNCONSCIOUS

David J. Gordon

Louisiana State University Press   *Baton Rouge*

Designer: Dwight Agner
Type face: VIP Aldus
Typesetter: The Composing Room of Michigan, Grand Rapids
Printer and binder: Kingsport Press, Kingsport, Tennessee

LIBRARY OF CONGRESS CATALOGING IN PUBLICATION DATA

Gordon, David J
    Literary art and the unconscious.

    Includes bibliographical references and index.
    1. English literature—History and criticism. 2. American
literature—History and criticism.   3. Psychoanalysis and literature. I. Title.
PR408.P8G6   820'.9   75–27662
ISBN 0–8071–0197–4

To Maureen

CONTENTS

PREFACE

IS THERE a connection between literary art and the unconscious? Can any aspect of literary meaning in works of undeniable art be brought into relation with processes in the writer's mind that are barred from his awareness? May the language of a work ever suggest that an artist has misinterpreted his own feelings, or may its effects ever constitute evidence of imaginative error or unconscious insincerity? These are several phrasings of the central question to which this book—first theoretically, then practically—provides an answer.

The question would not require such extensive theoretical consideration if modern criticism made room for it. But it is difficult to fit the concept of a repressed unconscious into prevailing pictures of the imagination. Equally difficult is to refurbish the concept of sincerity in the current intellectual climate. One must challenge an array of formalists and Freudian revisionists to secure the right to interrelate text and mind, language and feeling. And those who do make a point of the unconscious are inclined to depreciate art. Because Part 1 sets the question into so full a context, it offers more than a particular resolution of a particular problem. It also presents a general affective theory of literary art, one that steers between the Scylla of nineteenth-century expressionism and the Charybdis of twentieth-century formalism, including the inverse formalism of the structuralists.

Part 1 might also be briefly described as an essay in the spirit of those principles of literary criticism promulgated by I. A. Richards fifty years ago and, for the most part, sidetracked since then. His emphasis on the importance of the difference between science and poetry has its counterpart in these pages. So does his emphasis on the problematics of communication; although Richards stressed the unreliability of the reader, saying little about the unreliability of the writer, the two ideas are practically inseparable. And his belief that the critic must deal with values—values implicit in the work rather than external standards of judgment—is also reformulated here.

Part 2 consists of five analytic essays on major works or oeuvres. Although the choice of subjects includes only a few of the great literary psychologists, it does illustrate the range of ways in which an artist either incorporates insight or lets the reader arrive at insights inconsistent with his design. At the same time these five essays are linked together as an outline of a new estimate of the modern heroic tradition, in which are characteristically found both depth of insight and problematic effects.

I have provided reference footnotes for the ranging, allusive discussion in the Introduction and in Part 1, but not for Part 2, where it seemed more helpful simply to incorporate references into the text, adding an occasional note, marked by an asterisk, for special information.

The long labor of preparation has been lightened by the interest and help of many friends. It is a pleasure to thank some of them here, though I must add a more than perfunctory disclaimer of their responsibility for any of my opinions. The interest shown by Martin Price and Paul Pickrel in what is now a chapter of the book was my first real incentive to broaden its conception. I am very grateful to Mary Price for providing me with opportunities to write about literary theory in the *Yale Review.* My special thanks go to Thomas Steiner and Porter Abbott, for dialogic stimulation during a year at the University of California in Santa

Barbara; to my sisters Naomi Lebowitz and Ruth Newton, who exercised their privilege as my oldest critics to help me improve an early draft; and to Harold Bloom and Helen Vendler, whose valuable suggestions spurred me to a final revision that may have made a great difference in the published result. Over the years I have often benefited intellectually and personally from the friendships of colleagues at Hunter College and the CUNY Graduate Center. Recently I have incurred a debt to my editor Marie Carmichael, whose clean sense of style has made this a more readable book. By far my greatest indebtedness is to the dedicatee, as imaginative and intelligent and sympathetic a friend as she is a writer.

Grateful acknowledgment is made to the *Yale Review*, copyright Yale University, and to *Literature and Psychology* for permission to reprint revised versions of articles that first appeared in those journals.

INTRODUCTION

WHEN THE literary critic of our day functions as a biographer or as an investigator of the creative process, he finds the psychological concept of unconscious mind difficult to avoid. But, when he functions as an interpreter of art, he finds it difficult to use. The title of this book is meant to suggest an incongruity. Art signifies design and, inevitably, a designing consciousness, so what connection can be established between a work of literary art and those portions or processes of the artist's mind barred from consciousness? His correspondence, journals, rough drafts and the record of his speech may exhibit the kinds of discrepancies and disproportions that permit us to perceive an alien inner influence. But a highly integrated verbal structure would seem to repel any such intuition.

I use the term *unconscious* in the basic Freudian sense of the repressed or repressing, which sometimes thrusts toward consciousness but becomes conscious "only [with] considerable expenditure of energy or possibly never at all."[1] The

---

1 Sigmund Freud, *New Introductory Lectures on Psychoanalysis* (New York: Norton, 1965), 71. Freud proceeds to comment on the ambiguities arising from a mixed use of descriptive and dynamic conceptualizations of the unconscious and to adjust them by means of the structural scheme of id, ego, and superego. It will not be necessary in this essay on literary theory to go so deeply into psychoanalytic theory, but I will quote later from Freud's essay "The Unconscious" concerning the role of language in the distinction between conscious and unconscious, and I recommend Chapters 1 and 2 of *The Ego and the Id* for further clarification.

term is, of course, often used by literary critics in a less strict sense, to denote mental events that are merely removed rather than barred from awareness, that are not fully conscious but capable of becoming so without much resistance. To describe such thought as spontaneous or instinctive or imaginative (as we might well do) indicates both why critics favor this broader sense of the word and why it sooner or later becomes hard to distinguish from consciousness itself. When E. D. Hirsch asserts that "the principle for excluding or accepting unconscious meanings is precisely the same as for conscious ones," he is using the term unconscious in this sense (*i.e.*, preconscious) rather than in the sense of repressed. Similarly, the author of *Structuralist Poetics*, though he takes a very different view of literary meaning— opposing Hirsch's commitment to strict determinacy with an ideal of maximum indeterminacy—writes that in art, "as in most other human activities of any complexity, the line between conscious and unconscious is highly variable, impossible to identify, and supremely uninteresting." I see no need to challenge this dismissive statement except to add that he also is referring to the line between conscious and preconscious and not confronting the special problems which the unconscious poses for criticism.[2]

We do not clarify these problems when we describe as unconscious those implications of a work that are "covert" or "latent" but nevertheless consistent with the general design. No one would say that the artist has consciously calculated every effect which the discerning critic can perceive, but when all of the effects harmonize, when the various implications enrich one another, we do naturally suppose that, in some prereflective fashion, the artist has planned and coordinated them. We may say that he has built better than he knows and can explain our paradox by crediting the faculty of imagination with the capacity for both purposiveness and spontaneity.

2 E. D. Hirsch, Jr., *Validity in Interpretation* (New Haven: Yale University Press, 1967), 51; Jonathan Culler, *Structuralist Poetics* (Ithaca: Cornell University Press, 1975), 118. Culler illustrates unconscious activity by the practice of skills such as chess and diving.

Similarly, we receive an impression from a work before we
reason it out, but we can produce our reasons at will.

What connections can be established, then, between literary art and the unconscious? The most obvious is by way of
the work's own dramatized insight into unconscious processes, as when the writer creates characters who are shown to
resist (perhaps only partially or up to a point) the recognition
of certain wishes and fears apparent to the reader. In a sense
nobody's unconscious mind is involved here, since the unconscious mind of a literary character is only an artful illusion
conveyed from a knowing writer to an alert reader. But any
particular instance does involve an intuitive understanding of
unconscious processes shared by both partners of the aesthetic
transaction.

Writers notable for this kind of characterization can be
found at least as far back as Shakespeare and up to our own
day: among them, Hawthorne, Melville, Dostoevski, Ibsen,
Hardy, and Lawrence. I compose the list almost casually, but
it must be admitted that critical agreement on individual cases
(*e.g.*, Hamlet) is far from unanimous, even though the insight in question is the author's own and enhances rather than
compromises the coherence of the work. And therefore I must
sometimes query arguments that undermine the possibility of
a psychological theme. One distinguished critic, for example,
after justly correcting T. S. Eliot's formulation—"Hamlet's
state of emotion is inexpressible because it is in excess of the
facts as they appear"—on the grounds that we can only surmise this from the expressed effects, goes on to say, strangely, "That Hamlet himself or Shakespeare may be baffled by
the emotion is beside the point." [3] Beside the point? If Hamlet
alone is baffled, then this illusion of bafflement must be
Shakespeare's artistic means (and I think it is) of suggesting
unconscious conflict; if Shakespeare is baffled, then we must
conclude, as Eliot does, that the play is flawed.

Eliot regards the unbalanced effects in the play, particularly
the absence of an objective equivalent to Hamlet's feelings, as

3 W. K. Wimsatt, Jr., *The Verbal Icon* (New York: Noonday, 1958), 35.   XV

a purely dramaturgical problem. But, if the unbalanced effects of a work are not coherent by themselves yet do make sense if we connect them to a missing and presumably repressed idea, then we can legitimately refer to the influence of the artist's unconscious mind. The sense we make would necessarily be incongruous with the sense we have made of the perfectly coherent effects. We could call it unconscious meaning or intention if we clearly understand by such a phrase an interpretation that is incompatible with our interpretation of the artistic intention. But the analysis of the unbalanced effects themselves, which led us to the hypothesis of unconscious distortion, is orthodox critical procedure. And this constitutes the second connection I propose to establish between literary art and the unconscious, less obvious and certainly more complex than the first, but important and greatly needing clarification.

There are in many works—and not least in the greatest, if only because they take larger risks—discrepancies and disproportions which seem to be due not to carelessness or the inherent difficulties of execution but to some sort of disturbance in the balance of affective currents, as if the emotion belonging to one no longer visible idea got displaced onto another expressed idea. In D. H. Lawrence's striking image, it is as if the author "puts his thumb in the scale to pull down the balance to his own [unconscious] predilection."[4] The expressed idea or effect may be called problematic, for it contains a false note or irrational component which prompts the reader to frame an interpretation that cannot have been intended by the writer.

In other words, though we cannot really describe problematic effects as themselves unconscious, they may fit together into a counter-intended meaning if we presume the agency of a specific unconscious process of distortion. What we perceive are imbalances that might plausibly be accounted for according to a hypothesis of unconscious influence.

4 D. H. Lawrence, *Phoenix: The Posthumous Papers of D. H. Lawrence*, ed. Edward D. McDonald (London: Heinemann, 1936), 528.

We acknowledge the existence of problematic effects when we speak of discrepancies between tone and statement, demonstration and allegation, intention and effect. More simply and commonly, we describe them by any of a number of familiar evaluative adjectives—sentimental, self-pitying, spiteful, coy, arrogant, evasive, embarrassing, priggish, strident, etc.—implying that in the tilt of some effect we perceive a potentially subversive implication that is not artistically developed and brought into antithetical or qualifying relation to the rest of the work. From such effects of language we may infer that the consciousness of the writer has to some degree been corrupted, that an error has been made not in the process of reasoning but, more fundamentally, in the process of imagining or creating.

A few examples of problematic effects will help to make more concrete my necessarily abstract presentation, though I must confess to some reluctance in offering them. It might well be thought hypercritical to find flaws in a work that achieves on the whole a high level of formal integration. More important, there is the question of the reader's reliability, which is bound to arise when we talk about the unreliability of the writer. All a reader can do to offset this danger is to make allowances for certain responses that he recognizes—with uncertain accuracy—as prejudiced. But there can be no guarantee that he himself is not deceived, that *his* consciousness is not at that point corrupt. There can only be an increasing probability of objective judgment as there is a wider measure of agreement among others, especially others from different places and times. I see no reason, however, to believe that these perceptions of incongruity are as idiosyncratic as preferences of taste. With my scruples noted, here are four among innumerable examples, arranged by increasing complexity.

One kind of fiction, perhaps typically middle-brow and best illustrated as a type, dramatizes a sobering theme such as the transience of love yet panders surreptitiously by means of a glamorous background to fantasies of wealth, power, fame, and beauty. The type is described perfectly in *Sister Carrie:*

Introduction   "The play was one of those drawing-room concoctions in which charmingly overdressed ladies and gentlemen suffer the pangs of love and jealousy amid gilded surroundings. . . . They have the charm of showing suffering under ideal conditions. Who would not grieve upon a gilded chair?" Any moviegoer should be able to supply more examples. Three films that come readily to my mind are *Darling, Two for the Road,* and *A Touch of Class.* They leave a general impression of insincerity because the subversive implications are undeveloped or, since we are assuming a correspondence between the formal and the psychological, unacknowledged. There is, however, an exploitative aspect of such works that makes one wonder how much of the insincerity is merely calculated and cynical. For my purposes it is important though somewhat difficult to make this determination, for problematic effects do not become an issue unless a piece is sufficiently imagined.

Appreciably more sophisticated because it to some extent sets the contrary currents of passional life and renunciatory Christianity into dramatic relation is Charlotte Brontë's *Jane Eyre.* Yet, as Lawrence glancingly perceived, the scene of Jane's gladly consenting to marry the blinded and burned Rochester suggests to our minds an idea that the author does not presumably intend, namely, that these handicaps license an open sexual interest by partly denying it. Rochester's wounds seem to give Jane a satisfaction not fully accounted for by the honorable idea that she can be more useful to him; she seems to love him because of, as well as in spite of, them. The fact that elsewhere in her novel Brontë makes vigorous claims for the passional life against renunciatory Christianity makes more plausible the inference that, when she composed this scene, her consciousness underwent some degree of corruption, influenced by the Victorian climate of opinion which she could not altogether escape.

Thomas Hardy's poem "Hap" implies by its tone and imagery an anthropomorphism that undermines the logic of its statement. The poem states that chance rules all, that a malevolent deity no more exists than does a benevolent one, and that therefore even the comfort of rational suicide is de-

nied us. But the too forceful images of "the best hope" never
blooming, of "dicing Time ... cast[ing] a moan," of "pur-
blind Doomsters," who would "as readily" strew "Blisses
about my pilgrimage as pain," show that Hardy felt fate to be
a treacherous seducer whatever he thought of it. The element
of pathos in the poem contains a just perceptible degree of
self-pity, the element of satire a degree of spite, and these
problematic effects permit us to infer the influence at some
point in the creative process of an inadmissible grievance.
Although I must call this an individual grievance, perhaps I
should add that it is evidently one Hardy shares with others.
In fact, my judgment of this poem is partly based on the
perception that my own pleasure in it is too gleeful, *i.e.*,
excessive or irrational.

Finally, there is the very complex example of Joseph Conrad's *Heart of Darkness*. The story dramatizes Marlow's confrontation with the "wilderness" and the corrupted spirit of
Kurtz. Its intended theme, roughly speaking, is the narrator's
mingled attitude of attraction and revulsion and the implication that this partial identification is a moral victory less direct
but comparable to Kurtz's own in finally recognizing his degradation. But Marlow's kinship with Kurtz, on which this
theme turns, is not altogether clear on the emotional-
imaginative level. The characterization of Kurtz is a com-
pound of the spirit of imperialism (idealistic in principle,
barbaric in practice) and of heroic, romantic adventure, but
Conrad decisively rejects the one and, as it were, projects the
other from Marlow himself, who is always sober and responsible, to the harlequin figure whose adoration of Kurtz is
either very naïve or vaguely expressed. The fear that Marlow
constantly emphasizes is only symbolically associated with a
temptation to give way; it is repeatedly asserted to be a fear of
the unknown, the incomprehensible. And Marlow's rhetoric
in these assertions is inflated and coercive enough to make us
ask, with a touch of impatience, What exactly is he afraid *of?*
Fears of sickness and of being killed would make sense, and
these are expressed in Conrad's "Congo Diary," but they are
strangely attenuated in the story. Marlow's critical illness at

the end, for example, seems sneaked into it. Almost like a Hemingway hero, though more complexly, Marlow does not want to know too much about the darkness of the heart ("the inner truth is hidden—luckily, luckily") yet asserts, "The most you can hope from [life] is some knowledge of yourself." In short, we may well sense in the story some missing, or "repressed," idea that would enable us to account for all its emotional weightings.

As my comments indicate, there is only a certain amount one can say about problematic effects without trespassing into the area of ulterior causes. It should be clear that we cannot justify, except as metacritical, such locutions as unconscious intention or unconscious meaning. A. J. A. Waldock rightly objects to E. M. W. Tillyard's facile reference to the unconscious meaning of *Paradise Lost* by asking, "Is the breakdown of a conscious intention the equivalent of an unconscious meaning?" [5] No, it is not. It merely points to and supports the hypothesis of some sort of unconscious distortion at work in the creative process.

The investigation of this process, fascinating in itself, is work appropriate to psychologists, sociologists, historians, and linguists—and to literary critics insofar as they choose to function in these roles. It is scientific work and as such assumes that there is a discoverable (though not of course perceivable) reality behind phenomena, that there are laws underlying a given set of phenomena and governing their behavior. Critical inquiry into unconscious processes might therefore be described as an aid to interpretation or as "a form of research," which is how Philip Rahv describes the metacritical portions of Frederick Crews's book on Hawthorne's psychological themes. [6]

Although the importance of problematic effects for the

5 A. J. A. Waldock, *"Paradise Lost" and Its Critics* (Cambridge, England: Cambridge University Press, 1959), 125. This kind of honest scruple helps to advance our understanding. Compare it with the snide remark of another Miltonist—"Milton was aware of the unconscious meaning of *Paradise Lost*"—which merely dismisses the critical problem.

6 Philip Rahv, review of Frederick C. Crews's *The Sins of the Fathers: Hawthorne's Psychological Themes*, in *New York Review of Books* (September 22, 1966), 22.

practical critic is somewhat reduced by the fact that tracking down causes is beyond his proper scope, their importance for the theoretical critic is greater than might be expected. They require us to reconsider the theory of mind, and particularly of imagination, that we make use of and to look at a number of standard critical terms (irony, ambiguity, paradox, sincerity) in a new light. Without some acknowledgment of the concept of a repressed unconscious, our theory cannot adequately account for the problematic effects. And to make room for that concept, we have to modify and revise some entrenched critical attitudes.

A clearing of the way might begin with the observation that errors of imagination are not the kind for which one can hold another person fully responsible, as Jean-Paul Sartre does when he speaks of inauthentic expression as "bad faith," a moral failing. F. R. Leavis takes a similar view. Although Leavis comes close to putting the matter as I would have it put when he equates sentimentality with incompleteness of context caused by a divorce of thought and feeling, he nevertheless thinks of it as an error of the conscious will; for him, sentimental language is "faked," in contrast to language that "comes from below and could not have been excogitated." [7]

This severity of judgment concerning a work's or writer's integrity is only partly appropriate. It is true that problematic effects (a phrase I prefer to the familiar term inauthenticity because the latter tends to lead us to a non-Freudian view of the unconscious) are not inevitable. The writer may recognize and alter them in the process of composition; probably he has done so with other effects we no longer see. Hence, although they point to the hypothesis of an unconscious conflict in the mind of the author, it does not follow that the presence of such a conflict must result in problematic effects. However, it is quite possible that whatever prompted the distortion in the first place may prevent the writer from recognizing it. Throughout a discussion of imaginative truth telling, a double

7 F. R. Leavis, *How to Teach Reading: A Primer for Ezra Pound* (Cambridge, England: Minority Press, 1932), 26. See also F. R. Leavis, " 'Thought' and Emotional Quality," *A Selection from Scrutiny*, XIII (1945), 215–16.

standard of judgment must be adopted: exculpatory insofar as the act could not have been avoided, inculpatory insofar as it could have been. The stance of evaluative criticism must be peculiarly flexible.

Another critical habit, perhaps more deeply rooted, hampers our welcoming the unconscious into the arena of literary theory. The psychological map usually relied on in critical discourse divides the mind into the two halves of feeling and thought; since we are as aware of our feelings as we are of our thoughts, there remains no room at all for the concept of unconscious mind! Nor is the matter mended by renaming these halves imagination and intellect; these terms simply distinguish two kinds of thought, one merged with feeling and one somehow distinct from it, and fail to point to any kind of feeling or thought barred from awareness. It is somewhat more helpful to think of mental activity as either rational or irrational—it is a small step certainly from irrational to unconscious—but one does not want to be obliged to describe fully integrated imaginative speech as purely rational. Although I applaud the efforts of Leavis and Yvor Winters to rescue emotion from a facile association with the irrational, it is too restrictive simply to equate it with rationality or, like Hirsch, to identify verbal meaning with willed meaning. We are left with the need for some middle term, like prerational or intuitive, for an admission of the idea that art, without being irrational, is the embodiment of a more than rational energy. If, as seems reasonable, we identify consciousness and verbal language, then we must postulate some sort of mental activity or preverbal language anterior to consciousness, and we must think of creation as taking place, to some extent, at the threshold of consciousness. I will present and defend this psychological picture in the pages ahead.

The various literary theorists who have taken a particular interest in both art and the unconscious I shall group as follows: those who focus on the individual unconscious; those who focus on the cultural unconscious; the Freudian revisionists (mostly French); and assorted psycho-aestheticians (mostly English and American). Among these groups

much valuable work has been done in recent decades, and
much of that I have gratefully absorbed in the following
pages, but some of it, more than a little, undermines either
art or the unconscious as I understand those concepts. A
brief word here about each group will outline the direction of
my argument in Part 1.

The critics who have endeavored to apply the concept of an
individual unconscious beyond the somewhat narrow limits I
have defined—I am thinking here of Freudian critics, for
Jungian psychology, as Edward Glover has conclusively
shown, is not a psychology of the *un*conscious [8]—have inevitably become involved in what Norman Holland calls
"metacriticism or . . . infracriticism." [9] That is, they study
either the genesis of the work or the reader's response, but
not only that part of the genesis which leaves visible marks
upon the text and not only that part of the reader's response
which is congruent with the artistic intention. Although
such studies are doubtless legitimate as a form of psychological inquiry, one may question their bearing on our
understanding of texts.

The writer's, or reader's, infantile conflicts are, I think,
too remote to contribute to that understanding. But the
more the critic relates art to later transformations of early
conflicts, the more he studies the artist's wrestlings with his
material and his predecessors, the more bearing his insights
will have on the interpretation of texts. Richard Ellmann
subtitles his study of these wrestlings "biographical speculations," which is what they are, but they capture more of that
elusive middle ground between what he calls "the fiery clay"
and "the wrought jar" than do more basic psychological
studies. [10] Harold Bloom's psycho-literary investigations

8 Edward Glover, *Freud or Jung* (London: G. Allen and Unwin, 1950).
9 Norman Holland, *The Dynamics of Literary Response* (New York: Oxford University Press, 1968), vii.
10 Compare, for example, Ellmann's "infracritical" comment on *Heart of Darkness* in
Golden Codgers: Biographical Speculations (New York: Oxford University Press,
1973), 17–19, with one by Frederick Crews in "The Power of Darkness," *Partisan
Review*, XXXIV (Fall, 1967), 507–25. Crews interprets the African continent as
"the maternal body," Kurtz as "a vindictive reconstruction of Conrad's father,"

may come closer still to illuminating the style and idea of works themselves—Bloom is a brilliant interpreter of texts when he chooses to be—although I find so far that his most persuasive evidence for his central insight that a strong poet must misread his precursors in order to achieve originality lies *outside* the poem. I may, however, be too much of a holist to follow Bloom's transgressions of the individual text, too unsure that the larger structure intimated by his method is an artistic one.[11]

When an essay overtly using psychoanalytic ideas is really perceptive about the visible structure of the work, such as Ernst Kris's "Prince Hal's Conflict,"[12] the critical value of that essay is likely to be quite independent of those ideas. Kris would not have been one jot less persuasive if he had stripped off the psychoanalytic apparatus and presented his comments simply as an analysis of Shakespeare's insight. In fact, he would have been more persuasive, for the theoretical support prompts the mistaken inference that insight is dependent on some system, that there really is such a thing as psychoanalytic (as distinct from psychological) insight.

My view of those critical positions which place the work in

---

and Marlow's journey as "voyeuristic and incestuous." I find all this, as Crews works it out, not so much wrong or absurd as simply too remote from the feel of the story to be illuminating. Ellmann, on the other hand, drawing on more accessible biographical material concerning Conrad's Congo journey and youthful suicide attempt, comments: "It would seem likely that young Korzeniowsky's suicide attempt was extrapolated as the self-abandonment and moral cowardice of the European Kurtz, and that the confrontation with Marlow, Captain of English ships and master of English prose, bearer of an indisputably English name, was symbolically rehabilitative. To commit suicide is to yield to the mind's jungle, to write is to colonize with the efficiency so highly regarded by Marlow. Kurtz and Marlow meet in the "heart of darkness" as in the recesses of Conrad's mind. One dies, the other contrives to be reborn." This comment remains infracritical, but it comes much closer to supplying what was earlier found to be the missing sense of the somewhat incoherent story—at the sacrifice, of course, of the story's indivisible meaning.

11 Harold Bloom, *The Anxiety of Influence* (New York: Oxford University Press, 1973); Harold Bloom, *A Map of Misreading* (New York: Oxford University Press, 1975); Harold Bloom, *Kabbalah and Criticism* (New York: Seabury Press, 1975); Harold Bloom, *Poetry and Repression: Revisionism from Blake to Stevens* (New Haven: Yale University Press, 1976).

12 Ernst Kris, *Psychoanalytic Explorations in Art* (New York: Schocken Books, 1952), 273–88.

relation to the unconscious conflicts of a culture is similar.
Insofar as the artist stands apart from them sufficiently to
dramatize these conflicts, the critic not only may but ought to
discuss them. But insofar as the art suggests that the artist is
himself their victim, the ambitious interpreter is likely to be
led beyond art. Books like Lawrence's *Studies in Classic
American Literature* and Leslie Fiedler's *Love and Death in
the American Novel,* though containing some sharp critical
perceptions, are in large part a kind of sociology or psycho-
history. The homoerotic aspect of *Huckleberry Finn* points to
something problematic in American culture but not really to
something problematic in the text, where it is simply recessive and nonfunctional. When Lawrence and Fiedler do convince us that a subversive implication is in the text, we see
that usually it is part of the book's design and that we are
dealing with antithetical rather than problematic effects. (I
avoid the terms ambivalent and dialectic for reasons to be
explained in Part 1.) But at least Anglo-American critics tend
to talk about literature concretely enough to keep the
psychological concept of the unconscious relevant; comparable European critics tend to discuss the discontinuities between abstract entities such as time and transcendence, effec-
tually nullifying the concept.

It is somewhat easier to talk about a cultural unconscious
than an individual one in that the supporting evidence is more
public and accessible—although in actual cases the two are
often hard to distinguish—but there is a greater temptation,
when we do so, to elevate the unconscious into a teleological
force, to give it historical direction, to let mythologizing sub-
stitute for scholarly inquiry.

My scruples in these two cases are based mainly on a concern for defining the limits of interpretative criticism. My
difficulties with the literary theories of the Freudian
revisionists—the structuralists and others—are more fundamental. These critics are so radical in their attack on the very
premises of criticism that, in confronting them, I have found
myself needing to justify principles I had taken as axiomatic:
that there is a correspondence between the language of litera-

ture and the life of the mind, particularly the affections; that a work of art implies the existence of a constitutive, coordinating selfhood; that the structure of art is not the same as the structure of such disciplines as psychology, anthropology, sociology, history, and linguistics. When I began seven years ago the study that resulted in this book, it seemed necessary to reconcile Freud's scientific determinism with literary humanism, but after the incursions of these literary antihumanists, Freud may be seen as a staunch defender of the dignity of man.

My project does not absolutely oblige me to engage structuralism because its literary theory pertains to something more fundamental than textual interpretation; it is concerned with what underlies art rather than art itself. It proposes, in fact, a dissolution of expressive and mimetic into semiological criticism, a shift of focus from meaning to how meaning is produced. But it shows so clearly how crucial the concept of the unconscious is to certain basic issues of literary theory that some consideration of it offers me the opportunity to gain a deeper control over my own argument.

Closest to my own view are those theories which might be classified under the broad heading of psycho-aesthetics. But the names I have in mind—I. A. Richards, F. R. Leavis, William Empson, R. G. Collingwood, E. H. Gombrich, Susanne Langer, Elias Schwartz, Geoffrey Hartman, Harold Bloom—make up a very heterogeneous list. Richards, despite his emphasis on conflicting impulses in art, on the differences between art and science, and on the corruptibility of communication, bypasses the unconscious in his appeal to neurology. Leavis tends to explain problematic effects as errors of intellect and will rather than of imagination. Empson, on the other hand, tends to explain all sorts of ambiguity by the nature of language rather than of mind. Langer, in *Feeling and Form*, and Schwartz, in *The Forms of Feeling*, develop their expressive and mimetic theories respectively with little concern for distortions of language and feeling. Hartman and Bloom are concerned with distortion, but are revisionists who

set the concept of a repressed unconscious into an anti-

Freudian, roughly Hegelian tradition. Collingwood and Gombrich, of all these theorists, have been the most useful to me, showing how some key issues brought to the fore by the challenge of psychoanalysis might be fitted into an aesthetic rather than strictly psychological frame of reference. The theory of imagination I will use to clarify the relation of feeling to language is drawn from Collingwood. My understanding of sincerity and of the relation between convention and originality—key topics in my presentation—owes a great deal to Gombrich. Collingwood's ability to use Hegel and Benedetto Croce discriminatingly (to winnow their psychological insight from their metaphysics) and Gombrich's resolute anti-Hegelianism have also been helpful to me in a less obvious way, strengthening my intellectual resistance to a temptation I am temperamentally prone to, that of trying to think all things into a unity. Yet, perhaps strangely, neither man, neither the philosopher nor the theorist of the visual arts, is in the least a *literary* critic.

What chiefly holds this heterogeneous group loosely together is their common emphasis on a few related principles that I too find essential. One is that art is not a *kind* but a *use* of language. Another, closely related, is that the self is the organizing agent of artistic structures. And a third is that, although conventions and forms are extremely important for the study of art (in this emphasis they are joined by New Critics, the school of Northrop Frye, structuralists, and almost everyone else nowadays), their importance must be appreciated in relation to, and not at the expense of, the importance of originality. Without the underpinning of these ideas, it would not be possible to demonstrate that the concept of unconscious mind must be seriously reckoned with in literary criticism. And to do so is my objective in Part 1.

The five essays on particular works and writers that make up Part 2 illustrate both the writer's own shaped insights and those peculiar reader's insights into repressed connections which follow from disruptions of the artistic surface. The former predominate because these essays are whole views of certain complex subjects in discussions of which the question of unconscious motives arises, whether the effects are wholly or only partly controlled by the artist. The works chosen might be said to run a gamut in the degree to which the psychological insights I develop are reconstructions of the author's own.

The essay on *Hamlet,* a substantially modified and extended version of the Sigmund Freud–Ernest Jones view (for I reject the relevance of the term neurosis to Hamlet's case and insist on the integration of a psychological with a political and philosophical level of meaning), is only occasionally concerned with problematic effects, but is of course centrally concerned with Shakespeare's insight and with the difficulties which the concept of the unconscious encounters in critical discussions of the play.

The essay on *Paradise Lost* probes Milton's very considerable insight as well as the ways in which his style and theme reflect, compared with Shakespeare's, a stiffening of moral posture that a little unbalances the weightings of the work. In its attention to these, the essay inevitably is influenced by the Romantics (with their distinction between human and poetic selfhood) and by Waldock (with his distinction between the poem's levels of allegation and demonstration). But I do not, like Blake, Shelley, Lawrence, and Empson, associate true art with the unconscious nor, like Waldock, do I explain all inconsistencies as clumsiness due to intractable subject matter. Perhaps the imbalances I focus on result in part from a half-conscious self-testing, for Milton takes risks he needn't have taken in dramatizing God and His strict justice and gives Satan greater latitude to speak his mind than the narrative requires. And certainly it is difficult to focus on them at all and render full justice to the poem's elaborate architectonics. But the points I make are neither trivial nor altogether derivative, and, as will be seen, they are central to the thematic development of Part 2.

The essay on *Billy Budd,* a story which is in many ways a post-Romantic *Paradise Lost,* takes advantage of the genetic text edited not long ago by Harrison Hayford and Merton

Sealts. This text affords us an exceptional view of a story that embodies without resolving the author's successive intentions. It thus contains what might be called incipient problematic effects, which Herman Melville more or less perceived but did not, perhaps for lack of time, entirely suppress.

The last two essays—on the oeuvres of Bernard Shaw and D. H. Lawrence and on Ernest Hemingway's fiction—are different from the first three in scope and from each other in style. One is a highly synoptic analysis of both intellectual and imaginative patterns in two copious writers, and the other is a survey in chronological order of fictional patterns as they develop during a career. In both I trace textual responses to an inferred unconscious conflict, showing how the heroic vision of these authors is related to it and showing also how writers of extraordinary energy and intelligence (Shaw and Lawrence as opposed to Hemingway) can, upon sensing subversive elements in their own work and as an alternative to eliminating them, choose to re-present them, purified, at a higher level. Their work thus evinces more complexity and coherence, though also more strain.

My choice of subjects in Part 2 is somewhat arbitrary but not altogether. *Hamlet* and *Paradise Lost* come close to being inevitable test cases in a discussion of literary art and the unconscious (that presumption may help to justify my temerity in venturing into these critical hornets' nests without the protection of specialized knowledge), and the other subjects, though less inevitable, do serve to test my focal concept's range of application. Moreover, all of the writers involved occupy cardinal positions in what might be called the modern heroic tradition, and Part 2 as a whole is a kind of introduction to that tradition, especially insofar as it contains suggestions for a history of the concept of unconscious mind.

A vital connection between the heroic tradition and the unconscious is captured in a particular insight of Freud's, which I use in these essays. In the story of Christ, Freud perceived not only the avowed idea of the Son's atonement with the Father but also the unavowed idea that by His martyrdom the Son replaces the Father and vanquishes the old law. It follows that the literary motif of either martyrdom or apotheosis, extreme self-denial or extreme self-assertion, might unintentionally suggest the presence of the opposite motif. And the crisis-minded writers of the modern heroic tradition, from Milton down through the Romantics to Ernest Hemingway, William Faulkner, and Norman Mailer, have been remarkable both for the depth of their insight and for their tendency to embrace, with varying degrees of awareness, one of these extremes, so that in their language we sometimes perceive a gap between what they think they are and what they are in imaginative fact.

My choices in Part 2 are also based on personal preferences, for I confess that the literary art that interests me most is the kind that moves searchingly toward a resolution of sexually charged inner conflict. I make this confession in the hope that what may appear to be my temperamental overcriticalness will be understood, in part at least, as a lover's quarrelsomeness. I expect a lot from literature—nothing less than the power to imagine my life better and to gain a larger measure of mastery over my own energies.

THE UNCONSCIOUS
IN LITERARY CRITICISM

AMONG sophisticated students of literature today, the ideas of Sigmund Freud less often provoke indignation than regret—regret that the human image has been irreversibly diminished. Freud himself acknowledged that his psychoanalysis was a blow to our pride and compared it in this respect to the work of Copernicus and Darwin. What is less well known, though equally important, is a complementary Freudian idea; namely, that the discovery of our repressed wishes and fears shows us to be better than we think we are as well as worse. Given what we are up against, we behave remarkably well. From there it is only a step to the realization that anchors this study: given the difficulty of telling the truth about our deepest experiences—for sincerity of intent does not guarantee truth of effect—every imaginative work that is profoundly truthful in most of its effects is a kind of marvel.

The idea of some kind of emotional dishonesty in a work which the artist himself has not recognized may seem a debasement of art. But it seems so only if we have assumed that imaginative truth telling is entirely within a writer's control. If the distortion comes about unconsciously, the artist is not completely responsible for it. In this light both his lapses and his triumphs attain a measure of genuine poignance.

Certain critical moralists who are concerned with truth telling in art—Leavis, Winters, Sartre—tend to hold the artist fully responsible for his "inauthentic" effects. At least they perceive the corruption of consciousness as, in part, a question of individual psychology, which leads us to a deeper understanding than simply tracing it (as do Richards, Kenneth Burke, and Edmund Wilson, among others) to the vulgarizing influence of popular taste. But their view is too strict. The corruption that we infer from certain problematic effects is to be understood as a natural psychological process occurring on the threshold of consciousness during the act of creation. Therefore, if we wish like Sartre to speak of inauthenticity and bad faith, we must not use these terms as synonyms for 3 insincerity or a failure of conscious will. The insincerity involved is, to some extent, unconscious.[1]

But Sartre's strict doctrine that bad faith is a moral failing, that an appeal to unconscious determination is itself a prime instance of bad faith,[2] contains a truth worth preserving. When it comes to being honest with ourselves, we sometimes *are* cowards, saying, in effect, "I can't" when we mean "I won't." A double standard of judgment is required for acts of unconscious insincerity. To some extent we are to blame for not confronting our feelings, for our complicity with our fears. But to some extent we are not to blame because of our lack of access to the unconscious process by which the distortion comes about. R. G. Collingwood, who has developed a satisfying theory of imagination around this important psychological crux, explains the point strikingly. He says our failure to admit certain ideas into consciousness without distortion resembles both a vice and a disease: compared with disease it is more like a vice; compared with vice it is more like a disease.[3]

The important point here is that we recognize the complex though familiar truth that art, on the one hand, entails conscious control and direction but, on the other, involves an imaginative process anterior to such control. Lacking the first, art is hardly distinguishable from dreaming, and it would make little sense to hold the artist responsible for the coordination of his effects. Lacking the second, art is hardly distinguishable from such practical uses of language as advertising or propaganda, and it would make little sense to say the artist was *not* fully responsible.

1 Lionel Trilling, in *Sincerity and Authenticity* (Cambridge: Harvard University Press, 1972), shows that the modern idea of authenticity is a more strenuous and demanding version of the older idea of sincerity. It implies not merely a congruence between avowal and actual feeling but a confrontation of the darkest and most subversive feeling. Yet it does so in order to circumvent, or undermine, the Freudian idea that our lives are governed by processes over which we do not have full control.

2 For Sartre's challenge to Freud, see particularly Chapter 3, "Bad Faith," in *Being and Nothingness*, trans. Hazel E. Barnes (New York: Philosophical Library, 1956).

3 R. G. Collingwood, *The Principles of Art* (New York: Oxford University Press, 1958), 220.

The psychoanalytic literary critics, committed to emphasizing the importance of someone's unconscious, the writer's or the reader's, are inclined to simplify this complex truth. One of their typical procedures is to imply that art, if it is somehow deep, is not compromised by incoherence. Frederick Crews, for example, recommends a study of Hemingway by saying that the critic "would like us to consider that a writer can be morbid and major at the same time—that a pathetic and at times sinister code of bravado and a desperate moral confusion can go into the making of brilliant art." Morbidity may be compatible with artistry, but is confusion? And if the critic's insights do not correspond to the artist's, if they are not near enough to the artist's awareness to be shaped into his design, what sort of "brilliant" art do we have? Crews goes on to say, "The Hemingway code is very much a part of his net effect, but it is only a part; his energy and urgency come from the deeper realm explored in this book." This seems to imply an acceptance of uncoordinated effects, for surely the critical question is how far the energy of a book is governed by its moral direction, whether the two are radically inconsistent.[4]

Norman Holland's discussion of "Dover Beach" illustrates a slightly different procedure. Holland fairly describes the theme of the poem as "an attempt to recreate in a personal relationship the sweet sight of stability and permanence which the harsh sound of the actual ebb and flow of reality negates." Then he adds, "This intellectual theme is a transformation of the fantasy content: an attempt to counter sounds associated with a mother's sexualized withdrawal from sight by creating the image of asexual lovers." But the so-called fantasy content is not visible in the poem. Whether or not it was part of Arnold's thinking as he composed, it is too remote from the actual feel of the verse.[5]

The question unasked here is whether "the intellectual theme" works on its own terms or whether it seems evasive. If it is fully convincing as it is, then we would have to say that

4 Frederick C. Crews, foreword to Richard B. Hovey, *Hemingway: The Inward Terrain* (Seattle: University of Washington Press, 1968), x.

5 Holland, *The Dynamics of Literary Response*, 115–33.

the sexual implications Holland discovers are not so much deviously present as transformed into a higher idea. An artist does not realize all aspects of his material. Some things are brought to the fore and others are, so to speak, left in the stone. And the interpreter of texts (as distinct from the psychologist) must adjust himself to this fact.

An alternate procedure of the psychoanalytically oriented critic is to emphasize the reader's rather than the writer's unconscious. Simon Lesser, in a quite perceptive essay on Nathaniel Hawthorne's story "My Kinsman, Major Molineux," incautiously asserts that Robin's encountering various obstacles while searching for his kinsman is the aspect of the story our conscious minds notice while our unconscious minds are taking in his inner resistance to finding him.[6] But this is to make Robin's mind identical to the reader's, and clearly Hawthorne is guiding us to understand Robin as a naïf. Indeed, the ironic discrepancy between what Robin thinks is happening and what is actually happening is crucial to the story. Oddly, a similar tack is taken by some antipsychological critics who overemphasize the reader's uncertainty. Thus we are told that Hamlet is about an *audience* that cannot make up its mind, as if Shakespeare has left us as bewildered as his protagonist, or that Satan is heroic in Books I and II of *Paradise Lost* in order to trap the reader in his own pride, as if Milton (as well as literary tradition) hasn't alerted us from the beginning that Satan's is the very type of corrupt will.[7]

The problems raised by the procedures of the Freudian literary critics can be traced to their commitment as critics to psychoanalytic theory. I sympathize with their frustration at not finding available literary theories that are hospitable and

6 Simon O. Lesser, *Fiction and the Unconscious* (New York: Vintage Books, 1962), 216–24.

7 See, for example, Stephen Booth, "On the Value of Hamlet," in Norman Rabkin (ed.), *Reinterpretations of Elizabethan Drama* (New York: Columbia University Press, 1959); Joseph H. Summers, *The Muse's Method: An Introduction to "Paradise Lost"* (Cambridge: Harvard University Press, 1962); and Stanley E. Fish, *Surprised by Sin: The Reader in "Paradise Lost"* (Berkeley: University of California Press, 1967).

responsive to Freud's chief insights, and I share their admiration for that theory as such, but I cannot share their confidence that it can serve the needs of criticism. It has, after all, been forged in response to that series of ongoing questions and answers which constitutes the discipline of psychology. Criticism has its own history, and its theory must grow out of that. The psychologist is looking for answers to questions about mental functioning, the critic for answers to questions about the meaning of texts, and although these aims sometimes overlap, they are far from coinciding.

Consider what happens to certain terms—repression, ambivalence, conflict, the unconscious—which are used in both psychoanalysis and literary criticism. The psychoanalyst understands these terms to refer in every case to unconscious mental processes and not merely to deep or strong or subtle conscious ones. But for the critic such a reference, like the psychoanalyst's inevitable reference to childhood and sexual development, is usually too remote or, in a genetic sense, too fundamental. He uses repression to mean suppression or oppression, ambivalence to mean mixed or contrary but conscious feelings (or simply verbal ambiguity), conflict to mean an opposition between body and mind or desire and reason, and unconscious to mean subconscious (removed but not barred from awareness). My point is not, of course, to chide critics for misuse, for no field has a restrictive right to terminology, and in any case all of these terms antedate the origin of psychoanalysis. But it is important to point out that the concept of the unconscious is almost invariably diluted even when the critic does not suppose he is diluting it.

Here is a typical instance, all the more striking because the critic is avowedly indebted to psychoanalysis. Speaking of Hemingway's famous story, he writes, "Wilson unconsciously represents for Macomber a surrogate father."[8] The statement sounds passable, but it cannot sustain analysis. If it is a question of Macomber's unconscious, the unconscious of a mere fictional character, then this could be a shorthand way of saying that Hemingway has so conceived him. But has he? Can we say that Macomber makes unwitting connections between Wilson and his own father, as Hamlet does in relation to Claudius? Or does the critic's statement refer to Hemingway's unconscious? Surely not that either, since he is speaking of conscious artistic design, of Hemingway's purposeful suggestion that Macomber's attitude toward Wilson resembles that of a son toward his father. There is, then, no question of unconscious mind here. It is a question, rather, of an analogy with a son-father archetype such as Christ the Son and God the Father: both "sons," one might say, reject woman, are accepted by the father, and exalted in death. We could frame an alternative interpretation of this archetypal pattern itself which *would* implicate the writer's unconscious, but there would be no point in doing so if the story is coherent. The implicit analogy with the archetype and the little allegory one makes of it add resonance to the image without themselves leading us to the unconscious.[9]

If we want to establish a satisfactory affective theory of literary art, we would do better to start from the other end, from a formalist rather than a psychoanalytic or expressive point of departure. It will be clear soon enough that art must be viewed as a thing of the mind and that aesthetics, as Geoffrey Hartman puts it, "should really be called *psychoesthetics,* for it investigates the relation of art to the life of the mind, and particularly the affections."[10]

We recognize a work of literary art initially by the presence of artifice. We perceive that the artist has created an illusion of

---

9 With this in mind, we can say that, when psychoanalytic terms themselves are used in allegorical fashion (*e.g.,* id-ego-superego, oral-anal-genital), they are bound to be troublesome, for allegorical meaning, when truly implied by the work, is nothing if not conscious on the writer's part. Of these two triads, the second is more objectionable, perhaps because it is descriptive categorization rather than theoretical construct and therefore less translatable. To equate id-ego-superego with passion-reason-conscience is inexact, but, granted the equation, the terms could conceivably correspond to a pattern in a literary work. But I cannot imagine a writer organizing an artistic structure on the basis of the psychosexual stages of infantile development.

10 Geoffrey H. Hartman, *The Fate of Reading and Other Essays* (Chicago: University of Chicago Press, 1975), 20.

actuality, an imaginary and formally unified world distinct from the world of practical interest. The artifice constitutes a frame, which relieves us of the more or less anxious concern we must give to information not so set off, and in so doing stimulates our sense of play. From the time that art has been distinguishable from myth, it has notified us of its own gratuitousness and thereby induced in us an expectation of imaginative license.

In narrative forms, the illusion is usually signaled by the introduction of at least partly fictitious persons, places, and situations. In lyrical and meditative forms, the artifice we first perceive is likely to be that of rhythm, phonology, and diction: a movement of words that is unlike the movement of discourse, an arrangement of sounds that calls attention to the words themselves as well as to their meanings, a use of words that is normatively metaphoric rather than literal. The voice we hear in all cases is not that of an actual "I" or "he" or "she" about whom unorganized associations cluster but that of a literary self, organized and conventional, which is to serve as the agent for a particular, highly integrated experience. Whether the experience be shallow or profound is not so readily apparent, but we do expect, as we begin to read, that a coherent design will emerge in which no part will seem irrelevant and each part will acquire significance from its relation to the whole.

Like discourse, art gives us knowledge of the external world but gives it to us for a nondiscursive purpose: to render a certain way of looking at the world rather than to establish the propositional truth of a viewpoint. The facts an artist uses are also qualities and, unlike the facts of an essay, lose most or all of their significance if removed from their context—hence, the awkwardness of trying to state what a genuine work of art is *about*. The distinction between art and discourse is not, of course, absolute. Just as looser forms of fiction may include passages that are virtual essays, whose separation from their contexts entails negligible loss, so the argument of an essay may well have such essentially artistic qualities as implicitness of design and meaning, stylistic elegance, and expressive force. But these counter characteristics are secondary in each

9

case. The governing purposes of art and of discourse are different. As Susanne Langer and Elias Schwartz have taken pains to point out, literary art is best understood not as a certain kind of language but as a certain use of language. "Poetry is not genuine discourse at all," says Langer, "but is the creating of an illusory experience . . . by means of discursive language." She adds that so-called poetic language is simply "language which is particularly useful for this purpose, [but] what words will seem poetic depends on the central idea of the poem in question." [11] We know that the language of a poem is functioning artistically, writes Schwartz, "not from any feature inherent in the words, but from our sense of the total poetic structure and our perception of the relation of parts to whole within this structure." [12]

The choice of an art concept over a language concept of literature has been challenged by the formalist Monroe Beardsley on the grounds that it requires the assumption of an *intention* to compose a work. [13] So it does, but his attempt to discredit this assumption only strengthens it. He observes that a poem may fail to come into being despite an intention to compose one or may be realized, as by a computer, in the absence of a human intention. But the fact that one aims and fails is hardly decisive, for no one claims that intention alone, without the requisite skill and energy, is enough. And, as for the computer, one could easily argue, as Beardsley himself seems to concede, that the emergence of a real poem by such means could be accounted for by the will of the programer. He does not cite a more interesting example of "unintentional" composition—the poetic creation that has been known to occur in sleep—which would indicate that intention is a more complex psychological phenomenon than the simple distinction between man and machine permits us to see.

The famous Intentional Fallacy, formulated by Beardsley

11 Susanne K. Langer, *Feeling and Form* (New York: Scribners, 1953), 252.
12 Elias Schwartz, *The Forms of Feeling: Toward a Mimetic Theory of Literature* (Port Washington, N.Y.: Kennikat Press, 1972), 28.
13 Monroe C. Beardsley, "The Concept of Literature," in Frank Brady, John Palmer, and Martin Price (eds.), *Literary Theory and Structure: Essays in Honor of William K. Wimsatt* (New Haven: Yale University Press, 1973), 23–27.

and Wimsatt, refers to one sense of the word *intention* (what one plans to write as distinct from what one writes) that ought never to have been confused with another sense of the word (the design or implicit purpose of what one has written) which is critically essential. And, since a design implies a designer, any distortion in it may logically refer to a motive in the mind of the designer. I press the point because it highlights the fact that art, even when approached formalistically, cannot remain for long a purely objective, nonmental phenomenon. A psychological perspective, however complex, is inevitable. But can we not get around the idea of the mind of the artist (hence, the unconscious mind) by saying with the Wittgensteinians and structuralists that there is no reality beyond language and so no legitimate referential meaning?

It will take me a number of pages to develop an adequate answer to this very sophisticated and challenging question. But the answer will come a little more easily if I begin agreeably by saying that the emphasis in contemporary criticism on the institutional rather than individual character of the artistic enterprise and particularly on the necessary mediation of conventions (linguistic, artistic, and social) is welcome and has proved fruitful. One can find support for this formalist emphasis in a wide variety of critical camps. (Indeed, I cannot think of any substantial dissenting opinion, except perhaps among the armies of naïve students who tend to look upon mediated expression as compromised or insincere.) For my purposes, E. H. Gombrich's formulation is especially helpful, as it permits the development of a complementary expressionist emphasis which I want to combine with it. "Unless reader and writer share a knowledge of the conventions of artistic representation," writes Gombrich, "messages will die on the way from transmitter to receiver, not because we fail to be 'attuned,' but simply because there is nothing to relate them to. Neither communication nor expression can function in a void." It is, in fact, through the use of conventions that expressiveness becomes possible. "No emotion, however strong or however complex, can be transposed into an unstructured medium. Both the transmitter and the receiver need the right degree of guidance by an array of alternatives within which choice can become expressive."[14]

It is, then, the use of conventions that determines the effect of originality. Originality is impossible without a knowledge and use of precedents. The point has been made more aggressively by Northrop Frye and others, and I have no wish to dispute it. But no fine art can be *purely* conventional. Even poets with orthodox attitudes in stable societies must make changes in the verbal combinations they have learned in order to produce anything more than cliché.[15] Their language, in other words, conveys the effect of a voluntary acceptance of those attitudes just as the language of poets we call rebellious conveys the effect of a voluntary defiance of them.

Students of classical, as opposed to Romantic, literature speak of the mind of the maker as somehow eliminated from the work, effaced or fully absorbed by the medium. But this is only a manner of speaking to indicate the relative emphasis of convention and originality or, perhaps better, the relative weight of the convention that is made to come alive. In no art is the mind of the maker—the constitutive self—truly eliminated. What we call classical literature contains at least some degree of self-assertion if it has achieved a style and voice, just as what we call Romantic literature has effaced or conventionalized the self to some degree if it is intelligible. When we complain that a writer *merely* expresses himself, we simply mean that he has failed to submit himself sufficiently to the necessary mediation of conventions.

Critics whose central concept is type or form or symbol may try to eliminate the self in the aesthetic transaction by separating art altogether from life and the real world: "Those who confuse dramatic characters with real people are likely . . . to consider Bassanio [in *The Merchant of Venice*] a

---

14 E. H. Gombrich, *Meditations on a Hobby Horse and Other Essays on the Theory of Art* (London: Phaidon Press, 1963), 68.

15 In this connection, Helen Vendler has brilliantly shown in *The Poetry of George Herbert* (Cambridge: Harvard University Press, 1975) how verbally and attitudinally daring even so devout and "traditional" a poet as George Herbert actually was.

materialist and opportunist; those who see that art creates its own world with its own emphases will take him for what he is meant to be—a symbolic quester for love and the Golden Fleece who has the wit to find them in the leaden casket."[16] We may not wish to assert baldly that Bassanio is a materialist and opportunist, but in a full response to the play we would certainly want to judge him in terms of social conventions—Elizabethan and our own necessarily, since our understanding of the past must be filtered through our present experience of life. To let the real world bear on art symbols in this way does, admittedly, introduce a measure of inexactness (for the conventions governing the art of past times and different places are not fully recoverable), but not to do so must result in a hollow formalist victory.[17]

Paradoxically, a too pure expressionist aesthetic may lead to the same end. To Langer, for example, forms themselves—or symbols—are inherently expressive: they have a psycho-biological rather than historical base. I think there is some truth to her view, for how else can we explain the fact that some conventions are extraordinarily similar among widely separated societies? And Gombrich, evaluating her theory with reference to music and the visual arts, concedes that, for example, the association of rapid movement and bright color with gay moods and of slow movement and dark color with grave ones does seem to be independent of historical considerations. Nevertheless, as Gombrich emphasizes, most artistic communication depends, like any other kind, on the mediation of historically rooted conventions.[18] The intelligibility of art is probably similar in this respect to the intelligibility of dreams. Some dreams or parts of dreams are typi-

16 Brents Stirling, introduction to William Shakespeare, *The Merchant of Venice* (Pelican ed.; Baltimore: Penguin Books, 1975), 22.
17 Compare a statement of Martin Price's: "What strikes me about much recent criticism is its rather puritanical fear of character, as if a reader who shows interest in a character of any complexity must be irresistibly drawn into regarding the characterization for its own sake or as a real person." From "The Logic of Intensity: More on Character," *Critical Inquiry*, II (1975), 377. The sentence is part of a brilliant, beautifully balanced discussion of the contrary claims in literary art of reflexiveness and reference, configuration and representation.
18 Gombrich, *Meditations on a Hobby Horse*, 56–58.

cal and can therefore be immediately understood to some degree by everyone, but the majority require for their interpretation a particular knowledge of the dreamer's situation and history.

The question of genre is at issue here. To agree with Croce that genres are historically evolved concepts rather than archetypes possessing a reality independent of our minds does not require us to belittle them, to see them as mere designations imposed upon the end products of imaginative activity. They are crucial to composition. Elias Schwartz compares genres to meter in verse, a norm from which the poet departs to obtain an actual rhythm. Generic forms are, similarly, sets of expectation in the minds of both writer and reader which the writer departs from in certain definite and limited ways to express an individual vision and voice.[19]

I think a certain suspicion attaches to the idea of individual expression because it is confused with personal or so-called self-expression. We know that the experience conveyed by literature is either a much transformed version of personal experience or may be only imagined. But this knowledge does not entitle us to describe any poem as "pure convention," which is how Northrop Frye describes Thomas Campion's lovely lyric, "When thou must home to shades of underground." Frye's follow-up is revealing: "It's a complete waste of time trying to find out about the women in Campion's life—there can't possibly be any real experience behind it. . . . He was a busy man, who didn't have much time for getting himself murdered by cruel mistresses."[20] That the poem is based on imagined rather than actual experience is not really the question. Hardly any poem is a transcription of the poet's personal situation; as Gombrich points out, "We could hardly ever recognize an artist whom we knew only through his work."[21] But we do not need to drag in a personalist theory of self-expression in order to assert that imagined experience is, however indirectly, *felt* experience. Frye throws out the baby

19 Schwartz, *The Forms of Feeling*, 43–92.
20 Northrop Frye, *The Educated Imagination* (Bloomington: Indiana University Press, 1964), 48.
21 Gombrich, *Meditations on a Hobby Horse*, 28.

with the bath water; in repudiating a partly erroneous idea too zealously, he cuts art off entirely from the mind of the individual artist.

The indirectness of purely imagined experience is certainly important but not, in its bearing on an affective theory of literary art, decisive. Oscar Wilde observes shrewdly that the type of all arts as to form is music and that the type of all arts as to feeling is acting. The remark is suggestively relevant here. The artist enters into certain roles or attitudes. He necessarily involves his own emotions but he remains their master and director. (It is the detachment implicit in this idea of acting that we tend to forget when we label "neurotic" the artists who favor morbid subject matter.) Role playing creates an all-important, though sometimes fragile, barrier between a state of mind in which one controls an emotion and a state in which one is controlled by it. Shakespeare was assuredly not overcome with Hamlet's or Lear's anguish or he could not have written so well (or at all) about it. He *entertained* their anguish in the controlled form of imaginative ideas and was interested in the artistic use he could put them to. The ability to convert emotions from something one is controlled by to something one controls by means of imaginative comprehension is not a bad definition of inner freedom, and evidently Shakespeare (to judge from the extraordinary range of emotions in his plays and from the extraordinary tolerance accorded negative emotions before moral judgments are applied) had this ability in a superlative degree.

Not only does the artist enter into the various feelings he dramatizes. He also coordinates them. It is a question of structural integrity and, since this coordination is psychological as well as formal, a question also of mental integrity or sincerity. The word *sincerity* derives from *sincerus* (pure, sound) or possibly from *sine cera* (without wax) but in either case contains the root meaning of whole or unflawed. In ancient times, as Lionel Trilling points out, the word referred to things rather than people,[22] but there may be a deep wisdom in its evolution into its modern psychological meaning, for

22 Trilling, *Sincerity and Authenticity*, 12–13.

there is a vital connection between the integrity of artifact and of artist. Without doubt its plain modern sense—direct congruence between avowal and personal feeling—cannot be applied to the complex phenomenon of art, and the word has in fact been effectively discredited as an aesthetic term. But a writer's ability to coordinate all of his effects, which emphatically includes the perceiving and eliminating of unintended effects, requires an integrated, uncorrupted consciousness. The "convincingness" of the work is prima facie evidence of the "sincerity" of the artist. We will return to this crucial and tricky concept of sincerity later in the light of Collingwood's theory of imagination.

The effect of unity in works of art is achieved most immediately by style or by the authority of the writer's presence inherent in style. This, I take it, is what Mark Spilka calls "the necessary stylist" and Richard Poirier "the performing self."[23] It is both the force inherent in eloquence or sustained rhythm, which probably determines our attraction to literature more than we know or say, and a coordinating power virtually indistinguishable from our sense of the unity of structure. In the words of Leo Tolstoi: "The cement which binds together every work of art into a whole and produces the effect of life-like illusion is not the unity of persons and places but that of the author's independent moral relation to the subject. . . . Whatever the artist depicts, whether it be saints or robbers, kings or lackeys, we seek and see only the soul of the artist himself."[24]

I want to spell out one not so obvious implication of this idea so that its force may be felt. If all the attitudes present in a work of literary art are thought of as distributed from a

---

23 Mark Spilka, "The Necessary Stylist," in Walter Sutton and Richard Foster (eds.), *Modern Criticism: Theory and Practice* (New York: Odyssey Press, 1963), 328–34; Richard Poirier, *The Performing Self* (New York: Oxford University Press, 1971). Poirier goes somewhat farther than I would. For him writing is "an act of keeping alive *rather* [my emphasis] than an image of life or of living" (111), as if style is itself subject. I demur from this extreme formulation on the grounds that it is a subtle form of self-expressionism, conceiving of art not as a transcendence of the personal self but as a glorification of it.
24 Quoted in Miriam Allott, *Novelists on the Novel* (London: Routledge and Kegan Paul, 1959), 131.

coordinating selfhood, if they are shapes in what the phenomenological critics like to call an interior landscape, then even the negatively charged idea or image in satire must correspond to some portion of the artist's mind. In the form of imaginative art, not even a repudiative attitude can avoid being reflexive. Perhaps the closest it can come to being so in successful art is illustrated by the rather gently ironic portrait of the neighbor in Robert Frost's poem "Mending Wall." This morally stupid figure who repeats, "Good fences make good neighbors," is not perceived as an aspect of the poet's self, but his defects are nevertheless described with the kind of tolerant humor that suggests they are all too understandable and familiar. When it comes to repudiative satire, effectiveness has much to do with whether we can perceive through the ironic shadings the author's awareness that he is opposing something in himself. Irony establishes an aesthetic distance, to be sure, but must not mark off an attitude as utterly alien. A note of self-righteousness or spite is likely to be struck when moral judgments are too sharply drawn.[25]

If all ridicule is a form of self-ridicule, the corollary is just as true: all idealization is a form of self-idealization. And the effectiveness of these attitudes in literature depends a great deal on whether the writer seems sufficiently aware of these transformations, whether he appears to conceive of his imaginings as extended from, rather than apart from, his own identity. Of course this does not condemn him to dramatizing one role. He may be able to give of himself to many roles, and in fact the greatest writers are those who have not only the most vivid but also the most divisible selfhood.

My emphasis on the mind and self of the writer in the work is a response to the conspicuous tendency among contemporary critics and aestheticians to conceive of literary art not simply as the transcendence of the private self, which it as-

---

25 Compare the nicely turned comment of Morris Dickstein, review of Philip Roth's *My Life as a Man*, in *New York Times Book Review* (June 2, 1974), 2: "Even a satirist must love his characters a little, especially if he also loathes them. He must be drawn to them a little in an animating way, must need to give them life. He can't use novels simply to settle old scores."

suredly is, but as a separation from the self altogether: thus
the long authority of the Intentional Fallacy; thus Frye's picture of Campion or his similar picture of Shakespeare as a
man who "wrote two plays a year until he'd made enough
money to retire, and spent the last five years of his life count-
ing his take";[26] thus Langer's attempt to take feeling out of
the mind and attach it to the objective symbol; and thus above
all in recent years the fanatic aesthetic objectivism, the ruthless campaign against self and personality promoted under the
auspices of structuralism. Leo Bersani observes that, for Roland Barthes, literature may be defined exactly as Claude
Lévi-Strauss defines myth: "a type of discourse from which
the subject of the enunciation (the person, the author, the
individual history and psychology) has been eliminated."[27]
How far we have come in all of this from what Henry James
in "The Art of Fiction" calls "the very obvious truth [!] that
the deepest quality of a work will always be the quality of the
mind of the producer."

The principles of structuralist poetics are extreme, but they
are sophisticated and not easily dismissed. At the least they
have given the act of reading a new importance for criticism
that it is not likely wholly to lose. It was I. A. Richards who
introduced into Anglo-American criticism the question—or
questionableness—of the reader's response. But, although he
was sensitive to the corruptions of demotic art, he did not
challenge the inviolability of the superior text; rather he
sought to expose deviant readings of it in the confidence that
they were corrigible. The New Critics who followed him cor-
doned off from the interpretable text the consideration of any
distortion that might arise from the writer's or reader's mind.
In doing so, they discouraged one salutary direction that
Richards' influence might have taken; namely, the absorption
of certain psychological insights, enabling critics to allow for
some distortion at both ends of the aesthetic transaction so
that the ideal of an approximately objective literary meaning,
arrived at by consensus, could be preserved.

26 Frye, *The Educated Imagination*, 88–89.
27 Leo Bersani, "Is There a Science of Literature?" *Partisan Review*, XXXIX (Fall,
1972), 545–48.

Some of the main trends of literary theory since 1950, in reaction to the New Criticism, have entailed a drastic subordination of the once preeminent text. It is not the text that matters here but what the reader can do with it. Like Frye he may place it in a vast, enclosed system with other texts or, like Sartre and Barthes, he may dissolve it into a systematic ideology or semiology. The critic in effect replaces the artist. It used to be said that no one would be a critic if he were able to be an artist, but I wonder how many critics would rather have written, say, *Anatomy of Criticism* than any poem, play, or novel composed in the third quarter of our century.

What seems most significant about these newer critical theories, which find myth everywhere and tend to glory in imaginative misreadings or meta-readings of literary art, is that they seek a totally aesthetic view of knowledge, pointedly including scientific knowledge. The quest goes back by way of Nietzsche and Hegel all the way to Vico, and in fact the structuralists' *les sciences humaines* is a concept very similar to Hegel's *Phänomenologie des Geistes* and Vico's *La Scienza Nuova*. Science, in these systems, is not so much dismissed as co-opted, made over or revised into another myth. The element of justification in these audacious attempts is the fact that the arts and sciences alike must start from a metaphysical base of undemonstrable assumption. But of course the procedures of two intellectual activities are quite different, the one seeking to convince by an appeal to the faculty of empathy, the other by an appeal to sensory perception and reason. And when this difference makes itself felt, as in the use of language, then the omni-aesthete's deep hostility to science emerges. Barthes, in an essay called "Science Versus Literature," declares, "The destruction of the instrumental use of language"—without which, of course, no science, not even linguistics, is possible—"must be at the center of the structuralist program."[28]

Such trends create a climate that makes a criticism derived from Richards, which seeks to bring a scientific spirit into

28 Roland Barthes, "Science Versus Literature," in Michael Lane (ed.), *Introduction to Structuralism* (New York: Basic Books, 1970), 410–16.

discussions of literature without compromising what is distinctive and valuable in literary art, difficult to pursue. The semiology of the structuralists is less a science than a weapon to undermine the idea of the person, the appeal to human experience, and the expressive and mimetic functions of language on which they depend. Coleridge's words, "You feel [Shakespeare] to be a poet, inasmuch as for a time he has made you one," are now reduced by the new French-inspired criticism into "every man his own poet." It is perfectly possible for a reader with a different value system from Shakespeare's to find Claudius more admirable than Hamlet or with a different value system from F. Scott Fitzgerald's to find Tom Buchanan no worse than Gatsby, but to grant full sanction to such an unhistorical reading can lead only to the end of criticism as a worthwhile enterprise. Without historically based standards for judging the relative merits of different readings, we may kill the meddling spirit of science but only at the cost of emptying our own treasury. The pity of it is that these correctives to the old New Criticism might well, in their emphasis on the reader, stimulate a dialogic vividness and add human interest to reader-writer confrontations, but, pushed to extremes, they drive out the person once again.

But all of this needs to be restated less polemically. What the structuralists have to say about, or against, the idea of feeling in literature is sophisticated and deserves a philosophic response, not simply a commonsense dismissal.

From a commonsense point of view, both of the following statements are readily acceptable, even though they point toward opposite aesthetic orientations: (a) a work of literary art is made out of words and nothing but words; (b) a work of literary art expresses and elicits feeling. Common sense is not so much unsound as limited and incurious. Dr. Johnson kicking the stone was only enforcing a proper manner of speaking, which Berkeley himself had no intention of flouting;[29]

29 "I am not for disputing the propriety but the truth of expression. If therefore you agree with me that we eat and drink and are clad with the immediate objects of sense, which cannot exist unperceived or without the mind, I shall readily grant it

he was not refuting the philosophic proposition that objects of sense cannot exist unperceived. Modern philosophy has refined this Berkeleian proposition to read, in effect, that perceptions cannot exist unmediated by language. And so we are prompted to wonder—if we are thinking philosophically rather than sensibly—how we can ever get from the prison house of language to some reality, psychological or physical, which is presumed to lie beyond language; how, in short, we can reconcile statements *a* and *b*.

It is to the credit of the linguistically oriented critics, structuralists and Wittgensteinians primarily, that they do make us wonder about this question. I confess that their philosophic purity (particularly that of the French, who have a distinctive, antiempirical style of intellectual radicalism) sometimes tires my patience. One would hardly guess from their work, for example, that linguistics is a branch of cognitive *psychology*, as Noam Chomsky points out repeatedly.[30] But it does make us reconsider some fundamental aesthetic issues (including the role of the unconscious in literary theory) and is well worth the effort of an uncommonsensical response. I seek here to correct the antihumanistic bias of the structuralist position that seeks to eliminate the constitutive self in the aesthetic transaction and of Wittgenstein's comparable and characteristic denial that aesthetic argument is about human beings.

The relation between words and psychic or inner reality is basically the same as that between words and physical or outer reality. Since neither subjective nor objective reality exists except as it is perceived and since consciousness is inseparable from language, words must be said to bear a symbolic relation to both.[31]

---

is more proper or conformable to custom that they should be called things rather than ideas." Quoted in Edwin A. Burtt (ed.), *The English Philosophers from Bacon to Mill* (New York: Modern Library, 1939), 535.

30 See, for example, Noam Chomsky, *Language and Mind* (Enlarged ed.; New York: Harcourt Brace Jovanovich, 1972), 1; and Chomsky, quoted in Israel Shenker, *Words and Their Masters* (Garden City: Doubleday, 1974), 237.

31 Claude Lévi-Strauss argues that even historical facts do not enjoy an independent reality. They too must be mediated by language, so that history, like all other "superstructures," is essentially a myth. Claude Lévi-Strauss, *The Savage Mind*

Whatever words refer to—ideas or objects—seems therefore to lack priority compared with language itself. Barthes speaks of liberating the verbal sign from its reference. The sign consists of a signifier and a signified, the latter being the literal meaning of the word but not what it refers to. He does not exactly deny the symbolic property of language but merges it with the literal: if all words are symbolic, reference has no independent authority and all symbols might as well be treated literally. From the structuralist point of view, it is at best unsophisticated to adopt a thematic rather than semiotic approach to literary interpretation. We should seek to understand not meaning but how meaning is produced, how the text resists, in fact, the mimetic and expressive (*i.e.*, referential) functions we are disposed to look for. There is no need to invoke experience to explain a text because experience does not really lie behind language. (And, Wittgenstein would add, we should not say "explain," because that word implies a reality behind phenomena; he frequently insisted that philosophy does not seek to explain anything.)

Such a view certainly tends to eliminate mind and world from aesthetic consideration, but to some sophisticated students of literature, the restriction seems not only valid but exciting. One major reason for this is that, though it seems to negate "experience" and "life," it really readmits these ideas on a higher level, purged of vulgar association. It does this by aestheticizing all those contextual disciplines which have been felt by critics to threaten the autonomy of their enterprise. (Wittgenstein said directly that psychoanalysis was "aesthetics rather than science." [32]) By asserting that no system is more privileged than another, structuralists can make a sublime republic of all the arts and sciences: they are all, equally, mythologies. In this happy land, there is no longer any need to be defensive—or indeed anything but

(Chicago: University of Chicago Press, 1966), 245–69. An adequate answer to this argument was given some time ago by Croce and is given again by E. H. Gombrich in "Canons and Values in the Visual Arts," *Critical Inquiry*, II (Spring, 1976), 395–410.

32 According to G. E. Moore. Quoted in John Casey, *The Language of Criticism* (London: Methuen, 1966), 19.

tender—toward scientific disciplines, for all are unprivileged: none can claim to know any reality beyond language.[33]

The social sciences are thus made respectable for criticism, but at a price. It is not only the prejudice against science that falls away in this rapprochement but science itself. It loses its nature if not its name when it is left with only verbal equivalents and cannot pursue a rational inquiry into phenomena themselves in the hope of gaining insight into their connections and of formulating unperceivable laws that can be said to govern their behavior. Art seems to me a loser here too. Surely the glory of literary art all along has been that its language is more resistant to the ravages of time than the language of discourse. There is, to be sure, some sort of intellectual humility in saying that no knowledge is privileged, but there is subtle arrogance too. If there is no reality beyond verbal structures, then there can be no truth about ourselves which we do not know, for language and consciousness are inseparable. And this arrogance becomes overt when the structuralist polemic distinguishes (as it does) between those spirits who have the courage to acknowledge the utter nothingness beyond and those who remain shrouded in bourgeois illusions.

We may initiate an alternative picture of the relation between language and feeling by questioning an inference drawn from the fact that words merely symbolize what they refer to. Symbols are necessarily conventional, but are they always arbitrary? One remarkable thing about the conventions of reference and representation is that, though they are conventions, they are sometimes very similar among peoples of different times and places. It looks as if there were some common denominator which prevents them from being wholly arbitrary or customary, and that common denom-

---

33 I have implied that this tenderness, carefully examined, is the soft glove over the iron fist. But it looks like tenderness indeed, even like a religious movement, to plainer observation. In the words of Robert Scholes: "Structuralism... is a methodology which seeks nothing less than the unification of all the sciences into a new system of belief." See his *Structuralism in Literature: An Introduction* (New Haven: Yale University Press, 1974), 2.

inator must be the human mind, the psychobiologic aspect of human destiny.

This does not take us very far, for most conventions are historically conditioned, are counters for communication which only become intelligible if the transmitter and receiver share a knowledge of certain codes. But, we may then add, intelligibility requires *more* than mechanical accuracy in coding and decoding. A message to be understood by human beings must have human significance, human interest. When conventions are not inherently expressive, they become expressive insofar as a mind modifies or extends them for a discernible purpose: they become expressive, in short, when language is used creatively.

I seem to be talking about literary creation as an activity that is partly anterior to verbalization and connects words with feeling. Can anything in our consciousness, the structuralist would ask, be anterior to language? As far as we can see, ideas of any kind (whether we call them thoughts or feelings) must take a verbal form. We may answer by saying that the postulate of preverbal mentation is not at all farfetched. For one thing, we begin to learn verbal language at about the age of two, when the mind has already been functioning in some manner for a considerable and, needless to say, important time. For another, as Chomsky emphasizes, in even ordinary speech—and all the more in art speech—we create language; we do not simply deal it out from a memory bank like a computer, but produce it—often with hesitation, unsureness, and lapses—from somewhere. To suggest that *mind* is more extensive than language does not challenge the identification of *consciousness* and language. What we are forced to question and to reject is the idea that consciousness is the whole of mind.

This is a crucial point. And it is easy to undermine. For example, a Wittgensteinian critic argues to a conclusion— "Logic, therefore, precedes experience"—which seems to assert only that consciousness is not separate from language, but by using the word *experience* instead of *consciousness*, he subtly wipes out the idea that verbalization may be preceded by bodily sensation anterior to consciousness, that there is a threshold to consciousness.[34]

I am implying neither that creativity is unconscious, if by unconscious we mean what is barred rather than removed from consciousness, nor certainly that thought is conscious whereas feeling is unconscious. The notion of unconscious feeling, though sometimes used as a shorthand, is illogical. "It is surely of the essence of an emotion that we should feel it, i.e. that it should enter consciousness. So for emotions, feelings and affects to be unconscious would be quite out of the question." I quote Freud, who goes on to explain that the repressed unconscious is best understood as a process that distorts the expression of emotion: "It may happen that an affect or an emotion is perceived, but misconstrued. By the repression of its proper presentation it is forced to become connected with another idea, and is now interpreted by consciousness as the expression of the other idea. If we restore the true connection, we call the original affect 'unconscious,' although the affect was never unconscious but its ideational presentation had undergone repression." This is intricate but important, so it will be helpful to quote another passage from later in the same essay, "The Unconscious":

> What we could permissibly call the conscious idea of the object can now be split up into the *idea of the word* (verbal idea) and the *idea of the thing* (concrete idea). . . . now we know what is the difference between a conscious and an unconscious idea. The two are not, as we supposed, different records of the same content situate in different parts of the mind, nor yet different functional states of cathexis [an accumulation of energy in any one part of the mind] in the same part; but the conscious idea comprises the concrete idea plus the verbal idea corresponding to it, whilst the unconscious idea is that of the thing alone. . . . [The preconscious] originates in a hyper-cathexis of this concrete idea by a linking up of it with the verbal ideas of the words corresponding to it. It is such hyper-cathexes, we may suppose, that bring about higher organization in the mind and make it possible for the primary process to be succeeded by the secondary process which dominates [the preconscious]. . . . Repression denies to the re-

34 Casey, *The Language of Criticism*, 63.

jected idea . . . translation into words which are to remain at-
tached to the object. The idea which is not put into words or the
mental act which has not received hyper-cathexis then remains in
the unconscious in a state of repression.[35]

There is no hope, Freud admits elsewhere (acknowledging
the truth that some of his revisionists start from), of our ever
being able to reach the unconscious reality itself, "since it is
clear that everything new that we deduce must nevertheless
be translated back into the language of our perceptions, from
which it is simply impossible to set ourselves free."[36] But the
revisionists do not appear to welcome the hypothesis of unconscious mental processes whatever concessions Freud has
made. They have devoted considerable energy to showing
that his key terms are translatable in such a way that language
can reassert its priority over experience.

Jacques Lacan, the revisionist psychoanalyst, has put forward in direct challenge the idea that the unconscious itself is
linguistic in structure: "It is neither primordial nor instinctu-
al; what it knows about the elementary is no more than the
elements of the signifier."[37] On the basis of this questionable
premise, Lacan can translate those unconscious processes
named by Freud condensation and displacement into the
rhetorical terms metaphor and metonymy. Without the
premise, however, these substitutions are only analogies,
striking and suggestive but no more persuasive as argument
than analogies can be.

It seems essential to the revisionist enterprise that all of the
key psychoanalytic terms be translated to accord with a concept of the unconscious that does not denote any reality beyond language. Jacques Derrida has thus translated anxiety
("anxiety is invariably the result of a certain mode of being

35 Sigmund Freud, *Collected Papers*, trans. Joan Rivière (5 vols.; New York: Basic
Books, 1959), IV, 109–10, 133–34. See Sigmund Freud, *The Ego and the Id*,
trans. Joan Rivière, rev. James Strachey (New York: Norton, 1962), Chaps. 1, 2,
for further clarification.
36 Sigmund Freud, *An Outline of Psychoanalysis*, trans. James Strachey (New York:
Norton, 1963), 105.
37 Jacques Lacan, "The Insistence of the Letter in the Unconscious," in Jacques
Ehrmann (ed.), *Structuralism* (Garden City: Doubleday, 1970), 130.

implicated in the |verbal| game") and repression ("writing is unthinkable without repression"), but a Freudian would find some anxiety irrational and ungovernable and would find the survival of childhood, let alone writing, unthinkable without repression—though by repression Derrida apparently means something as un-Freudian as the implicit resistance of a text to the mediation of writing.[38] Harold Bloom has not only converted anxiety, repression, and sublimation into literary terms but has devised an elaborate map of misreading which aligns the psychoanalytic mechanisms of defense with the ratios of poetic influence.[39] Geoffrey Hartman, the subtlest of revisionists because he attempts to draw an improved theory out of undeveloped implications in Freud himself, postulates a compulsion to communicate on a par with libido, which was for Freud the whole of the instinctual drive.[40]

In the thirties and forties, humanist critics (Kenneth Burke, John Crowe Ransom, *et al.*) used to oppose Freudian "determinism," mistakenly understood as an empirical compulsion rather than as an a priori assumption of universal cause. The new strategy of challenge is more sophisticated and bold: to show that Freud was right after all if his ideas are lifted from their mundanely sexual context and put into a sufficiently philosophic frame of reference. With considerable temerity Lacan concedes that the resistance to psychoanalysis makes good sense but not because it emphasizes sexuality, "which is after all the dominant object in the literature of the ages," but rather because it exposes "an abyss open before all

---

38 On anxiety, see Jacques Derrida, "Structure, Sign, and Play in the Discourse of the Human Sciences," in Richard Macksey and Eugenio Donato (eds.), *The Languages of Criticism and the Sciences of Man: The Structuralist Controversy* (Baltimore and London: Johns Hopkins Press, 1970), 249. On repression, see Jacques Derrida, "Freud and the Scene of Writing," in *French Freud: Structural Studies in Psychoanalysis*, Yale French Studies (New Haven: Yale University Press, 1972), 73–117, esp. 113. The context of the quoted remarks does not make clear whether "writing" for Derrida is actual written language or, simply and broadly, anything that impinges on the psyche. In any case, he is the most ruthless of the structuralists, seeking rather fantastically to destroy all of those concepts in the Western literary tradition (essence, existence, subject, man, God, etc.) that imply a self to which art or any human activity can be referred.
39 See particularly, Bloom, *A Map of Misreading*, 84.
40 Hartman, *The Fate of Reading*, 21–40.

thought."[41] Bloom strictly enforces a distinction between sexual and creative anxiety and then freely talks about anxiety, repression, and Oedipal relationships as purely poetic problems.[42] Barthes, in *The Pleasure of the Text*, politely sneers for a few pages at "neurosis," "inconsistency," and "self-contradiction" and then, having as it were disarmed the mundane sexualists, launches into a highly erotic yet absolutely complacent lyrical meditation on the act of reading.[43]

The disarming or "revision" of psychoanalysis, which in France is almost an intellectual obligation, is a remarkable feature of contemporary literary criticism. I have cast doubts on its cogency, but I believe there is some critical value in the structuralist emphasis on the reader's uncertainty during the act of reading. The uses of such uncertainty are doubtless most evident in discussions of modernist literature, although some interesting attempts have been made to show how improvisatory and self-conscious earlier literature also was. I suspect that what is now called structuralist literary criticism will, in accordance with its base in linguistics, merge eventually with other schools of criticism oriented to information theory and cognitive psychology.

I hope these corrective comments do not suggest the conclusion that we must examine literary texts in terms of how minds work *rather* than how language works. But I do suggest that in criticism the concept of mind or self cannot be displaced by the concept of language. The accidents of language, like the conventions of literary forms, provide the possibilities and sets of expectation, but it must be the human mind, the "constitutive self" (the reports of whose death have been exaggerated), that determines the choice of meanings and the shape of the whole.

That is as far as I can go in answering the question I posed some pages back: can we not get around the idea of the mind of the artist (hence, the unconscious mind) by saying that

41 Lacan, "The Insistence of the Letter in the Unconscious," 131.
42 Bloom, *The Anxiety of Influence*, 36.
43 Roland Barthes, *The Pleasure of the Text*, trans. Richard Miller (New York: Hill and Wang, 1975).

there is no reality beyond language? But I believe I can throw a little more light on the whole question by tracing the premises of both Freudian science and revisionist criticism to their common origins in Romantic thought and by suggesting how they diverged into rival traditions.

Nineteenth-century artists and critics were better disposed than we are toward a psychological perspective on art, for it was then new and venturesome rather than mutilated and vulgarized as now. It would be a bad generalization to say that twentieth-century theorists ignore feeling whereas nineteenth-century theorists ignored form, because every serious theorist is concerned with both; but it is fair to say that twentieth-century critics have tended to take art as their central concept whereas Romantic critics took imagination as theirs. The Romantics saw *poetry* where we see the *poem;* they took an essentialist position deriving ultimately from Plato, and we tend to take a formalist position deriving ultimately from Aristotle. The Romantics no doubt overrated the capacity of the artist to be original, to build new forms exempt from what Shelley called "custom's evil taint." Yet their orientation led them to a valuable idea that gets pushed aside today—namely, that art is a mental activity, not merely the activity of applying a technique or even of devising models and hypotheses but also of expression, of self-discovery. To call this coming to awareness a process of self-knowing would not be incorrect, but the phrase suggests too private a mental act, more like dreaming than creating. It is also a process of self-making. Collingwood, who has brilliantly developed and carried forward some nineteenth-century aesthetic insights, describes the artist as someone whose "knowing of himself is |also| a making of himself" and very suggestively compares the creative process to children's play.[44]

The Romantics understood that the mind's capacity to invent and synthesize—the faculty of imagination—was basic not only to art but to all intellectual endeavor, not the least to

44 Collingwood, *The Principles of Art,* 291, 80.

science. The imaginative element in scientific thinking, first
appreciated by Kant, has very properly been stressed in recent
decades, for instance by Karl Popper, who tells us that "science corroborates theories whose origins are the same as those
of myth."[45] Although many Romantics did not fail to realize
that scientific thinking drew from the sacred fount of imagination, their trust in the primacy of that faculty prompted them
to make another distinction which was bound to eventuate in
the depression of science. They distinguished between imagination and intellect or, more exactly, between two kinds of
knowing: imaginative or associative and intellectual or analytic. Their enemy was not science precisely but a certain type
of reasoning—consecutive or logical—which science, however imaginative first and last, cannot do without.

Science does not confine itself to experience and untested
intuition. It deals in probabilities whereas art, like religion,
deals in certainties (*i.e.*, the experience of certainties).
Cause-and-effect reasoning, as Hume observed long ago,
cannot be conclusive, and it has therefore been regarded by
some poets as a false path to knowledge. D. H. Lawrence
speaks for them in the memorable exchange reported by Aldous Huxley on the theory of biological evolution. Huxley,
trying to convince his skeptical friend, said, "But look at the
evidence," whereupon Lawrence, pointing to his solar plexus,
replied, "Evidence doesn't mean anything to me. I don't feel it
here."[46] More than indifference to cause-and-effect reasoning
is expressed here. Many artists and critics fasten onto what

45 I am unable now to locate this particular sentence in Popper's work, but the idea
recurs frequently. See, for example, Karl Popper, *Conjectures and Refutations:
The Growth of Scientific Knowledge* (New York: Harper Torchbooks, 1968), 127,
257. Compare it with Freud's own statement, in his open letter to Einstein: "It
may perhaps seem to you as though our theories are a kind of mythology. . . . But
does not every science come in the end to a kind of mythology like this? Cannot
the same be said to-day of your own Physics?" From Sigmund Freud, *The Standard Edition of the Complete Psychological Works of Sigmund Freud*, trans.
James Strachey (24 vols.; London: Hogarth Press, 1953–74), XXII, 211. I am
aware that Popper questions whether psychoanalysis is a science, but his reasons
have more to do with the difference between social and natural science than with
the difference between science and art.
46 Quoted in Aldous Huxley, introduction to D. H. Lawrence, *The Letters of D. H.
Lawrence* (London: Heinemann, 1932), xv.

they call "determinism" as if it were a dragon to be slain. But the concept of determinism in science is not the antithesis of the free will they are anxious to defend. The true antithesis of free will is compulsion or necessity (*i.e.*, the *experience* of unfreedom), whereas determinism is simply the hypothesis that all effects have causes, without which science could not develop.[47]

The distrust of science by many literary humanists may be prompted by insufficient self-regard. True, an imaginative enactment proves nothing compared with an argument but, if the two are of comparable merit, has more force. Imaginative as opposed to cooler intellectual conviction is a kind of contagion, akin to belief. Not that we believe in a dogmatic sense; we believe in Dante's believing, whatever we may think of his beliefs as such. Art appeals much more directly to our affections than does scientific discourse, and that is a major reason we value it.[48]

Since the Romantics were so centrally concerned with mind, with consciousness, feeling, and imagination, it was the science of psychology and particularly the hypothesis of unconscious mind (which, of course, had a history before it came to scientific maturity in the work of Freud) that they wanted—and that their modern heirs still want—to undermine. Psychoanalysis is sometimes said to be fundamentally different from other sciences, but Freud made it clear that, although it specifically investigated the phenomena of consciousness, it was no exception:

> In our science the problem is the same as in the others: behind the attributes (i.e. qualities) of the object under investigation which are directly given to our perception, we have to discover

47 Paul Roazen, *Freud: Political and Social Thought* (New York: Knopf, 1968), 297, quotes two statements which are pertinent here. One is from P. H. Nowell-Smith, *Ethics:* "To discover the cause of something is not to prove that it is inevitable. On the contrary the discovery of a disease is often the first step towards preventing it." The other is from J. A. C. Brown, *Freud and the Post-Freudians:* "The principle of causality is not ... strictly a scientific law but rather a necessary assumption without which no science would be possible."
48 This paragraph adapts ideas developed in William Righter's suggestive little book, *Myth and Literature* (London: Routledge and Kegan Paul, 1975).

something which is more independent of the particular receptive capacities of our sense organs and which approximates more closely to what may be supposed to be the real state of things. . . .

We have discovered technical methods of filling up the gaps in the phenomena of our consciousness, and we make use of these methods just as a physicist makes use of experiment. In this manner we deduce a number of processes which are in themselves "unknowable" and insert them among the processes of which we are conscious.[49]

Freud admitted that we are "not constitutionally disposed" to "apply this method of inference to ourselves," but he said also that doing so "does not depart a single step from our accepted mode of thinking," since "the assumption of a consciousness [in others] rests upon an inference and cannot share the direct certainty we have of our own consciousness."[50] The Romantics seized upon the fact that analytic thinking about anything requires a division between subject and object—between self and world or, if the object is the mind itself, between one part of the self and another. This dualism seemed to them the source of our misery as human beings. There is, however, considerable ambiguity in Romantic thought over whether this division was inherent in the biological fact of consciousness and therefore capable of being only temporarily healed by the unifying action of the imagination or whether it was a "fall" within history from an original lost unity (prevailing, perhaps, before the time of Descartes) and therefore could be recovered or even exploited as a necessary step of progression to a higher state of consciousness.

Given this ambiguity, I leave the question of whether or in what degree this division accounts for our misery. What is important to note here is the close relation between the Romantics' profound psychological insights and their specific aversion to the hypothesis of an individual unconscious mind. Like Saint Augustine much earlier—who keenly understood the perversity of the will but recoiled in self-reproach when he "miserably imagined there to be some unknown substance of

49 Freud, *An Outline of Psychoanalysis*, 105–106.
50 Freud, *Collected Papers*, IV, 101–102.

irrational life ... not derived from Thee, O My God"—they drew back from the conclusion that some of their boldest insights were pointing toward. They perceived that a poet may unknowingly subvert his own poem; but, in order to escape the hypothesis of a repressed unconscious, they took an idealistic view of the poem, in which the real poem was not the one actually written but the one that a sufficiently imaginative reader would recover by perceiving apparent discrepancies as a dialectical path toward a higher unity.[51]

The Romantics averted the conception of an individual unconscious in two ways. One was the way of Augustine, Milton, and Christian tradition generally. This was to postulate a divine, collective mind of which individual minds were a part so that anything anomalous in experience could be attributed to divine will and either rationalized or left a mystery. Although the Romantics seldom adopted an all-around orthodox position on matters of theology, they more than flirted with such an idea. For our purposes, Coleridge's famous formulation of the Primary Imagination is an important instance. It incorporates the psychological insight of Kant (which leads to Freud) that the structure of our minds is involved in our every perception of the outer world. But it also equivocates at just this point and allows us to think of the involuntary organizing of perception not as a purely naturalistic but as a supernaturalistic phenomenon.

The second way, that of Blake and others, most systematically of Hegel, is more subtle. It pictures mind as individual consciousness but as metaphysically expandable. It is a dynamic conception like Freud's, but its goal is to abrogate or transcend conflict rather than to reduce it. All fears are capable of becoming conscious; all conflicts are resolvable. Hegelian dialectic has influenced a succession of literary movements and presents at the same time a formidable obstacle to an explanation of how the concept of a Freudian unconscious might pertain to such study, so I must take a moment to question its usefulness.

51 See the brilliant and sympathetic discussion of this critical idealism by Charles Rosen, in "Isn't It Romantic?" *New York Review of Books* (June 14, 1973), 12–18.

The psychological term for opposing emotions is the noun *conflict*. Insofar as this conflict is rational (*i.e.*, "derived from the actual situation, proportionate to the real circumstances, under the complete control of the conscious ego"[52]), we may expect it to be resolved by a conscious choice or compromise. If it does not seem capable of being so resolved, then we may suspect the presence of an unconscious conflict underlying it.

Now, Hegelians describe opposing emotions not with the psychological term *conflict* but with the logical term *contradiction*. That is, they transform a subjective, psychological idea into an objective, linguistic one. Yet they retain a psychological frame of reference, for they mean a contradiction in consciousness. Contradiction properly refers to statements in discourse, and when we encounter it we expect something to be discarded. As Gombrich shows, that is indeed how intellectual progress is made: hypotheses are proposed, tested, and, if need be, discarded. But the way of the dialectician is inclusion only. As Gombrich sarcastically comments, "If the dialectician finds a hypothesis confirmed by some evidence he is happy; if other evidence seems to conflict he is even happier, for he can then introduce the refinement of 'contradiction.' "[53]

The goal of Hegel's phenomenology is to break down division in the mind. Toward this end it protests that the methodology of science (of science so-called, opposed to the *true* science of phenomenology) is false because it combines incompatible modes of knowing, empirical and rational. The two do not indeed overlap, but Hegelians ignore the fact that in every science there is a definite method for moving between them. The unconscious as developed in the science of psychology is not a blank check for motivation as modern Hegelians have said: psychoanalysis entails particular, painstaking methods for filling the gaps among the phenomena of our consciousness.

Of course dialectical criticism, if this means simply criti-

---

52 Freud, *Collected Papers*, II, 232.
53 Gombrich, *Meditations on a Hobby Horse*, 88–89.

cism responsive to antithetical implications, is entirely unobjectionable, for such implications are characteristic of complex imaginative art. Often a writer will make an artistic structure by holding opposing forces in balance without resolving them and may run into the danger of seeming to impose a resolution if the dramatized conflict is taut.

One might say that antithetical effects become precarious, approach the condition of problematic effects without necessarily turning into them, when the artist dramatizes an unstable, unresolved balance of contrary attitudes toward a focused character, image, or idea. At the end of *Women in Love*, Lawrence establishes a balance between his hero's need for heterosexual and homosexual affection—an uneasy balance and one that is not always successfully maintained earlier in the novel. Purer but also more rigid examples are *Lord Jim* and *The Great Gatsby*, in which the narrator of each strenuously maintains a double attitude of contempt and admiration for the title character, conscious always of the difficulty of holding counter emotions together.[54] And the tension of opposites is brilliantly condensed in Dostoevski's *Notes from Underground*, where the comprehending observer is himself the oppositely charged central figure whom he observes.

Although these opposing attitudes cannot themselves be called unconscious, for they are openly held in view, it is not farfetched to suppose the existence of a potentially troublesome unconscious conflict in the mind of the writer. We perceive a tension between the centripetal force of his judgment trying to hold things together and the centrifugal force of his imagination. One must emphasize that the presumable presence of an unconscious conflict in the mind of the writer is not as important as the fact that he contains the potentially disruptive effects of such conflict in his art, that he prevents the inhibiting consequences of conflict from resulting in incoherence and an impression of insincerity. It is always possible for

---

54 See F. Scott Fitzgerald's remark, "The test of a first-rate intelligence is the ability to hold two opposed ideas in the mind at the same time, and still retain the ability to function," quoted in Lionel Trilling, *The Liberal Imagination* (New York: Doubleday Anchor, 1957), 238.

an energetic and disciplined artist to become aware of incongruous elements in his art and to either eliminate them or work them into a more complex synthesis, thus converting potential weakness into actual strength. But in a taut fictional balance, especially if the central consciousness of the story is not clearly removed from the writer's own, the writer is bound to feel a pressure to let one or the other contrary take over; if he finds a form that holds the balance, as Conrad does in *Lord Jim* and Fitzgerald in *The Great Gatsby*, that form is likely to seem brittle, as if opposing energies are stiff from being so tightly held. Not surprisingly, neither writer found another formal structure which was so successful.

The inherent instability of polarized attitudes, the tendency of each contrary to shun the presence of its opposite and clamor for exclusive recognition, is what the psychoanalysts call ambivalence. The word has acquired a weaker meaning in general usage which somewhat obscures the present issue. One might well hear it said that Marlow is ambivalent toward Jim or that Nick is ambivalent toward Gatsby. But their mixed feelings are wholly conscious. That is quite different from saying that Hamlet is ambivalent toward Claudius because his hostility is disproportionate and leads us to infer the unconscious presence of a positive attitude toward Claudius in Hamlet's mind.

The difficulty of maintaining a balance is naturally increased when the pressure for social and psychological change, in whatever direction, is intense—as it has been during the last two hundred years. Hence Romantic and post-Romantic artists, with revolutionary orientations, are notable both for the problematic aspects of some of their most impressive achievements and for the extraordinary mental energy that seems to have gone into offsetting such effects. We are only partly convinced, for example, that the renunciation of vulgar sexuality in so many fictions of Lawrence and Shaw is motivated by moral idealism, yet the charge of unconscious hypocrisy is certainly weakened by their amazing resourcefulness in making the heroic stance plausible and by their keen insight into unconscious hypocrisy in the works of

others.

Lawrence's procedures as a critic are especially revealing, for they illustrate the revolutionary critic's urgent need to formulate an alternative conception of the unconscious. His *Studies in Classic American Literature* provides sharp glimpses into the subversive implications of some American classics: the implication in Poe that death is the price of idealized love; in Hawthorne that the Puritan ethic is more honored in the breach than the observance; in Melville that the "white consciousness" is forging its own doom. But, when Lawrence attempts to formulate these perceptions into something like a theory, he tends to impose rather than discover imbalances in the works' imaginative energies. The theory consists of his often quoted distinction between the "tale" and the "artist," between the "alien undertone" of the work and the moralized intention. The tale's moral, more urgent because it is suppressed, is to be honored; the artist's moral, "the love and produce cackle," is to be dismissed as a screen: "Never trust the artist. Trust the tale."[55] This theory clearly neither respects the artist's success in balancing antithetical implications (which is surely part of the truth in "Ligeia," *The Scarlet Letter*, and *Moby-Dick*) nor focuses on what I have called problematic effects (perhaps a certain smugness in Poe or coyness in Hawthorne) that invite explanation in terms of a repressed unconscious. Prompted by the need to make the unconscious itself purposeful—in Norman Mailer's phrase, to make it "the navigator at the seat of our being"[56]—Lawrence, like Blake and Shelley before him, divides the work into progressive and regressive segments and implies that this judgment is aesthetic as well as moral.

It is apparent that, despite Lawrence's numerous insights into unconscious motives in his fiction and his criticism and despite even an occasional formulation consistent with them (like his "thumb in the scale" image alluded to previously),

---

55 This slogan does not mean, as it is so often made to mean in citations, either a distinction between the knowable intention of the work and the unknowable intention in the mind of the artist (*i.e.*, a version of the Intentional Fallacy) or a distinction between what the artist tells us imaginatively in his fiction and what he tells us discursively elsewhere. Lawrence meant something considerably bolder, a distinction between competing meanings *within* the work.

56 Norman Mailer, *Advertisements for Myself* (New York: Putnam, 1959), 386.

his distinction between the tale and the artist will not help us illuminate the relation between art and the unconscious. I had hoped to use "the tale and the artist" as a title, but realized this phrase must cause confusion; it rests on the validity of the notion of unconscious intention or unconscious meaning, which, as I noted earlier, makes sense only if one means by these phrases an interpretation or logical chain which is completed from outside the work and which must be incompatible with an interpretation fully implied by the text. When these phrases are used as if they were critically valid, we discover that "unconscious" is taken to mean preconscious or that "intention" is taken to mean an idea only potentially present in the work. The latter critical tactic for getting around the idea of problematic effects requires further comment.

The tendency to think of intention in an elevated sense, to gather and unite discrepant effects into a higher idea of what a poem means, is characteristic of Romantic criticism, and M. H. Abrams discusses it admirably in *The Mirror and the Lamp* under the heading "Romantic polysemism." It persists in our day and deserves to be understood and evaluated as a contemporary phenomenon.

Consider Empson's recently published discussion of "The Rime of the Ancient Mariner."[57] Empson finds the poem (especially the first version, before the marginal notes were added and other changes made) to be deeply antireligious, concerned with guilt and revulsion from life far greater than any possible motivation and hence an unconscious protest against the way we are made, an attitude he misleadingly calls "neurotic." But does this satisfactorily account for the disparity between the crime of shooting the albatross and the subsequent horrors visited upon the Mariner? It points clearly to the difficulty of the Christian view of the poem (Empson notes, for example, that the horrors do not really cease when the Mariner feels love and the albatross falls off), but there is some truth to that view. The poem does affirm the idea of

---

57 William Empson, introduction to William Empson and David Pirie (eds.), *Coleridge's Verse: A Selection* (New York: Schocken, 1973), 27–81.

justice, love, and unity with godhead as well as the idea of irrational terror, and affirms both ideas not merely through authorial commentary but through concrete presentation. The essential difficulty is that Coleridge does not bring these ideas into firm relation with one another. "The Ancient Mariner" remains a strong poem because its effects are strong—and doubtless a vivid yet unresolvable work exercises a special fascination for its interpreters—but it is not finally coherent.

Instead of trying to show that the poem's effects are not really problematic or that they are best explained by the hypothesis of an unconscious conflict in the mind of the poet which interferes at a certain point with his management of the poem, Empson adopts an idealistic or Romantic tactic: the poem is really the idea that the text seeks to realize; if the poet has in some sense betrayed this idea, as the critic admits, then this betrayal becomes part of his intention. Empson actually uses the tricky word *intention* in this enlarged sense. Thus, what Collingwood calls "corruption of consciousness" is thought of as a stage in a dialectical progress to a higher unity. The unconscious is bypassed; unconscious meaning is on the same plane artistically as conscious meaning.

By such reasoning we are led not to depth psychology but to metaphysics, not to individual minds but to composite mind. The word *problematic* is often used by critics in the Hegelian tradition but, as a rule, not in a mundane enough sense to lead them to make the sort of differentiations I have attempted. For example, they describe as problematic the gulf between words on the one hand and objects, feelings, and events on the other; that is, they see reading and writing themselves, not merely local effects, as problematic. I stress the contrast because what is involved here is not simply different but rival traditions, each forced to define itself against the other.

It is not entirely surprising, then, that the theory of imagination I have found most useful is one developed by an aesthetician who has learned to use the insights of Hegel and Croce without their metaphysical framework and to develop 39 these within the alternate framework of British empirical philosophy. He is therefore able to make pointed use of the Freudian concept of a repressed unconscious.

In the middle section of his *Principles of Art,* Collingwood addresses himself at once to the elusive distinction between feeling and thought. Thought, he observes, is always bipolar, always divisible into true and false, whereas feeling seems to admit of no contradiction. Yet all we can ever discover about feeling, though it seems to arise independently of thought, is *through* thought. The terms are opposed, yet they overlap. He then reminds us that feelings may be subdivided into sensations, which are in flux, and emotions, which are stable, and he devises this extremely useful three-part scheme: (a) the preverbal level of fluctuating sensa; (b) the level of consciousness at which, through language, sensa are capable of being held in view or imagined; (c) the level of intellect at which feelings are placed in relation to one another (and at which, at a further remove, the thoughts about imaginative ideas admit of being thought about). In this progressive scheme each level modifies the preceding one, so that the second level of consciousness (or imagination, defined as "the new form feeling takes when transformed by the activity of consciousness") will show features of both the first and third levels. We will see how helpful this description is in clarifying the imagination's peculiar relationship to feeling on the one hand and thought on the other.

If we take seriously the familiar idea that sensa are in constant flux, the question arises, How can any sensum last long enough for its relation to another to be studied? We usually blur this question by speaking illicitly of sense *data* that one can appeal to or be acquainted with. But there is something in the mind which is *like* "lasting sensa." When one becomes aware of a sensum, one seems to liberate it from the flux and perpetuate it, to convert it from "impression" to "idea," in Hume's terminology. The activity of consciousness gives a new form to feeling (*i.e.,* to sensa plus the inevitable emotional charge upon them), and this new form is *imagination*.

To think about relations among sensa, then, is really to

think not of sensa or impressions but of imaginative ideas. As Hume said, the immediate concern of thought is with ideas, not impressions. But the level of consciousness is not yet the level of intellect. Only intellect can interpret, can determine whether these "lasting sensa" or imaginative ideas are true or false.

We can formulate the modification from first to second level this way. A conscious being is not free to decide what feelings to have but he is able to dominate them. In becoming aware of my feelings, I do not yet know what I am—for placing feelings in relation to one another is the work of intellect—but I do know that I am something to which a feeling belongs, not something belonging to it.

Turning to the modification from second to third level, Collingwood observes that consciousness, though distinct from intellect, is a form of thought and so will exhibit some of the bipolarity characteristic of all thought. When we attend to what we see and hear, we divide the feelings present in the mind into part we are conscious of and part we are not conscious of (the part removed from attention).

And this enables us to explain how imagination can become infected with falsity. In a sense imagination cannot be divided into truthful and erroneous segments. What feels true *is* true, as the Romantics insisted. But the assertion "This is how I feel" does in fact admit of an opposite, namely, "This is *not* how I feel." A feeling can be *disowned,* and an idea one seeks to express can seem falsified when certain elements essential to it are disowned. Collingwood's description of the process of corruption is like Freud's account of repression with which, in fact, it is explicitly associated:

> If a given feeling is . . . recognized, it is converted from impression to idea, and thus dominated or domesticated by consciousness. If it is not recognized, it is simply. . . left unattended to, or ignored. But there is a third alternative. The recognition may take place abortively. It may be attempted, but prove a failure. . . .
> First we direct our attention towards a certain feeling, or become conscious of it. Then we take fright at what we have recognized: not because the feeling, as an impression, is an alarming impression, but because the idea into which we are converting it

proves an alarming idea. We cannot see our way to dominate it, and shrink from persevering in the attempt. We therefore give it up, and turn our attention to something less intimidating.

I call this the "corruption" of consciousness; because consciousness permits itself to be bribed or corrupted in the discharge of its function, being distracted from a formidable task towards an easier one. So far from being a bare possibility it is an extremely common fact. . . .

This process is sometimes called self-deception. Collingwood discourages use of the word, noting that a man cannot literally lie to himself. He calls it instead a form of self-mismanagement: "It is a misdoing, a pretending that the given emotion is a different emotion or the emotion of a different person or both. And this pretense, since it cannot be simply conscious or unconscious, must be understood as taking place on the threshold. It is the malperformance of the act of converting impression to idea, the result of one's wishing to think of himself as too innocent or too broadminded to be horrified." *Horrified* may seem too specific a word, but it is precise. Collingwood shares with Freud the idea that fear is always the cause of the mind's submitting itself to division.[58]

This theory of imagination, based upon the idea of a corruption of consciousness, highlights as an aesthetic issue the question of candor or of sincerity, to use the word that literary critics have debated. As we noted earlier, despite the deserved disrepute of the term, there does seem to be a deeper connection between the integrity of a poem's effects and the integrity of the artist's consciousness, a connection not generally appreciated.

René Wellek charges that "there is no relation between 'sincerity' and value as art. The volumes of agonizingly felt love poetry perpetrated by adolescents and the dreary (however fervently felt) religious verse which fills libraries, are sufficient proof of this."[59] The statement is useful for reminding us that an earnest tone does not necessarily make for a

58 Collingwood, *The Principles of Art*, 157–224.
59 René Wellek and Austin Warren, *Theory of Literature* (3rd ed.; London: Penguin Books, 1973), 80.

better poem than an ironic tone and that simplicity and directness are not inherently superior to complexity and indirectness. It is useful also for calling attention to the fact that it is certainly possible to write badly by not knowing enough about using words to secure the desired effect. But how is the desired effect achieved? How does one make sincerity convincing? Has it nothing to do with feeling rightly, with caring about truth telling?

W. K. Wimsatt makes a more pointed objection to the term and leads us farther. He says there is no equation between the expressionists' key term "sincerity" and the formalists' key term "unity."[60] But I believe there is. It is true that merely trying to be sincere is not enough, that the artist must also be convincing. But expression is convincing precisely when all the means of expression are coordinated. Gombrich puts it well:

> The feeling of "sincerity" we have in the face of certain masterpieces cannot be disputed, any more than of "nobility," "purity," or "discipline." The suspicion arises that they are all metaphors pointing to a similar centre. When we find a teacher's frown "expressive," we are not concerned (unless we are the pupils) whether his rage is "real" or only "put on." We rather mean that it is convincing, because it is not merely a symbol in isolation (that would strike us as false), but that it is co-ordinated with other symbols of anger, a scornful voice, a tight lip, and set in the proper curve of rising anger. It is possible that most people will perform more convincingly if they talk themselves into real anger, but surely it is not this that would make it more moral. And so we are led to the conclusion that once more it is the submission of the part to the whole, the element of control, of bridled emotion rather than disconnected symptoms, that is responsible for the intuition of "honesty," and that may make art analogous to a moral experience.[61]

In other words, it is not a question of truly expressing one's real feelings, which is what sincerity commonly means. But it is a question of caring enough about what one has to say, of being sufficiently committed to it, to coordinate all the effects.

60 Wimsatt, *The Verbal Icon*, 9.
61 Gombrich, *Meditations on a Hobby Horse*, 26.

This is true even when the sentiments of a poem are handled with obvious irony (as in Donne's *Songs and Sonets*) or with obvious artifice (as in Sidney's famous sonnet where the sudden effect of sincerity in the final line—"Fool, said my Muse to me, look in thy heart and write"—is plainly contrived). Such poems merely prove that the mind is complex enough to be detached and committed at the same time.

If the effect of sincerity depends on the coordination of all effects, it follows that there must be no unintended effects to undermine the others. The existence of these, whether or not we track down their causes to unconscious influence, is not much discussed in literary theory, and, as we have seen, they are not easily managed with the customary tools. Yet problematic effects are important enough to make even our standard critical terminology (*e.g.*, irony, ambiguity, paradox) look a little rusty.

We are accustomed to describing all sorts of discrepancy as irony, all sorts of alternative meaning as ambiguity or ambivalence, all sorts of apparent contradiction as paradox. In every case we imply a fully controlling artistic consciousness. But how far can one carry the debate over whether Melville presented Captain Vere ironically if Melville is perceived as having felt both positively and negatively about Vere and as being unable to resolve these conflicting attitudes and deciding finally to shift the focus of his story? Can we really use the term ambiguity as Empson does to refer to the subversion of intention in *Paradise Lost*? He states, "That |Milton's| feelings were crying out against his appalling theology in favour of freedom, happiness and the pursuit of truth was I think not obvious to him. . . . The poem gets its great merit from presenting the real *ambiguity* |my emphasis| of its theme with such dramatic and insinuating power." [62] And how apt is the term paradox to describe, say, Hemingway's title *Winner Take Nothing*? The term is formally apt but, insofar as the stories convey the idea, in spite of their avowed theme, that

---

62 William Empson, *The Structure of Complex Words* (London: Chatto and Windus, 1951), 104.

losing is indeed satisfying because winning entails too much guilt, the paradox dissolves into a literal truth.

Two conclusions may be drawn from all that has been said so far. One is that the nearer the artist comes to avoiding problematic effects, the less valid are any claims that the work contains evidence of a counter-intended or unconscious meaning. This conclusion lends support to those critics who have resisted the application of this central psychological concept to the study of literature. The second conclusion, however, points in the opposite direction. It is that many literary effects, even in great works, may be called problematic because they strike the competent reader (whose reliability cannot be taken for granted) as partly unintended. These are not exactly failures of objectification, resulting from a deficiency of energy and/or skill, nor are they simply traceable to intractable material. They are rather imbalances in the emotional weightings of the work, which remain puzzling until we connect the broken chain of implications in the work with an idea assumed to have been repressed by the artist. And these problematic effects must be the primary evidence for establishing the importance of the concept of the unconscious in literary criticism.

I have sifted and combined elements of what may roughly be called formalist and expressionist aesthetics in order to establish in literary criticism the importance of mind and particularly of unconscious mind. It is evident that the analysis of problematic effects, which I have concluded to be the principal basis for justifying this importance, implies an act of evaluation in some sense of that troublesome word. And I think it would round off this essay to inquire what kind of evaluation we are talking about and why a certain opprobrium attaches to the term.

Like *intention*, the word *evaluation* really contains and confuses two different meanings, one of which is alien to the spirit of interpretation and one inseparable from it. I have said that intention may refer either to the plan in the mind of the artist as he writes, which is inaccessible to the critic, or to 45

certain qualities of the work—its coherence and artifice—
which must have been caused by an intender. The distinction,
in fact, seemed so plain that I wondered whether the word had
become scandalous in order to avert an inference that must
sooner or later be drawn from the second meaning—namely,
that certain kinds of formal disunity must correspond to a
psychological disunity. The case of evaluation is similar.

The meaning of the word which is alien to the spirit of
interpretation postulates a separable judicial standard. As Frye
rightly points out, the kind of evaluation that ranks poets
one-two-three according to such a standard is at best unnecessary because it will soon enough be apparent that some texts
yield to the critic a greater richness of implication than others.
But there is another kind of evaluative judgment that is, as
Richards puts it, empirical rather than idealistic or, in Leavis'
phrasing, implicit in realizing and describing.[63] When we say
how a poem holds together or when we indicate where or
how it does not, we do not fall back upon a separate judicial
standard. Again the distinction seems sufficiently plain to
make one wonder whether some critics have obscured it to
avert the inference of unconscious motivation which might
well be drawn from the observations of discontinuities and
disproportions.

One of the most impassioned modern denunciations of
evaluation was published in 1930 by G. Wilson Knight, and a
brief look at his argument will give us a better understanding
of the term's bad reputation. Knight distinguished sharply
between criticism or evaluation and interpretation or elucida-
tion. The one he called "a judgment of vision," the other "a
reconstruction of vision." Although acknowledging that "the
greater part of poetic commentary pursued a middle course,"
he says that, in regard to the greatest work, "criticism beats
against it idly" and that commentary on it "must necessarily
tend towards a pure interpretation." We should "submit ourselves with utmost passivity to the poet's work" because

63 I am indebted to John Casey, *The Language of Criticism*, 167 and elsewhere, for
   citing these relevant passages from Richards and Leavis and developing this distinction.

"when we think 'critically' we see faults which are not implicit in [it] . . . but merely figments of our own minds." [64]

As an introduction to Shakespeare, these statements are sound enough. And indeed my own essays on major writers in the pages to follow are, for the most part, interpretation in Knight's sense. But his attack on criticism is more sweeping and harsh than the case of Shakespeare suggests. It is tied in with a certain psychological theory according to which intellect and imagination are sharply divided and intention does not at all pertain to imagination (hence, to artistic design) but only to the judgmental intellect:

> In those soliloquies where Brutus and Macbeth try to clarify their own motives into clean-cut concepts, we may see good examples of the irrelevance born by "intentions" to the instinctive power which is bearing man towards his fate: it is the same with the poet. Milton's puritanical "intentions" bear little relevance to his Satan. "Intentions" belong to the plane of intellect and memory: the swifter consciousness that awakens in poetic composition touches subtleties and heights and depths unknowable by intellect and intractable to memory. [65]

I too have been irritated by censorious critical judgments, but I consider the principles Knight outlines unsound, even a little insidious. The reference to Milton suggests that his view is the simple opposite of C. S. Lewis'. Where Lewis can see nothing of Milton in Satan, Knight can see nothing of him in the puritanical intentions. Neither critic perceives any discrepancy in the poem's effects. And this is *Milton*, who can after all sustain pure interpretation to a very considerable degree. Imagine submitting with utmost passivity to the vision of a Faulkner, in whose work, for all its power, the currents of feeling are often awry, or to the vision of Norman Mailer, in whose work so many vivid and energetic effects are tainted with vanity and spite. Imagine submitting with utmost passivity to the vision of Ian Fleming or subscribing to a method which, as one antireferential American critic candidly

---

64 G. Wilson Knight, *The Wheel of Fire: Interpretations of Shakespearean Tragedy* (4th rev. and enlarged ed.; London: Methuen, 1949), 1–3.

65 *Ibid.*, 7.

puts it, "shows to best advantage on unpromising material."[66] We may suspect that, when the mind of the critic is appreciably more sophisticated than the mind of the artist, submission is in truth a subtle form of domination. The refusal to judge any effect as crude, clumsy, or problematic is a mock humility permitting the critic to absorb the artist.

There is something unpleasant, perhaps authoritarian, in being told that when we think critically about a great artist we are bound to see faults which are not in the work but only in ourselves. It is surely dangerous to assert as a principle that a work of genius is necessarily free of faults. Our theory of mind and imagination indicates that no one, not even a great poet, is immune from faultily interpreting his own feelings and that everyone, even a critic, may possess some intuition of the unconscious processes of others. Someone who doesn't begin to share the poetic gift of a Milton, but who is differently situated (*i.e.*, who has different insights and different blindnesses), may see things in Milton's poems that the poet himself did not so clearly see. Such intuitions may be wrong, but they are not presumptively so; they derive from our intuitive understanding of our own mental processes. No doubt criticism exposes the critic's limitations, but an honorable wrestling with a text is surely preferable to a passive surrender to the perfect faith that the artist cannot err.

We can still preserve the idea that art represents a superior "ordering of what in most minds is disordered." Richards, who defends this idea in these words, goes on to explain its consistency with our recognition of the artist's "*failures* to bring order out of chaos." That they are more conspicuous than those of other men, he says, "is due in part at least to his greater audacity; it is a penalty of ambition and a consequence of his greater plasticity."[67] I add to this the observation that most of us are capable of candor in dealing with indifferent matters, but we find it much more difficult to be engaged and truthful at once. One of the reasons we honor the serious

[66] Stanley Fish, "Affective Stylistics," *New Literary History*, II (Autumn, 1970), 124.

[67] I. A. Richards, *Principles of Literary Criticism* (New York: Harcourt, Brace, 1949), 60.

artist is that, with his rhetorical skill, he so often finds a way to be or to seem to be both, to hold (in W. B. Yeats's fine phrase) reality and justice in a single image.

I am not of course saying that every defect in a completed work of art can be traced to an unconscious process in the artist's mind. Often, especially in lesser work, defects are most apparently due to intractable subject matter or to insufficient energy and skill. But these causes have limited application. Intractable subject matter could help to account for a certain clumsiness even in major work, but it is not difficult to distinguish this probable cause from that of unconscious distortion. For example, the awkwardness of using the eating of an apple to dramatize a massively consequential sin against divine law is very probably evidence of Milton's practical difficulty in adapting primitive narrative material to seventeenth-century literary needs. Surely this problem in *Paradise Lost* is different from the problem of Satan's degradation. Or so it seems to me, although Waldock, the critic most responsible for calling attention to this questionable degradation, traces the defect to intractable subject matter and is diffident to a fault about granting critical sanction to the concept of unconscious mind.

As for art lacking in energy and skill—that is, underimagined art—it does not by definition go deep enough to yield problematic effects: we cannot hypothesize a corruption of consciousness except in connection with art of a certain imaginative energy. Hence, although faultfinding is admittedly not one of mankind's most lovable traits, the kind of faultfinding we have been concerned with here is unusual. Given the medial position of the imagination among our mental faculties, truthful and untruthful artistic effects are closely intertwined. Separating them is a complex act of evaluation, which does not at all resemble a censure.

In a famous letter, Lawrence speaks of the "blood" as being "wiser than the intellect": "we can go wrong in our minds but what our blood feels and believes and says, is always true."[68] It is the same distinction Knight urges upon us when he

68 Lawrence, *The Letters of D. H. Lawrence*, 64.

scorns intentions as belonging to the plane of intellect and honors the swifter consciousness at work in creation. This essentially Romantic idea—that the imagination is necessarily truthful whereas the intellect is unreliable—is certainly valid up to a point. Imagination does have an intimate connection with feeling and like feeling harbors no negations but only contraries. But Lawrence and Knight do not recognize any overlap between feeling and thought, imagination and intellect, hence do not recognize, at least in theory, any way in which imagination can err. In the process of self-knowing, we can err before the intellect proper is brought into play. Moreover, the intellect, for all its limitations, is the only instrument we have for disentangling the special kind of error made in this process. Intellect helps preserve the truth of the imagination by rationally accounting for its excesses.

Finally, the exercise of critical judgment, based on the assumption that an artist's imagination is capable of error, helps to keep in balance the delicate question of the reader's reliability. If the critic thinks he ought to submit entirely to the vision of the artist, the suppressed moralist in him will probably find another, more questionable outlet. Critics like Knight and Lawrence tend to build their own systems and judge the works of others not only with the force of their individualities but ideologically. If the critic circumvents the responsibility of judgment by rejecting altogether the idea of validity in interpretation—and this is the position taken nowadays by many of those attracted to structuralism—then he implies inevitably that the reader cannot be wrong. Nor of course can the writer.

This extreme relativism or skepticism, like the extreme piety of the Romantic critic, is the reduction to absurdity of what I take to be Freud's principal instruction for the literary critic. What psychoanalysis teaches the critic above all is that, although any writer may communicate to some degree with any reader despite the differences in their circumstances, the blindnesses and limitations on both sides will always result in a margin of error. In other words, the question of the reader's reliability is inseparable from that of the writer's, and to eliminate the question of the writer's reliability is to eliminate the only standard by which the reader's can be measured.

When we think of practice rather than theory, we do not have to state these points so contentiously, for acts of implicit evaluation are common to the point of inconspicuousness. And this essay as a whole might be described as an attempt to contribute a measure of logical rigor and psychological sophistication to the universally practiced if not universally approved act of evaluation.

THE UNCONSCIOUS
IN LITERARY ART

Part 2

PARRICIDE, REGICIDE, AND DEICIDE IN *HAMLET*

SEVERAL references were made in Part 1 to the unconscious mind of Shakespeare's Hamlet. I am well aware that this manner of speaking assumes more than many critics are willing to grant. Therefore I shall preface my interpretation proper with some comments on the resistance to using the concept of the unconscious in critical analyses of the play. My aim is to winnow out the rational component of that resistance—for there is one—and expose the irrational part for the prejudice it is.

Freud's penetrating brief explanation of Hamlet's delay in killing Claudius, turning on the idea of his unconscious identification with the man who did away with his father and took his father's place with his mother, has been brought into disrepute by several objectionable features of Ernest Jones's famous elaboration of it (although, in fairness to Jones, one must admit that hints of these are present in his mentor's comment). One of them is Jones's extended discussion of Hamlet's childhood, his case-history approach to fictional characterization, which gives us a chapter called "Tragedy and the Mind of the Infant." Another is his blurring of our sense of the play as an artistic structure by discussing it in terms of the author's personal life ("The Hamlet in Shakespeare") and in terms of mythology as distinct from literary art ("Hamlet's Place in Mythology"). And a third is his use of the label neurotic, his implication that Shakespeare was dramatizing an individual problem *rather* than a culturally representative one.

The first two of these objectionable lines of inquiry are the less objectionable when we realize that Jones indicates, roughly at least, that he knows they are metacritical. Although his book mixes in a good deal of criticism proper, much of what annoys students of literature about *Hamlet and Oedipus* is simply the result of his coming to the text with psychological rather than critical questions.

The description of Hamlet as a neurotic troubles me somewhat more. For one thing, it shuts us off from the political and philosophical dimensions of the play, which are nearly as prominent as the psychological dimension and, I will show, closely bound up with it. For another, the term neurotic implies a weaker Hamlet than the one we find in the play. Perhaps the use of the term here can even be challenged on psychological grounds, for neurosis refers less to the mere presence of unconscious conflict, or even to its intensity, than to a particular way of solving such conflict, a way characterized by what Freud calls "moral masochism," or the deriving of pleasure from renunciation itself. Hamlet does not shy from his fears this way. He strives to the utmost of his powerful will and intelligence to discover the fears that prevent him from doing what he believes he ought to do. The fact that he fails (although evidence suggests that he begins to succeed toward the end of the play) testifies to the difficulty of his quest but does not indicate any weakness for which he can be held responsible.

There is another aspect of Jones's book which I find more objectionable than any of these, although little is said about it. This is the idea that Hamlet's unconscious conflict—despite the fact that it is shown by the text to be artfully created—was not consciously understood by Shakespeare himself. He was "unaware of its nature," as is the audience (except, presumably, those who possess the "psycho-analytical solution"). "We reach the apparent paradox that the hero, the poet, and the audience are all profoundly moved by feelings due to a conflict the source of which they are unaware." But can so much artful elaboration really be credited to the unconscious mind, in a sense of the word not covered by the term imagination? And when an audience is profoundly baffled, is it also profoundly moved? Jones offers us a picture of the aesthetic transaction as something that passes from the unconscious mind of the poet to the unconscious mind of the audience without going through the consciousness of either, much like the famous description of the university lecture that passes from the notes of the professor to the notes of the student without going through the mind of either. Such psychoanalytical purism is reminiscent of formalist purism; both quite separate art from the life of the mind.

This notion of unconscious art leads Jones to some curious inferences. For example, he cites the passage from Hamlet's third soliloquy describing life's "fardels"—"the whips and scorns of time / Th' oppressor's wrong, the proud man's contumely, / The pangs of despised love, the law's delay"— and comments that these do not fit Hamlet's personal circumstances, as they do not, or at least not closely. But instead of supposing that Hamlet is here talking as he often does about the human condition generally, Jones surmises that these fardels crept into the play unconsciously because they were Shakespeare's personal difficulties. He is heedless of the objection that, if we can account for them only in this way, we must be talking about an artistic fault.

So much for what I call the rational resistance to employing the concept of unconscious mind in discussions of *Hamlet*. I do not believe, however, that this silences the opposition which the Freud-Jones view of the play has aroused. The sticking point, after all, is the unconscious itself. And when it comes to that, even critical argument of a very high level is often conducted with a remarkable illogicality.

Consider for illustrative purposes Reuben Brower's recently published *Hero and Saint: Shakespeare and the Graeco-Roman Heroic Tradition*, a book that presents, intelligently and reasonably, a thesis that is readily acceptable as far as it goes—namely, that Shakespeare was trying to harmonize the Homeric tradition of a hero of blind impulse with a new heroic image of man governed by reason and touched by Christian kindness. But Brower, influenced by E. E. Stoll, establishes his position with the following curious statement: "Shakespeare . . . was not making psychological studies, he was interested rather in what happens when actors are placed in a plight which for the most part is not of their own making." Is a psychological conception, then, only one in which characters are wholly responsible for what happens to them, in which their plight is entirely of their own making? It isn't that Brower views Shakespeare as altogether unpsychological. He freely admits that what is new in Shakespeare's tragic characters, in comparison with those of ancient dramatists, is an "inwardness of the passions, the war with the self." He even admits that the essence of Hamlet, in contrast to one of the heroes of Corneille, "lies in his trouble, his confusion as he faces the conflict." But he evidently balks at the idea that Shakespeare is presenting a character who is moved inwardly by forces not within his own control.

Brower's description of the play's basic conflict follows accordingly. He says, "The ghost that haunts Hamlet is the ghost of the ancient hero in its more primitive forms, Homeric and Germanic. How to be both hero-avenger and the just hero of the Renaissance—that is the question." What the critic does not see is that the idea of killing the king his uncle is excruciating for Hamlet not because he is straining to be just, for he unquestionably regards this vengeance as just, but because it is bound up in his mind with the idea of killing the king his father. King and father, as the play shows, are for him emotionally inseparable, and the queen serves as a vital link between the two ideas. Jones shows well—it is his most valuable addition to Freud's insight—that Hamlet's feelings toward her are more irrational than those toward Claudius. Shakespeare is not pitting Christianity against revenge. He is pitting one kind of revenge implied in regicide against another implied in parricide, knowing that the two actions (or the two impulses) are compounded of the same psychological stuff. In sum, despite some extravagances and incompleteness in the Freud-Jones view from the standpoint of criticism proper, I regard as a prejudice the widespread antagonism to the idea that Shakespeare was knowingly attributing to his hero an unconscious conflict resulting in the inhibition of Hamlet's obvious desire to carry out the assigned task of revenge.

The sources of Shakespeare's *Hamlet* are melodramatic tales of revenge in which the hero cunningly delays killing his fratricidal and incestuous uncle for the sake of both personal safety and a more exquisite satisfaction. His interim behavior, especially his feigned imbecility, puzzles the other characters —except the friend, mother, and wife in whom he confides— but does not puzzle the reader, who is invited to admire his mingling of craft and candor. This is true at any rate of the story told in the medieval *Historia Danica* of Saxo Grammaticus and amplified in the *Histoires Tragiques* (1570) of Belleforest. To assess the contribution of the Elizabethan revenge play is more difficult, for its key link with *Hamlet* is a Hamlet play now lost whose existence must be accepted on the basis of contemporary references. But from various kinds of evidence—the tenor of those references; other revenge plays, especially Kyd's *Spanish Tragedy;* and a later German play which seems to be based on a pre-Shakespearean version of the Hamlet story, perhaps the lost play—scholars have fairly confidently concluded that the lost play must have closely resembled *The Spanish Tragedy* and that its contribution to *Hamlet* must have consisted basically of the ghost, the play within the play, and the tragic denouement in which the avenger dies along with the object of his revenge. Presentation of the delay as a crucial mystery was probably Shakespeare's contribution to the old legend.

Some critics, though a decreasing number, still find no mystery in Hamlet's delay and emphasize the practical difficulties of his task, particularly his doubt of the Ghost's "honesty," which he must settle by means of the play within the play, and his scruple shortly thereafter about killing Claudius at prayer, this being his only private opportunity to do so. But many have raised the objection, surely a decisive one, that these are not the central, emotionally weighted subjects of Hamlet's concern. It is clear enough that his chief worries are his father's death and the idea of his own, his mother's conduct and sexuality in general, his uncle's treachery and lechery, and his own bewildering delay in claiming revenge.

> I do not know
> Why yet I live to say 'This thing's to do,'
> Sith I have cause, and will, and strength, and means
> To do't (IV, iv, 45–48)*

Hamlet could not be more explicit both about his own inability to understand why he cannot fulfill his task and about the plain possibility of doing so, and these lines are spoken after the Ghost-confirming play scene and after the prayer scene. Brower curiously omits the "I do not know" when he quotes this passage.

Moreover, the practical difficulties are introduced in such a way as to make them appear very much like rationalization. Doubt of the Ghost's honesty is stated only once in a soliloquy:

> Why what an ass am I! This is most brave,
> That I, the son of a dear father murdered,
> Prompted to my revenge by heaven and hell,
> Must (like a whore) unpack my heart with words
> And fall a-cursing like a very drab,
> A scullion!
> Fie upon't! foh! About, my brain! I have heard
> That guilty creatures, sitting at a play,
> Have by the very cunning of the scene
> Been struck so to the soul that presently
> They have proclaimed their malefactions;
> For murder, though it have no tongue, will speak
> With most miraculous organ. I'll have these players
> Play something like the murder of my father
> Before mine uncle. I'll observe his looks,
> I'll tent him to the quick; if he but blench,
> I know my course. The spirit that I have seen
> May be a devil; and the devil hath power

---

* Quotations are from William Shakespeare, *Hamlet*, ed. Louis B. Wright and Virginia A. LaMar, Folger Library Series (New York: Washington Square Press, 1958).

T'assume a pleasing shape; yea, and perhaps
Out of my weakness and my melancholy,
As he is very potent with such spirits,
Abuses me to damn me. I'll have grounds
More relative than this. The play's the thing
Wherein I'll catch the conscience of the King.   (II, ii, 590–613)

We observe first that Hamlet, before raising the question of testing the Ghost, reproaches himself bitterly, which would make no sense if he were seriously uncertain about it; second, that the tone of his remaining words is noticeably less troubled and more fluent, as if he has come upon an emotionally safer topic; third, that the very next speech we will hear from him is the "To be or not to be" soliloquy in which the Ghost question is quite forgotten; and finally that, although the king more than blenches, the prince does not thereafter know his course.

The scruple raised in the prayer scene is equally unconvincing. Hamlet will soon send Rosencrantz and Guildenstern to their deaths without "shriving time" and will tell Horatio, "They are not near my conscience" (V,ii,51,64). Then why should the king's death be? Laertes would "cut [his enemy's] throat i' the church" (IV,vii,141), and Hamlet himself spoke in this vein just before coming upon the praying Claudius: "Now could I drink hot blood / And do such bitter business as the day / Would quake to look on" (III,ii,397–99). But now he is stopped by a Christian scruple. Or is it a revenger's scruple? But does a revenger heed scruples?

Let us not belabor the objections to the practical view of Hamlet's delay. It is a lazy viewpoint, making the play trivial and simple, and is not very seriously held any longer. Most of us can agree that Shakespeare intended to suggest more obscure and profound reasons for the delay, though there is considerable disagreement over whether these are psychological reasons.

One of the recent trends in *Hamlet* criticism is the endorsement of a philosophical perspective at the expense of a psychological one. We are told that Hamlet is not so much a character as a condition, not so much a perplexing personality as a state of perplexity into which we enter; that the play asks   61 endlessly receding questions; that it seeks to affirm the all-embracing will of providence. There is of course a strong generalizing or philosophical tendency in Hamlet's speeches, but the advocates of these views seem to ignore the fact that the play is conspicuously about a son, a mother, and a father, about questions of sexuality, guilt, and responsibility. They write as if the psychological slant of Goethe and Coleridge, and later of A. C. Bradley, Freud, and Jones, had to be diverted at all costs.

There is a similar bias among politically oriented critics, who emphasize the rottenness of the state and Hamlet's isolation. This is also important, but it doesn't exclude the possibility of inner conflict. The suspicion seems to prevail that, if the character of Hamlet is a psychological problem of some kind, the prince of Denmark ceases to be representative or heroic. But Shakespeare's breadth and balance are nowhere better seen than in his coordination of all three dimensions. I give the psychological meaning priority because in its concreteness it seems the most illuminative of the others. Hamlet is a son encased in a prince encased in a philosophic man.

In only one respect does the text stymie an approach to *Hamlet* that would emphasize guilt and responsibility. And that is the Ghost. The difficulty posed by his very presence (I don't mean the difficulty posed by such comparatively minor questions as whether the Ghost is to be understood as Catholic or Protestant) is seldom confronted by any critics, mainly, I suppose, because the rhetoric and theatricality of his role contributes to the atmosphere of menace and mystery appropriate to the play from just about any perspective. It has also been pointed out by Maynard Mack, Jr., in *Killing the King*, that the Ghost's speeches effectively establish a thematic contrast between a pristine past and a corrupt present, which allows us to think of Hamlet's conflict not merely as individual but also as cultural and even religious. But the fact remains that questions of human responsibility must begin to look comical in a world where supernatural visitors may intrude with essential information and obligatory commands.

This is not a general argument against supernaturalism in

literature. The gods in Homer and the God of the Bible belong to a sufficiently naïve universe to be understood metaphorically. The oracle in Oedipus and the witches and ghost in Macbeth, though supernatural, do not specify or command and can generally be accepted as psychological projections, if not simply as atmosphere. Ernest Jones is content to think of the Ghost in Hamlet in this way because its commands strongly suggest the function of conscience. So they do, but the Ghost is positively presented as another being seen by others, at least in Act I, and not hallucinated by Hamlet. We do not feel that the Ghost as conscience quite corresponds to Shakespeare's intention, though we might well feel that his intention in this matter is too casual altogether.

In general, of course, Shakespeare is relaxed enough ideologically to avoid the problems Milton gets into by insisting on both absolute divine will and absolute human freedom. Hamlet can talk about heaven and hell, human and divine, without becoming illogical. But, in creating the Ghost, the artist uses a bit of folklore so literally and obtrusively as to perplex the serious critic. The only way I can think of for a ghost as literal and morally obtrusive as this one to coexist in an artistic structure with a theme of guilt and responsibility is the way of Henry James's The Turn of the Screw, where the point is precisely the possibility of both naturalistic and supernaturalistic readings. James's story is an epistemological puzzle, which the author, if not his critics, described tactfully as an "amusette." But the naturalistic aspects of Hamlet are so dominant and searching that the Ghost finally has a trivializing effect on the play. Let us acknowledge the weakness of Shakespeare's imaginative logic at this point and accept the Ghost, as far as we can, in terms of atmosphere.

Psychological interpretation of Hamlet was launched in earnest by Goethe and Coleridge, whose views were favored by many critics during the nineteenth century and are still popular with laymen today. In Goethe's words, "a beautiful, pure, noble, and most moral nature, without the strength of nerve that makes a hero, sinks beneath a burden which it can neither bear nor throw off." Coleridge saw Hamlet as a man endowed with "a great, an almost enormous intellectual activity, and a proportionate aversion to real action consequent upon it." Critics in our century have energetically discredited these conceptions of a weak or indecisive Hamlet with the solid argument that he is shown to be capable of daring and even remorseless action at least twice: when he stabs the eavesdropper behind the arras and when he exchanges the king's letters, thus sending Rosencrantz and Guildenstern to the death intended for himself. Goethe and Coleridge idealize Hamlet's reluctance to kill Claudius—Goethe forgetting Hamlet's resistance to passivity and Coleridge failing to see that excessive intellectual activity makes more sense as a symptom than as a cause of such irrational reluctance.

Digressing briefly in *The Interpretation of Dreams*, Freud brilliantly strengthens the "inhibition" view of Hamlet's delay. He would have us see that it is neither the task alone nor Hamlet's character alone that prevents him from obeying the Ghost's command and that of his own conscience but a specific relation between the two, which he calls "the peculiar nature of the task." Since what is valuable in Jones's book is primarily what he took from Freud's comment, the core of the latter will serve as a nucleus for a somewhat different kind of elaboration: "Hamlet is able to do anything—except take vengeance on the man who did away with his father and took his father's place with his mother, the man who shows him the repressed wishes of his own childhood realized. Thus the loathing which should drive him on to revenge is replaced in him by self-reproaches, by scruples of conscience, which remind him that he is literally no better than the sinner whom he is to punish. Here I have translated into conscious terms what was bound to remain unconscious in Hamlet's mind."

Hamlet's self-accusations, not to mention his references to bad dreams, clearly indicate that he feels guilty about something; in the absence of misdeeds, something may well mean wishes or intentions which, because they are unknown to him, can be called unconscious. This sounds subtle when spelled out, but the evidence suggesting it is strongly dramatized. For example, it is strange that Hamlet should refer to himself as "revengeful" and "ambitious" in his well-known speech to Ophelia: "Get thee to a nunnery! Why wouldst thou be a breeder of sinners? I am myself indifferent honest, but yet I could accuse me of such things that it were better my mother had not borne me. I am very proud, revengeful, ambitious; with more offenses at my beck than I have thoughts to put them in, imagination to give them shape, or time to act them in. What should such fellows as I do, crawling between earth and heaven? We are arrant knaves all; believe none of us" (III,i,131–39). He believes his task of revenge to be honorable, not sinful, so his sense of being revengeful by nature seems to reflect an unadmitted envy, the emotion widely regarded in the Renaissance and today too as the parent of revenge. As for ambition, he is strangely reticent throughout the play about even his legitimate ambition to be a king like his father, strangely because it would seem to be such a rational motive for wanting to be rid of Claudius. It is as if all ambition is guilt ridden in his mind because it contains some inadmissible component. Freud suggests that Shakespeare's conception is as follows: Claudius' deeds have aroused comparable wishes in Hamlet's mind, and his guilt is related to these wishes. That is, Hamlet feels envious of his uncle but energetically bars his envy from awareness. This is implied in the text of the play by Hamlet's inadvertent equations between himself and Claudius, by his almost insane horror at the thought of his mother in his uncle's arms, by his incomprehensible sense of guilt, and by the persistent inhibition of his strong will to revenge. Considerable evidence in the play justifies Freud's translation into conscious terms of what was bound to remain unconscious in Hamlet's (but not Shakespeare's!) mind.

Observe how Shakespeare suggests Hamlet's tendency to link himself with his uncle: "My father's brother, but no more like my father / Than I to Hercules" and "Remorseless, treacherous, lecherous, kindless villain! / O, Vengeance! / Why, what an ass am I!" (II,ii,158–59,588–90). In the first passage the linkage is obscured only by the repudiative force of the negatives. In the second, the short line with its implied 65 pause between two bursts of anger prompts us to surmise that a subtle connection is being established between the two objects of Hamlet's anger. But the most emphatic evidence is in the famous third soliloquy:

> To be, or not to be, that is the question:
> Whether 'tis nobler in the mind to suffer
> The slings and arrows of outrageous fortune
> Or to take arms against a sea of troubles,
> And by opposing end them. To die—to sleep—
> No more; and by a sleep to say we end
> The heartache, and the thousand natural shocks
> That flesh is heir to. Tis a consummation
> Devoutly to be wished. To die—to sleep.
> To sleep—perchance to dream: ay, there's the rub!
> For in that sleep of death what dreams may come
> When we have shuffled off this mortal coil,
> Must give us pause. (III,i,64–76)

The most natural reading of this passage aligns the positive-sounding "to be" with the negative-sounding "to suffer" and the negative "not to be" with the positive "to take arms." This doesn't seem to make sense, but it is sound emotional logic. To act means to kill Claudius, and to kill Claudius means (if Hamlet identifies with him) to kill himself. The act of revenge is felt as an act of suicide. Hamlet can no more kill Claudius than he can kill himself—or he can kill Claudius, as the play shows, only when he himself is dying. Hamlet has nowhere to turn. "To be" means to suffer or remain inactive, the continuation of tormented consciousness. So he turns to "not to be," which he feels at first as an end to consciousness, death as sleep, a consummation devoutly to be wished. But to sleep implies to dream, and to dream implies to dread. So this road also leads to suffering and death in life. It is a vicious circle. Hamlet is "passion's slave." The only way he can break out is to relieve the obstructing guilt by bringing part of his underlying conflict into consciousness, where it will lose some of its force. This he accomplishes in the last act, as we shall see.

The close connection between Hamlet and Claudius can also be demonstrated in terms of the movement of the plot, in which context it is rich with ironies. Hamlet begins as an

innocent, Claudius as a practiced Machiavel. But, in their

seesaw battle, Hamlet is forced to fight on his adversary's terms of ruthless cunning and is finally responsible, immediately if not ultimately, for most of the play's deaths. At times, as in the fifth soliloquy, " 'Tis now the very witching time of night" (III,ii,395), he sounds quite like a Richard III confirming himself in hatred whereas only a moment later we hear the conscience-stricken Claudius repenting his misdeeds, quite like a once noble Macbeth: "O my offense is rank, it smells to heaven" (III,iii,39). The intertwining of their fates is again suggested in the dueling scene where Hamlet, untroubled by the irony, fights as the king's champion against Laertes and where, of course, they all die together.

These connections have prompted a few readers to wonder if the antithetical labels hero and villain are too crude in this case, but the connections call our attention to what are actually the crucial moral differences between the two figures. One is that Hamlet, until provoked by indecent spying, is guilty only of criminal wishes whereas Claudius is guilty of criminal deeds. Another is that Hamlet's conscious will remains noble despite his bloodthirsty self-exhortations, but Claudius' conscious will remains corrupt despite his attempted penitence. Hamlet (as even Freud and Jones failed to see, intent as they were upon correcting Goethe) is not really capable of ruthless cunning or planned murder. He stabs Polonius impetuously, instigates the deaths of Rosencrantz and Guildenstern "rashly," kills Laertes and the king as a climax to a quick series of unforeseen "accidents." The king is correct when he tells Laertes that Hamlet will not examine the foils because he is "most generous, and free from all contriving" (IV,vii,150). At least one critic, Thomas McFarland in *Tragic Meanings in Shakespeare*, has observed the ironical fact that, whereas Hamlet is prevented from taking direct action against Claudius by the fear of his own criminal wishes, Claudius is prevented from taking direct action against Hamlet by the fear of losing his wife's love. He tells Laertes:

The Queen his mother
Lives almost by his looks; and for myself,—
My virtue or my plague, be it either which,—

67

She's so conjunctive to my life and soul
That, as the star moves not but in his sphere,
I could not but by her. (IV, vii, 13–18)

But the irony points to a deeper contrast: Hamlet's inhibition is unconscious, Claudius' is conscious; Hamlet seeks to preserve his noble ideals, Claudius his criminal gains. Like most tragic heroes Hamlet is noble in will but deficient in self-knowledge; like most tragic villains Claudius is self-knowing but corrupt.

Some critics are troubled by Freud's idea of Hamlet's unconscious identification with Claudius because it seems the precise opposite of the truth. "If this be the case," writes Harry Levin, "it must be said that Hamlet conceals his sympathy for his uncle from the audience more effectively than he conceals his hostility to, and from, Claudius." But that is the point. We infer Hamlet's unconscious sympathy from the fact that his hostility is so violent and so inexplicably inhibited. Laurence Olivier spoiled a similar Shakespearean insight by suggesting onstage that Hamlet's sexual interest in his mother was overt rather than to be inferred from an exaggerated revulsion. One notes in support of both dramatic points that Hamlet has to whip himself up into hatred of Claudius but his hostility toward his mother is so ready and profuse that several times he must be wrenched into a recognition of where his duty lies.

This line of interpretation provides a natural explanation for other puzzling features of the play, particularly Hamlet's disproportionate reactions to his father's death and mother's hasty remarriage. I realize that many persons, among popular audiences especially, do not find the reactions disproportionate. I am thinking of the loud applause, more like relief than simple approval, which night after night greeted the following glib speech in the Broadway production of Tom Stoppard's *Rosencrantz and Guildenstern Are Dead:* "To sum up: your father whom you love dies, you are his heir, you come back to find that hardly was the corpse cold before his younger brother popped onto his throne and under his sheets. . . . Now why are you behaving in this extraordinary manner?" No doubt these are unusual and distressing events, the more distressing because his mother's remarriage was apparently regarded by his society as more or less incestuous, although no one but Hamlet, not even Horatio, makes a point of this. But it is not sufficiently clear on the basis of these events why a very capable and intelligent young man, a month or two later, should be plunged into a melancholy and disgust so profound that his first free words, "O that this too too solid flesh would melt" (I,ii,135), express a yearning for suicide. To say that Hamlet is also upset by the frustration of his political ambitions or by his suspicion of murder, "O my prophetic soul! / My uncle?" (I,v,47–48), only invites us to wonder further why he does not at this point mention these matters. We can hardly help wondering, in any case, why he continues to brood on suicide and on his mother's fault even after his father's ghost has set him the task of revenging a murder and specifically enjoined him to leave his mother to heaven.

Hamlet's feeling about his mother is so strong and so irrational that it leads repeatedly to a generalized disgust with women and sexuality, at one point to a cruel attack on the beloved and innocent Ophelia, which almost everyone recognizes as shockingly inappropriate. (Ophelia, of course, is "guilty" of obeying her conniving father but only of that. The libidinal outpourings in her mad scene, as Jones points out, indicate the habitual modesty of her sane demeanor. Her counterpart in Saxo and Belleforest clearly had relations with Amleth. Shakespeare suppresses this.) Some try to explain the attack as prompted by the practical need to put on an antic disposition. But this hardly explains why the need must be expressed in this form, and in any case the antic disposition ("less than madness and more than feigned," as Eliot aptly remarks) itself requires explanation. For, aside from its self-expressive function, it serves more to warn than to fool the king.

Although Hamlet's attitude toward his mother is particularly suggestive of irrational motives, there is also rather neglected evidence that his attitude toward his father is unrealis-

tic in the opposite way, that it is idealized. We are accustomed
to taking his words at face value when he compares his father
to the godly Hyperion and his uncle to a bestial satyr. But
there seems to be distortion on both counts. Hamlet de-
nounces his uncle as a swinish carouser and lecher, but we
never see him drunk or anything but very effective in his
work, and we have reason to believe he genuinely loves Gertrude. The play affirms his criminal usurpation, but it also
implies some striking parallels between the past and present
kings of Denmark. Hamlet tells his friends disapprovingly of
the warlike preparations of the present king, but warlike
preparations apparently were characteristic of the former king
too. The Ghost appears in "warlike form" and "martial
stalk," reminding Horatio and the sentinels of the elder
Hamlet who fought "ambitious Norway" and "smote the
sledded Polacks on the ice" (I,i,57,73,75). Both kings contended with a Fortinbras. Hamlet's father killed the elder
Fortinbras, and Claudius skillfully diverted young Fortinbras
from war—which suggests that he is, if anything, less belli-
cose than his predecessor. In Saxo and Belleforest, Hamlet's
father, named Horwendil, was a pirate. Shakespeare suppresses this as inappropriate to his design, but nothing in the play
quite supports the pitch of young Hamlet's admiration. The
cautious Horatio refers to the father as "a goodly King,"
which the prince promptly heightens to, "I shall not look
upon his like again" (I,ii,196–98). It is noteworthy that the
Ghost, who is emphatic enough about murder and incest, is
silent about the queen's love and devotion to her former husband. Nor does Gertrude herself say anything admiring about
him; the guilt Hamlet makes her feel in the bedroom scene
concerns her incestuous infidelity and is not clearly a
confirmation of Hamlet's polarized contrast of the two hus-
bands. Harold Goddard points out in this connection the
play's several references to the dead king's "sins" and "crimes"
(I,v,17,83; III,iii,84). These could be interpreted as a con-
ventionally Christian way of talking about an unshriven life,
but the repetition is suggestive. Suffice it to say that there is a
perceptible degree of idealization in Hamlet's attitude toward
his father.

We may say, then, that Hamlet's repressed feelings—father-hate and mother-love—resemble the complex of feelings we associate with the facts of the Oedipus legend. This is not to say that Sophocles, in his handling of that legend, conceived Oedipus as struggling with an unconscious conflict between wishful fantasies and inhibitory guilt. He does show us reactive horror, but the underlying wish is represented only in the affectively neutral form of an unexaminable past event. Swathed in myth, the ancient Greek hero is a more naïve characterization than the Renaissance prince. Only Hamlet shows us a conscious complex of feelings set over against another, opposite complex. And the conscious pattern resembles the attitudes we associate with the Orestes legend.

I have implied, following Freud and Jones, that the Orestes complex is best understood in dynamic terms as an attempt by Hamlet to keep the intolerable counterpart complex from awareness. But I must admit, out of fidelity to the complexity of Shakespeare's text, that this already difficult idea is burdened, probably overburdened, by another intricacy too important to ignore. T. S. Eliot writes that Hamlet "is dominated by an emotion which is inexpressible because it is in *excess* of the facts as they appear. And the supposed identity of Hamlet with his author is genuine to this point: that Hamlet's bafflement at the absence of objective equivalent to his feelings is a prolongation of the bafflement of his creator in the face of his artistic problem," which was "to impose the motive of a guilty mother upon the intractable material of the old play." For the most part, what Eliot accurately describes as emotion in excess of the facts as they *appear* does have, in my opinion, an objective equivalent in the inferences Shakespeare means us to make about the *unapparent* facts or unconscious dynamics of his character's mind. But, even when this is said, there is something more, something over the mark, and Eliot is right to say that it has to do with the question of Hamlet's relation to his mother. I think it too is capable of some degree of explication, but I offer this in the rather uneasy belief that Shakespeare the artist was not in full control of it and that, accordingly, it is more or less an artistic flaw.

Hamlet expresses his disgust with his mother not only in a

way that suggests denial of his own sexual interest in her but also in a way that suggests his identification with her in a sexual role, for he evokes several times a vivid picture of her receiving caresses. I cite the three most significant instances. (1) In the first soliloquy Hamlet paints a picture of his mother's sexual dependence on his father that has no contextual support and might fairly be called idealized: "Why, she would hang on him / As if increase of appetite had grown / By what it fed on" (I,ii,149–51). (2) Hamlet urges a player to speak lines from a play about the slaying of Priam and specifically requests him after a while to "come to Hecuba" (II,ii,507), as if Hecuba's lament for her slain husband is the feeling center of the play for Hamlet. This seems confirmed when he soliloquizes afterward on the player's eloquent representation: "What's Hecuba to him or he to Hecuba, / That he should weep for her" (II,ii,565–66). One would expect Hamlet to identify more readily with a son who has lost his father, given a story about the death of Priam. (3) In the bedroom scene, after Hamlet has shamed his mother, she asks him what she should do. We might expect him to say, "Avoid the king," but note how obliquely he couches his thought, as if he gets a masochistic pleasure from picturing his mother's sensuality:

> Not this, by no means, that I bid you do:
> Let the bloat King tempt you again to bed;
> Pinch wanton on your cheek; call you his mouse;
> And let him, for a pair of reechy kisses,
> Or paddling in your neck with his damnèd fingers,
> Make you to ravel all this matter out,
> That I essentially am not in madness,
> But mad in craft. (III,iv,203–10)

In sum, we have a repressed homosexual (or negative Oedipal) pattern in coexistence with a repressed heterosexual (or positive Oedipal) pattern. Such a complication is, I believe, common in life, but it may be too dense a meaning to be sustained effectively in a play.

It is difficult to believe that Shakespeare was quite oblivious to these implications but just as difficult to believe that he was fully aware or at least fully in control of them. Perhaps the unclearly motivated appearance of the Ghost in the bedroom is traceable to this difficulty. It would be as if at this point Shakespeare sensed some confusion in his conception of his hero's character and resorted to giving him an artificial push. That is speculation, but we do know that *Hamlet* is the longest and most worked over of Shakespeare's plays; it does not seem farfetched to suppose that the playwright was trying to create as dense a meaning as possible, but was not quite succeeding. We may note, in this connection, that male usurpation and female infidelity are the two strongest negative themes, or fears, in Shakespeare's plays and are dramatized more fully and more conjunctively in *Hamlet* than in any other.

If we give priority to the psychological theme of the play, we can say that, having established it, Shakespeare builds his meaning outward and upward in political and philosophical directions. The priority may be questioned, but reconstructing Shakespeare's design this way lights up two important anomalies that emerge in a broader view and that are seldom confronted with any directness. First, what are we to make of the fact that Shakespeare places his hero in a world which recognizes itself as Christian (the various allusions to a Christian frame of reference plainly depart from the explicitly pre-Christian setting of the Belleforest story) and then imposes a task of honorable revenge, an idea flatly incompatible with Christian ethics as propounded in numerous Elizabethan treatises? Second, what are we to make of the fact that Hamlet is enjoined as an act of piety to kill a king, when in play after play, especially those written about the time of *Hamlet*, Shakespeare dramatizes the impiousness of regicide and its inevitable termination in guilt? When Hamlet does finally stab Claudius, *all* cry "Treason!"

Hamlet unequivocally regards his task of revenge as an honorable and pious one. (Here lies the force of Shaw's seemingly cranky idea, in the preface to *Man and Superman*, that the prince of Denmark exhibits the morals of a bushranger. The limitations of such a judgment are obvious, but

Shaw clearly sees what some critics flinch from seeing, that Hamlet unequivocally regards *revenge* as *honorable*.) He never indicates that his plan clashes with Christian morality or with a strong secular taboo against regicide, even though he tries hard to understand why he cannot enact his revenge. I think it is misleading to see Hamlet's revenge as belonging to a primitive ethical code. It is clearly the expression of piety and is connected with the whole chivalric-heroic concept of honor and nobility centered on the authority of God-King-Father. But, as studies of the period show, these concepts or value systems were in the process of being subverted and defied. Fredson Bowers' *Elizabethan Revenge Tragedy* clearly shows, although its author seems to be claiming for the age a consistent position, that the idea of revenge in Shakespeare's day was both honored and scorned, that it inspired strong, irreconcilable feelings. Shakespeare apparently seized upon precisely this and created in Hamlet a broadly representative figure in whom the gathering force of rebellious defiance is thrown into conflict with a profound resistance to that force. The deeds of Claudius have intensified Hamlet's incipient impiety, and the injunction of the Ghost has intensified his rooted piety. Here we come to the nub of the tragic dilemma.

Shakespeare so contrives his play that Hamlet's revenge, on the one hand, supports the old idea of order and, on the other, violates it, for it involves the killing of a king and a desecration of the divinity that hedges a king. Hamlet wants to defend the old idea of authority represented by his father but cannot do so without destroying exactly that. Jones considers and rejects the idea that Hamlet is repressing a Christian prohibition against revenge on the psychological grounds that high ethics are not generally repressed. But Shakespeare is not pitting Christianity against revenge. He is pitting one kind of revenge implied in regicide and deicide against another implied in parricide. The first two are less personal ideas and are thus allowed to come closer to direct expression, but they are connected feelingly with the idea of parricide. Shakespeare knew that the three ideas are compounded of the same psychological stuff.

To appreciate the value of this insight, we need only remind ourselves of the eclipse it suffered during the three hundred years after Shakespeare. In the work of so profound a writer as Milton the eclipse is already underway. There, regicide is sanctioned, the taboo on deicide becomes more stringent, and the relation of both to parricide is obscured. I am not, like Eliot and other early modernists, deploring Protestantism, capitalism, and democracy. They are in some ways advances in civilization and in human freedom. But it is well to understand that they created a psychological strain, that the internalization of authority has meant also the internalization of judgment, that such a moral advance has increased our burden of guilt. Morally approved and disapproved elements are allowed considerable interaction in Chaucer's and Shakespeare's world. In Spenser's and Milton's less relaxed, more urgent world, they tend to be sharply separated. There is a distinct loss of flexibility. And it is the latter tradition which exerted the greater impact on "modernist" literature, particularly on the Romantics, who, with some sense of revolutionary violence, committed themselves to exploring the idea of an utterly naturalistic view of human freedom and found themselves exploring concomitantly the twists and turns of the mind-forged manacles.

Shakespeare's imaginative sympathies were deeply engaged by the old idea of freedom. In play after play he shows himself distrustful of lawless liberty, of opportunistic and prideful individualism. He embodies these attitudes in tragic villains (Claudius, Iago, Edmund), in comic villains (Shylock, Caliban), and most completely in tragic heroes, where it is accompanied by guilt, primarily conscious as in Macbeth or unconscious as in Hamlet. The most remarkable thing about the artist Shakespeare, from a thematic point of view, is his *openness* to his and his culture's fears. His villains are so plausible, and his heroes are so vulnerable. Frank Kermode notes that the attitude of "scepticism declining into naturalism and atheism, which was a strong Renaissance undercurrent," is always treated by Shakespeare as "degenerate"—to which I would add, but not before it is given generous room to state its case. It is as if Shakespeare does not want to separate feeling from thought, the real from the ideal, what I am from what I think I am, any more than is consistent with having a moral position at all. A moral position is maintained, but it does not give the effect of the author's having pushed his feelings into line.

Let us return to the play and observe how all of this is worked out dramatically. Hamlet is extraordinarily cut off, not only from himself but from others whose king he should now rightfully be. (Surely the play implies that election is a mere formality, modeled on Elizabethan government; there is no doubt that Hamlet is the rightful successor or that his dying recommendation of Fortinbras has the force of law.) In Saxo and Belleforest he enjoys the confidence and active support of his mother, friend, and wife. Even in Quarto 1, he has discussed his plans of revenge with the queen and Horatio and secured their promise of support. But in Quarto 2 the queen, Horatio, and Ophelia give little or no support. Gertrude and Ophelia are apparently too frightened and timid to do more than mean well, and Horatio is too passive. (Horatio is not clearly motivated. What everyone feels to be his woodenness may be the result of Shakespeare's having decided late to isolate Hamlet as much as possible by withdrawing Horatio's primary *raison d'être*, to give his friend active support.) Moreover, Claudius, unlike his prototype in Saxo and Belleforest who sought and obtained public justification for his fratricide, has made a secret of his crime and has built his state upon secrecy. In his court, lying and spying are the approved modes of procedure, and it is well for the modern reader, who is inclined to sympathize with victims, to remember that Polonius, Rosencrantz, and Guildenstern know this and choose to go along with it. (The same applies with lesser force to Ophelia and the queen.) The fact that their refusal to go along with Claudius would have been dangerous gives their situation a tragic cast but does not quite excuse them. In major political conflict, as we know, those who try for safety's sake to serve the tyrant, as well as those who must for the sake of their own integrity oppose him, may be fatally trapped.

These hard political facts make it impossible for us to regard Hamlet as a man caught up in a purely individual conflict. When corruption permeates a society, the isolated man will resemble a madman. But the point to emphasize is that conflict within the individual and conflict between the individual and society are not mutually exclusive. Difficult as is Hamlet's political situation, his task is not impossible, nor does he ever think it so *politically*.

Hamlet could hardly be unaware of the possibility, acted upon by Laertes, of arousing the people who love him and leading a rebellion against Claudius. Yet he never mentions this possibility. And he is almost as silent about the frustration of his presumable ambition to be king, though this frustration would provide strong support for his revenge. He alludes to the subject only twice in the first four acts, both times in response to Guildenstern and Rosencrantz, who have hit upon the idea of disappointed ambition as a clue to the prince's "distemper," and both times in such a way as to discourage us as well as them from thinking the right clue has been found:

HAMLET: Denmark's a prison. . .
ROSENCRANTZ: Why then your ambition makes it one. 'Tis too narrow for your mind.
HAMLET: O God, I could be bounded in a nutshell and count myself a king of infinite space, were it not that I have bad dreams.

. . . .

ROSENCRANTZ: Good, my Lord, what is your cause of distemper? . . .
HAMLET: Sir, I lack advancement.
ROSENCRANTZ: How can that be, when you have the voice of the King himself for your succession in Denmark?
HAMLET: Ay sir, but 'while the grass grows'—the proverb is something musty. (III,ii,260–72,345–52)

He mentions the subject for the third and final time to Horatio in Act V:

Does it not, think'st thee, stand me now upon—
He that hath kill'd my king, and whor'd my mother;
Popped in between the election and my hopes;
Thrown out his angle for my proper life,

77

And with such coz'nage—is't not perfect conscience
To quit him with this arm? (V,ii,70–75)

Here he is more straightforward, but this reflects the change
that has come over him in Act V, which I shall discuss later,
and hardly explains his previous melancholy. One cannot escape the conclusion that Hamlet, despite his strong sense of
princely responsibility, feels a profound reluctance to be king,
to replace the king, to do away with him. And this reluctance
is bound up with the inhibition of his parricidal impulse. The
words *king* and *father* are repeatedly interchanged in Hamlet's speeches, *e.g.*, "He that hath kill'd my king, and whor'd
my mother" (V,ii,71), where the word *father* would seem to
be more natural. The identification of past and present kings is
emphasized by the fact that the royal synecdoche, "the
Dane," is several times applied to each, and Hamlet applies it
to himself when he finally confronts Claudius and Laertes
with his own claim, "This is I, / Hamlet the Dane" (V,i,
255–56). In short, Hamlet's conflict about replacing the king
is inseparable from his conflict about replacing his father.

Hamlet's courageous willingness to look at dangerous
truths within and without is expressed also philosophically, for
he is a scholar as well as a courtier, an intellectual as well as a
prince. His philosophic questioning is in fact so searching that
he has with some justice been considered an early existen-
tialist, a man who perceives the nothingness that surrounds
our lives, the objective groundlessness of all values, the illusory nature of all metaphysical consolation: "There is nothing
either good or bad but thinking makes it so" (II,ii,265–66).

Here we must be careful, however, to avoid Coleridge's
error of making Hamlet's corrosive skepticism the cause of his
vacillation. An attitude of skeptical relativism such as we find
in Montaigne, a favorite of Shakespeare's, does not paralyze
the will. And a corrosive, Nietzschean skepticism (what the
temperate Horatio calls "considering too curiously") is, like
indecisiveness itself, probably best understood as a result or
symptom of an underlying emotional conflict. Questioning is
indeed central to the play, as critics have recently emphasized.
But to say that the meaning of the play is a question is

perhaps not to consider sufficiently the motive for such in-
temperate curiosity.

To be sure, Hamlet questions the meaning of life not
merely as an individual but as a broadly representative man
giving definitive expression to the ideals and fears of his age.
A generalizing style of thought, many have observed, is dif-
fused throughout the play, most notably in Hamlet's "What
a piece of work is a man" speech, in his advice to the players,
in the last half of his greatest soliloquy, and in the grave-
diggers' scene. The passage from the soliloquy is sufficiently
illustrative:

> For who would bear the whips and scorns of time,
> The oppressor's wrong, the proud man's contumely,
> The pangs of despised love, the law's delay,
> The insolence of office, and the spurns
> That patient merit of the unworthy takes,
> When he himself might his quietus make
> With a bare bodkin? Who would these fardels bear,
> To grunt and sweat under a weary life,
> But that the dread of something after death—
> The undiscovered country, from whose bourn
> No traveller returns—puzzles the will,
> And makes us rather bear those ills we have
> Than fly to others that we know not of?
> Thus conscience doth make cowards of us all. (III,i,78–91)

One would have to strain unduly to make these fardels specifically relevant to Hamlet's situation. They are rather the
burdens of the general human situation that Hamlet confronts as a representative man.

But the philosophical no less than the political dimension of
meaning is bound up with the psychological. Hamlet's culturally enforced individual conflict drives him toward a radical
questioning of values he had taken for granted. He has lost
not merely his father but also his king and not merely his
king but also the divinity-tinged idea of authority which
kingship represented. Product of an age in which atheism was
a fearful alternative to faith, Hamlet looks with the eyes of an
atheist into the stark nothingness of death. But, unlike the
Shakespearean villains (Claudius, Iago, Edmund) who take

pleasure from their philosophy of cynical egotism, Hamlet remains open to the experience of fear and conflict. He is too noble to be comfortable with an ignoble philosophy. He will not, like the villain, deal with his conflict by justifying his "evil" impulses. Nor will he, like what we now call the neurotic, deal with his conflict by making a virtue of passivity and inaction.

Fear of death is the crucial link between the psychological and philosophical dimensions of Hamlet's conflict. The passage just quoted is a good place to examine it. We remember that in his first soliloquy Hamlet withdraws from the temptation to suicide because "the Everlasting |had| fixed his canon 'gainst self-slaughter." That is, his view of the human situation is still theistic enough for him to invoke a Christian prohibition. But, by the time he reaches the middle act of his development, he no longer pictures death in recognizably Christian terms but as a dark unknown, an "undiscovered country, from whose bourn / No traveller returns." Moreover, his fear of death is now directly linked with his fear of bad dreams and finally with his fear of conscience. Now what is Shakespeare getting at? Is it fear of death or fear of conscience that pulls Hamlet back from the wish "not to be" to the suffering of being? And if there is a connection, what is it?

Men have long observed that the fear of death makes little rational sense. But I dare say that before Freud there was no satisfactory conceptual explanation of this irrational fear such as could be used to support the intuitive insight contained in Hamlet's lines. So I shall quote from the last pages of *The Ego and the Id*, urging the reader who finds the terminology puzzling or the excerpting abrupt to read the passage in full context:

> The high sounding phrase, "every fear is ultimately the fear of death," has hardly any meaning, and at any rate cannot be justified. It seems to me, on the contrary, perfectly correct to distinguish the fear of death from dread of an object (realistic anxiety) and from neurotic libidinal anxiety. It presents a difficult problem to psycho-analysis, for death is an abstract concept with a negative content for which no unconscious correlative can be found. . . . I believe that the fear of death is something that occurs between the ego and the super-ego.

We know that fear of death makes its appearance under two conditions . . . as a reaction to an external danger and as an internal process, as for instance in melancholia. . . .

The fear of death in melancholia only admits of one explanation: that the ego gives itself up because it feels itself hated and persecuted by the super-ego instead of loved. To the ego, therefore, living means the same as being loved—being loved by the super-ego, which here again appears as the representative of the id. The super-ego fulfils the same function of protecting and saving that was fulfilled in earlier days by the father and later by Providence or Destiny. But, when the ego finds itself in an excessive real danger which it believes itself unable to overcome by its own strength, it is bound to draw the same conclusion. It sees itself deserted by all protecting forces and lets itself die. . . .

These considerations make it possible to regard the fear of death, like the fear of conscience, as a development of the fear of castration. The great significance which the sense of guilt has in the neuroses makes it conceivable that common neurotic anxiety is reinforced in severe cases by the generating of anxiety between the ego and the super-ego (fear of castration, of conscience, of death).

Shakespeare did not go so far as to link fear of death and conscience to fear of castration. The imaginative grasp of that part of Freud's thought had to wait for a later age with a much more ironic view of man and is most articulate in very concrete writers, such as Hemingway. But he did perceive the connection which Freud reasons out between fear of death and fear of conscience.

So far I have alluded little to Act V because Hamlet's character and attitudes appear there significantly modified. This fact has come to be appreciated in recent decades, although interpretation has been posed too sharply in either Christian or existential terms.

Hamlet's dominant emotions—despair, anger, mania—persist but in modified form. He is still despairing, even somewhat morbid, when he talks to Horatio in the graveyard and when he accepts the dueling challenge, but the tone of his despair is more resigned and accepting. He wavers between fatalism and faith. He says with quiet horror, "To what base uses we may return, Horatio! Why may not the imagination trace the noble dust of Alexander till he find it stopping a bunghole?" (V,i,195–97). Yet, in describing the success of his rash, epistolary counterplotting, he alludes to divine will for the first time since Act I: "There's a divinity that shapes our ends, / Rough-hew them how we will" (V,ii,11–12). After accepting the challenge to duel, he observes, "How ill all's here about my heart" (V,ii,211–12). But, when Horatio urges him to heed such an inauspicious sign, Hamlet alludes, with an air of bravado, to a passage in Matthew: "We defy augury; there's a special providence in the fall of a sparrow." Then immediately he adds a fatalistic twist, closing with an allusion to Montaigne: "If it be now, 'tis not to come; if it be not to come, it will be now; if it be not now, yet it will come: the readiness is all. Since no man has aught of what he leaves, what is't to leave betimes? Let be" (V,ii,218–23).

He still expresses anger, at Claudius and Laertes, but the anger is more open and direct, less caustic and obsessive. He defies them publicly at the scene of Ophelia's burial, but soon agrees to duel as the king's champion, without commenting on his revenge, as if revenge is no longer his primary need or fear. And his outburst against the ostentatiously grieving Laertes (which is, by the way, Hamlet's first open declaration of love for Ophelia) is quickly followed by courtly apology, generous praise, and a request for friendship. Finally, a trace of mania persists in his high-spirited mockery of the affected courtier Osric, but it is more playful and goodhumored than his earlier mockery of Polonius.

In short, Hamlet has become more tolerant of himself and others: he is less the embittered ironist; he is closer than we have ever seen him to living up to his reputation as the "expectancy and rose of the fair state." His dying gestures reveal the true prince: he fulfills his revenge without ado, expresses a loving concern for his dying mother, and shows a responsible interest in the future of the state over which he is briefly the de facto king.

The turning point in Hamlet's spiritual development is the sea voyage to England which takes place offstage. (The trip to England in the sources served as a transition to a sequel of fresh heroics, but Shakespeare uses it to mark a psychological change and omits the second part of his sources.) Hamlet tells us what happened. "Feeling in [his] heart a kind of fighting," he got up from his cabin and with providential rashness groped toward the sleeping Rosencrantz and Guildenstern, on whom he discovered the king's sealed commission for his own sudden death. He then devised a new commission, which put them in his place, and was able to seal it officially—"even in that was heaven ordinant"—because he "had [his] father's signet in [his] purse, / Which was the model of that Danish seal." Finally, "a pirate [ship] of very warlike appointment gave . . . chase . . . and in the grapple [he] boarded them" and was returned, in the hope of favors, to Denmark (V,ii,5–60; IV,vi,13–29). How are we to interpret this crucial action? Let us review Hamlet's progress with this offstage action in mind.

We have seen that the injunction to revenge thrusts Hamlet into a profound dilemma. Killing the king is felt to be as a fulfillment of his own deep wish to replace his kingly father as Claudius has done, and this envious wish is strenuously barred from consciousness because of his reverence for his father and all he represented. He is drawn to the idea of death both to punish the Claudius in himself and to erase the anguish of separation from his father. But he has great fear of death and great will to endure, so he chooses "to be" even though to be means to suffer rather than to act. Hamlet is passive, however, only concerning the actual killing of Claudius. He is quite active, even cunning and daring, in verbal aggression against the king and in counteracting the king's aggression.

Hamlet's verbal or reactive combativeness becomes more and more overt throughout the play. At first (I,ii) it takes the subdued forms of *sotto voce* sarcasm ("A little more than kin, and less than kind"), of audible but cryptic sarcasm ("Not so, my lord, I am too much i' the sun"), and of obstinate melancholy ("Seems, madam? Nay, it is. I know not 'seems' "). After his meeting with the Ghost, Hamlet decides to put on an antic disposition, but this, though it ostensibly protects his plan of revenge from discovery (ostensibly because he has no plan), really serves to give his pranks fuller scope. It is a 83 compromise between his desire for revenge and his fear of actual revenge, which is to say that it is intended, almost consciously, to provoke Claudius. Hamlet senses that, although he cannot act deliberately against the king, he can act spontaneously in response to the king's aggression. As the play progresses, his own provocations become bolder. The play within the play and accompanying commentary hint so broadly at his knowledge of the fratricide and intention to revenge it that the shrewd Claudius could not possibly be doubtful any more, if he ever was. Then in his mother's bedroom he actually kills a man, the spy behind the arras. "Is it the King?" he asks, in mingled hope and fear. It might have been, and so we can say that Hamlet is at this point nearer to performing his task than ever before. But it is doubtful that he could have stabbed an unconcealed royal figure (he hadn't in the prayer scene a moment before), and the absence of any evident disappointment when he uncovers Polonius surely indicates relief as well as indifference. This tangible act, however, enables the king to justify, in Gertrude's eyes, his earlier decision to send Hamlet abroad. The prince significantly is unperturbed by the decision, even though he appears to understand it well enough: when the king lyingly protests that his purposes are good if only Hamlet knew them, the prince replies with aplomb, "I see a cherub that sees them" (IV,iii,52). He talks as if he has succeeded in some way, and he has: he has provoked Claudius to take direct action against him. Then in the offstage action he makes his boldest counteroffensive, which seems to mark a decisive change in his inner development.

On the sea voyage Hamlet has not only spoiled the king's plot by substituting the commission, but he has also, in an important symbolic action, begun to replace his father. He has used his father's authority, symbolized by the signet ring, which is "the model of that Danish seal," to alter a king's request to another king. Shakespeare points up the son-father interchange by altering the name of Hamlet's father in the sources, which is Horwendil, to Hamlet: when young Hamlet shows himself before the courtiers in Act V, identifying himself with the royal epithet, "This is I, Hamlet the Dane," the idea of the son-prince replacing the father-king is dramatic and unmistakable. A fascinating detail in this connection is "the pirate of very warlike appointment" that takes Hamlet on board, saves his life, and returns him with new pride to Danish soil. In the sources Hamlet's father was a pirate. Shakespeare apparently didn't want this fact in his play, but of course it was in his mind, and it may have influenced the artistic intention.

Looking at the whole pattern of his development, then, we are able to say that between his appearances in Acts IV and V Hamlet has broken the vicious circle of unconscious conflict. His rash action on shipboard has accomplished what introspection alone could not—salvaged from repression a portion of his legitimate desire to replace his father, to be a king like his father. Hence some guilt is dissolved, and his mind is eased. It is no wonder he should think of these actions as blessed from above:

> And praised be rashness for it; let us know
> Our indiscretion sometime serves us well
> When our deep plots do pall; and that should learn us
> There's a divinity that shapes our ends,
> Rough-hew them how we will. (V,ii,8–12)

This new if tentative faith becomes in turn a cause as well as being an effect of Hamlet's renovation. Since his father was the center of his moral universe, inseparable at the emotional level from both kingship and divinity, his death precipitated a loss of faith in an order of things external to his own will. So, to the extent that Hamlet can reaffirm his temporarily lost belief in a higher, benevolent will, he has *reconstituted* the image of the loving father and is further able to lighten the burden of total self-responsibility. He can love himself a little better (*i.e.*, his conscience is less punishing) and can be to that extent more loving toward others. Death is not so feared; it has lost some of its sting. He has recaptured a portion of his lost freedom.

But Shakespeare holds the balance between faith and

fatalism so delicately that in saying so much I have perhaps Christianized the last act of the play a little more than is warranted. The relaxation of Hamlet's conflict can be traced not only to a new faith but also to a new resignation, a greater acceptance of, a greater readiness for death. He has gone too far to recover his pristine faith. He is still fascinated and repelled by death; still despairing, angry, manic; still inhibited in the primary task of revenge. Prince Hal, in a significant symbolic action comparable to Hamlet's use of his father's ring, picked up the royal crown belonging to his sleeping father and tried it on for size. But Hamlet is a hero of tragedy, not romance, and his conflict cannot be completely resolved. That is, Shakespeare will not try to persuade us that guilt so deeply rooted can be annihilated. Hamlet can kill the king and reaffirm the moral order based upon a new king only at the price of his own death. Act V presents a modified, not a transformed, Hamlet.

The trouble with many Christian and existential interpretations of Act V is that they seek too complete, too perfect a resolution. Christianity is of course a very large idea, embracing a spectrum of attitudes ranging from a flexible, almost secular humanism to a rigid, puritanical fanaticism. There cannot be much objection to calling Shakespeare a Christian if one is thinking only of the humanistic side. He dramatizes extreme attitudes and extreme modes of resolving conflict with an astonishingly flexible empathy, but he does not endorse them. Hamlet is no Christ figure. It is misleading to talk of Act V in such terms as the atonement of son and father, the submission of human to divine will, the transfiguration of death into rebirth. So much does the play stress self-responsible human action in a world of ultimate uncertainties that it has also been claimed by existentialists. But, though Shakespeare explores the nothingness that surrounds and weighs upon us, he does not quite surrender the idea of pietas, of submission and accommodation to a moral order. Defiant self-sufficiency is always in his plays accompanied either by perverted will as in his villains or by guilt as in his tragic heroes. Shakespeare would have agreed with Pascal that atheists have powerful minds up to a point but only up to a point.

What we have in *Hamlet,* and indeed throughout Shakespeare, is something between, neither submissive fideism as in Milton's angels nor defiant rebellion as in his devils. The Shakespearean and Renaissance ideal of virtuous action, which Hamlet strives to follow, is nowhere equated with forgiveness and the remission of sins or, of course, with prideful egoism. Hamlet's revenge is not discredited any more than Claudius' is endorsed. The combination of "flights of angels" and military ordinance that attend Hamlet's death are suggestive, maybe not altogether successfully, of the Shakespearean compromise. Perhaps Prospero's handling of revenge in *The Tempest* comes closest to the Shakespearean ideal. He neither destroys his enemies nor (as is sometimes mistakenly claimed) forgives them; he has the power to humble them and the wisdom to restrain voluntarily his temptation to punish them further.

Hamlet belongs to the old heroic tradition in which the ideal, the noble, the good, is associated with power as well as benevolence. In tragedy Shakespeare tests the heroic code to the full by assigning his tragic hero as much fear as possible without perverting his will, by giving the "repulsive" as much energy as possible without depriving the "attractive" of superior energy. In the following centuries, goodness was more and more disassociated from power, taking the form either of heroic resistance to a power now regarded as evil or of innocent powerlessness.

There has been a corresponding persistent tendency in Shakespearean criticism to simplify the rich, complex mixture of strength and weakness, generosity and cruelty, that marks the character of the great tragic heroes. Critics during the eighteenth and nineteenth centuries tended either to be repelled by the bad qualities (as Dr. Johnson was by Hamlet's treatment of Ophelia) or to see only the good ones (like Goethe, who saw only what was beautiful, pure, and noble). Perhaps the tendency to separate human strength and weakness was strongest during those centuries, the heyday of sen-

timentalism. But it is present even today. One should remember that the protagonist of tragedy originated historically
as a scapegoat figure in whom the fears of the community
were embodied and through whom they were expelled. A
distinguishing mark of the greatest literature is how much
dread it can incorporate and transfigure.

The idea of weakness in Hamlet seems to irritate some
modern students of Shakespeare. But how could weakness of
some kind not be involved in any truly tragic dilemma? To
admit this is not to say that Hamlet is a coward in the least
degree, even though he calls himself one. He exerts his strong
will and exceptional intelligence to the utmost. The play
shows us weaker persons who serve the time or go really mad
or, at best, passively maintain their integrity. But Hamlet, a
true hero, will not compromise on the question of honesty,
which, as Harry Levin justly remarks, is always the main
issue between him and his interlocutors. Although Hamlet
deals with them ironically, his irony is pointed and penetrating, not self-protective. Nor does he resort to self-pity; his
conscious envy, as when he admires Horatio's freedom from
the slavery of passion, is dignified and controlled: "Something too much of this" (III,ii,75). Hamlet never questions his
responsibility to act, however insuperable his inhibition:
"The time is out of joint. O cursed spite / That ever I was
born to set it right" (I,v,215–16). He sets nothing right, but
not because he hasn't tried.

Thus the analogy with psychoneurosis is finally misleading. Although Shakespeare can certainly be said to have
created a character who suffers from an unconscious conflict,
he has not shown us a neurotic solution of conflict. Instead,
Hamlet is shown exploring his conflict to the limit of his very
great intellectual and conative powers, succeeding finally,
though too late, in modifying it.

The fact that these powers—the only ones we have for
effecting change—are insufficient is what tragedy is all about.
Tragedy shows us man when he is not fully master of his fate,
when he is opposed from within as well as from without by
powers too great for him. It makes good sense to call Hamlet

courageous for his demonstrable ability to wrestle so long and hard with his problems, to confront and explore so bravely and with such verbal resourcefulness the fearful space beyond his cherished idea of himself. And, since Hamlet is never anything more or less than *homo fictus,* despite our credence in the illusion of his actuality for purposes of critical reconstruction, this is at the same time a way of praising Shakespeare's own courage, which we, to our satisfaction, imaginatively recreate.

II ATTITUDES TOWARD AUTHORITY IN *PARADISE LOST*

A PREFATORY comment designed to ease the way for critical use of the concept of unconscious mind is even more needed for an essay on *Paradise Lost* than for one on *Hamlet*. In this case we cannot talk about a character's unconscious mind created by a knowing and artful author. Satan's conflict (only the characterization of Satan is in question here), although it corresponds phenomenologically to a conflict which to the modern reader suggests an unconscious basis, is not conceived by Milton as having such a basis. The characterization manages to display its creator's considerable psychological and moral insight but is flattened or allegorized in such a way as to prevent us, beyond a point, from perceiving a convincing motivation.

When we speak of the unconscious in relation to *Paradise Lost*, we therefore mean Milton's unconscious. We mean a certain constellation of problematic effects which suggests the presence of such a conflict in the mind of the poet. The idea of Hamlet's unconscious is less offensive to many critics because, properly understood, it is a tribute to Shakespeare's artistry. But to suggest a relation between Milton's unconscious and the meaning of his poem necessarily implies a degree of artistic imperfection.

The case against employing the concept of unconscious mind here is superficially strengthened by the fact that Milton
90 gives central importance to a concept absolutely incompatible

with it, an omnipotent and omniscient God who engulfs all human mind. This does not mean that any poet who dramatizes unconscious motivation must be an atheist. Shakespeare is proof to the contrary. But Milton's conception of God is strenuously rationalized. Like Augustine, Milton perceives that the idea of man's falling in spite of his own will and reason is bound to suggest some sort of irrational force within him. And like Augustine (who reproaches himself for "miserably imagin|ing| there to be some unknown substance of irrational life . . . not derived from Thee, O my God") he categorically rejects such a conclusion. The trouble comes from his insistence, born of a hunger for a perfectly rational universe, that there can be no force which excuses man, for if there is, then man's creator must himself be accused. The idea that God created man but did not create the fault in man that causes him to fall is aesthetically troublesome if it is insisted on. The idea is part of Christian doctrine, but its illogic hardly constitutes a problem except in the work of so earnest and uncompromising a conceptualizer as Milton. He wants in this poem to explain everything, and the result is a work of tremendous scope and resourcefulness marred by certain effects which appear to be not fully controlled.

It is a critical commonplace to describe Milton's ethical stance as both humanistic and authoritarian. But it is not commonly added that these attitudes tend to be polarized rather than simply combined. On the one hand, the narrator identifies readily, even heartily, with a punitive God; on the other, he presents with immense pathos the condition of his victims: of Satan, who is shown to be hopelessly trapped by inner conflict, and of Adam and Eve, whose punishment is dramatized far more realistically than their crime.

The emphatic confidence of the Miltonic manner is thus tinged with self-righteousness. Doubtless this confidence contributes to the strength of the poem's phrasing and the magnificence of its harmonies, but it is nonetheless problematic, as Leavis perceives. Harold Bloom has alerted us to the anxiety that strong poets must cope with in emulating their particular precursors. In that light one might say that the famous grand style is Milton's way of overriding his precursors. The style of his chief precursor, the author(s) of Genesis, is far less expansive and intense. Nor did Homer, Vergil, Dante, or Spenser sustain rhetoric at his pitch. The first sentence of the poem is a much more elaborate version of the epic invocation than any they attempted, and it ends with a show of pride in which, to my ear, confidence and arrogance are hard to distinguish:

> I thence
> Invoke thy aid to my advent'rous Song,
> That with no middle flight intends to soar
> Above th'Aonian Mount, while it pursues
> Things unattempted yet in Prose or Rhyme. (I,12–16)*

One must add that the poet bases his belief in the supremacy of his poem on Christian rather than personal pride—"What in me is dark / Illumine, what is low raise and support" (I,22–23), he asks of the Holy Spirit—but that makes little difference, for the speaker's stance and God's are scarcely distinguishable. Where Milton's style is grandest, it is also crudest in its embrace of power and most punitive:

> Him the Almighty Power
> Hurl'd headlong flaming from th' Ethereal Sky
> With hideous ruin and combustion down
> To bottomless perdition, there to dwell
> In Adamantine Chains and penal Fire,
> Who durst defy th' Omnipotent to Arms. (I,44–49)

I do not agree with Walter Raleigh's well-known charge that *Paradise Lost* is a monument to dead ideas. Despite the Latinate syntax and diction, Milton does not versify doctrine. But he does tend to abstract morality from its human context, to speak of good and evil not simply in relation to deeds, words, and attitudes, but as transcendental categories. I think it is significant that in *King Lear*, the play of Shakespeare's most often discussed by critics in terms of good and evil, the word *evil* is mentioned only once and then in an entirely mundane and unemphatic context.

---

* Citations are to book and line numbers. Since all modern editions of *Paradise Lost* are identical in this respect, there is no need to cite a particular one.

However, I do not intend to discuss Milton's personal problems. The unconscious conflicts which underlie the problematic effects in the poem appear to be cultural as well as individual and cannot, in a straightforward textual analysis, be sorted out with clarity or profit. I am concerned with Milton as a seventeenth-century poet of heroic ambition; for me this historical situation itself contributes a distinct poignance to the poet's enormous but imperfect effort to justify the ways of God to man.

More fully and concentratedly than any other work between the age of Shakespeare and the age of the Romantics, *Paradise Lost* records the arduous effort of the literary imagination to accommodate the increased sense of guilt and increased self-consciousness that were resulting from changes in men's attitudes toward authority. On the one hand, it is a rich last testament to Renaissance humanism. Puritanism has not yet, at least in Milton, put pleasure under official ban in the name of some ethical ideal, has not yet erected self-denial itself into a virtue: "For not to irksome toil, but to delight / He made us, and delight to Reason join'd" (IX,242–43). Nor has the classical ideal of moderation, though given a slight Puritan shading in Milton's preferred word "temperance," ceased to be valued as the basis of the good life: "Nor love thy life, nor hate; but what thou liv'st / Live well, how long or short permit to Heav'n" (XI,553–54). Nor has Milton's emphasis on obedience to the will of God subordinated an emphasis on human freedom, freedom of choice, as the cornerstone of a belief in the dignity of man.

On the other hand, Milton's poem is appreciably more burdened than *Hamlet* is with a sense of the general difficulty of the human situation. Lawful pleasure is approved, but one must quote passages describing the state of Adam and Eve before the Fall to illustrate this. Eden is viewed everywhere with nostalgia (hence, its poignance), and the "paradise within," the poem's ethical goal, is approachable only by way of a knowledge of the impulse to disobedience—i.e., of guilt, a consciousness of sin. God repeatedly asserts man's complete freedom of choice, but such freedom makes man utterly responsible for his own badness. Man is burdened by his freedom in *Paradise Lost* because Milton carefully identifies God with reason, will, choice, conscience, in short, with the Inner Light. Eve's declaration of self-sufficiency, with its existential ring to a modern ear, has the poet's approval: "we live / Law to ourselves, our Reason is our Law" (IX,653–54). Above all, the poem's most complex and interesting character is the one who is allowed to make the most effort, however doomed, to be autonomous, to live in defiance of Outside Authority, to struggle directly with his sense of guilt.

The world of *Paradise Lost* is more inclusive than the world of *Hamlet* but more predictable too, less subtle in its shadings. Elsinore, though only one small place, gives us the sense of being surrounded by huge and dark unknowns whereas the epic action, though filling all time and space, is enclosed in the mind of a not very mysterious God. Like other great writers in the Protestant-prophetic tradition, Milton is both tremendously ranging and monotonous, as if he must include everything but bend it to the shape of an obsession.

There is a greater stiffness of moral posture in *Paradise Lost*. Good and evil are more definitely separated and are invoked more often in abstraction from particular images and figures. Yet Milton is more earnest than Shakespeare about the moral responsibility of man. He does not dawdle with ghosts and other casual trappings of folk tradition. Nor does he compromise with the more primitive tradition of honorable revenge. (The war in Heaven glorifies arms, but Milton makes a special point of saying, however ineffectively he renders it, that this war is a representation of spiritual combat.) The God of *Paradise Lost*, because He contains nothing foreign to human sense, is less remote than is providence in *Hamlet*. This is especially true after the Fall. "Know to know no more" (IV,775), suggesting a distance between God's ways and man's, is prelapsarian wisdom. Afterward, men must learn to be as gods, knowing both good and evil.

Shakespeare comes nearer than Milton to admitting the concept of unconscious motivation, but Milton, in Satan, gives us a picture of a struggle with a guilty conscience that is even more immediate than Hamlet's. It is no easy matter to replace one long-established idea of authority with another, monarchism with republicanism, even if it is aristocratic republicanism. Milton's task was to fortify the conscience that had to take on the guilt incurred in toppling the older idea. The result was a new but problematic emphasis on self-esteem, for the self-esteem appears sometimes humanely realistic (as when Adam observes, apropos of Eve's dream, that we can have bad wishes without being bad) and sometimes arrogant and self-righteous.

Milton shares with Shakespeare a profound attachment to the heroic tradition but also expresses strong resistance to it. The Son is the "King of Glory in his powerful Word / And Spirit coming to create new Worlds" (VII,208–209), yet he is carefully praised by the Father for "being Good / Far more than Great or High; because in thee / Love hath abounded more than Glory abounds" (III,310–12). We are to admire the picture of Satan being defeated "at one sling of [Christ's] victorious Arm" (X,633–34) yet to deplore, with Michael, the age when "Might only shall be admir'd," when "to overcome in Battle . . . shall be held the highest pitch / Of human Glory" (XI,689–94). These oppositely charged attitudes pervade the poem and create some curious effects, for example in the characterization of Belial. Belial is the most scorned but the least vengeful of the devils. His great error is preaching "ignoble ease and peaceful sloth" (II,225), which may be a fault in a hero but hardly seems so in a villain. Some peculiar (*i.e.*, Miltonic) contempt for slackness seems to have intruded here, and, since Belial's sinfulness is associated with yielding to women, one is inclined to connect it with Michael's contempt for "Man's effeminate slackness" said to be responsible for "Man's woe" (XI,632–34).

Milton's contrary feelings about the heroic help explain why it has proved so difficult to agree on the hero of *Paradise Lost*. None of the major candidates can be supported without serious qualification. The story of Adam and Eve is a story of frailty and of a difficult, but hardly heroic, recovery. Satan has the strength of will and the strength of opposition belonging to a hero but is too tainted by deliberate envy and revenge. Milton wants to preserve the ideal of heroic action but to strip it of its morally objectionable association with worldly power and physical force; he wants a heroism based on *resistance* to power and on *spiritual* fight. This could lead to Christ, and Christ is certainly alluded to in the important passage from Book IX, where Milton distinguishes his idea of "heroic song" from previous ideas:

Since first this subject for Heroic Song
Pleas'd me long choosing, and beginning late;
Not sedulous by Nature to indite
Wars, hitherto the only Argument
Heroic deem'd, chief maistry to dissect
With long and tedious havoc fabl'd Knights
In Battle feign'd; the better fortitude
Of Patience and Heroic Martyrdom
Unsung. (IX,25–33)

But *Paradise Lost* is not about the martyrdom of Christ, and in fact Christ's role of viceregent to God the Creator and Judge is so closely identified with the absolute divine will that it cannot be called, in any meaningful dramatic sense, heroic. Logically, of course, God is the only hero of the poem, but dramatically this is impossible. The nearest Milton comes in his epic to embodying the avowed ideal of heroic martyrdom —and thus to projecting his sympathy least equivocally—is in the minor characterizations of Abdiel, Enoch, and Noah. Yet Abdiel is something of an afterthought, as he does not appear in early drafts of the poem, and the others are no more than brief moments of revived intensity in the rather fatigued narrative of the last two books.

These figures are essentially identical. "Among the faithless, faithful only hee" (V,897), we are told of Abdiel. Enoch is described thus:

The only righteous in a World perverse,
And therefore hated, therefore so beset
With Foes for daring single to be just,
And utter odious Truth, that God would come
To judge them with his Saints: (XI,701–705)

Noah is "the only Son of light / In a dark Age" (XI,808–809).

To this list may be added even Christ, who "shall endure

[Adam's punishment] by coming in the Flesh / To a reproach-
ful life and cursed death" (XII,405–406), and, finally, Milton
himself: "On evil days though fall'n, and evil tongues; / In
darkness, and with dangers compast round" (VII,26–27). The
striking fact about these figures is that they are underdogs,
even though they are of God's party. Milton wants the moral
advantage of opposition to power and, at the same time,
power itself. Abdiel heroically holds out against "revolted
multitudes" and stands unshaken "when thousands err"
(VI,31,148), but also has the confident authority to tell Satan
that the Lord "at one blow / Unaided could have finisht thee,
and whelm'd / Thy Legions under darkness" (VI,140–42). As
A. J. A. Waldock observes, Satan's rebellion is presented as so
real and formidable a threat that we are a little disconcerted to
be reminded that his forces numbered only one-third of
Heaven's hosts and that "far the greater part have kept thir
stations" (VII,145). Satan may be a fool for prosecuting a war
he cannot win, but Milton looks a little foolish too. It is not
just a question of the difficulty inherent in dramatizing
spiritual warfare. The difficulty also derives from Milton's
wanting it both ways and appealing to our sympathy in contrary directions. If we are not beguiled by good and evil as
mere labels, as merely asserted moral credentials, we can
begin to see why Satan is such a puzzle, for opposition to
superior power felt as tyrannical and certainly hostile is
nowhere so fully and forcefully dramatized as in him. Affectively, the distinction is unclear between Abdiel's defiance of
Satan and Satan's defiance of God and between Belial's and
Adam's spiritual laxity.

Unlike many Romantic poems, however, *Paradise Lost*
does not openly express doubt or question the authority in-
vested in traditional belief. On the contrary, it conveys almost
everywhere the sense of absolute self-confidence. The only
shadow of doubt appears in the invocations, where Milton
sees himself beleaguered, afflicted with blindness, fallen on
evil days, cut off from an audience, and fearful lest

> an age too late, or cold
> Climate, or Years damp my intended wing

Deprest; and much they may, if all be mine,
Not Hers who brings it nightly to my Ear. (IX,44–47)

Since the doubt expressed in the Romantic poem so often centers upon the sanctions of the creative act itself, our attention is caught by the disavowal of creative self-assertion in the final phrases of this passage. In the several eloquent passages where Milton raises the question of authorship, he is assertive regarding his advantage as a Christian over previous epic poets, but, when it comes to inspiration and invention, he will claim nothing for his own will. His Muse (Urania, "My Celestial Patronness," virtually identifiable with the Holy Spirit) has an inward quality but is still abstracted from the conscious will—which means from the self, since the poem doesn't admit the notion of an unconscious will.

Perhaps some of the freedom we sense in Milton's manner of writing about creation (one of the important current trends in Miltonic criticism is to emphasize the creative rather than judicial aspects of his God) has to do with his advantage as a Renaissance poet in being able to draw amply on tradition without an itching need to defy or alter it. His invocations, though more personal and inward than those of the Elizabethans, are still at a clear distance from such awed realizations as Wordsworth's "By our own spirits are we deified" and Keats's "I see and sing by my own eyes inspired." The Romantics could not evade the knowledge that gods and devils were creations of the human mind and necessarily corresponded to human aspirations and fears. For them creativity was more problematic, not only because they confronted a heavier weight of past example, but also because they questioned traditional authority more aggressively and hence with more guilt. In Milton, we may say, creativity is only incipiently problematic. With a great public myth still at his disposal, he could efface himself from the body of his poem and relegate all moral authority to a figure with the extremely impressive name of God.

But this leads directly to what is centrally problematic in the poem. Milton seems to claim nothing for himself, but he
98 speaks *for* God—a harsh God—with a readiness that at times

makes one wince. God's almost shrill insistence on man's freedom begins to sound as if some active doubt in Milton's mind were being suppressed, for a faith without conflict does not speak in this manner. Lawrence shrewdly observes, "Men are freest when they are most unconscious of freedom. The shout is a rattling of chains, always was." The formulation is perhaps extreme, but there is much truth in it. Insistent self-justificatory speech about right and wrong—Enoch, we are told, "spake much of Right and Wrong" (XI,666)—does suggest unadmitted or half-admitted scruples.

Some Miltonists would intervene at this point to say that any statements made by God must be exempt from aesthetic judgment. Stanley Fish says that God's judgment is "a scientific notation with the *emotional* value of an X or a Y." Merritt Hughes states that God speaks (must be understood as speaking?) "in the dispassionate voice of Truth itself." This is not criticism but a deadening historicism. Fish's book, *Surprised by Sin*, is fascinating because its very conscientiousness exposes the appalling assumptions of such a scholarly stance. In it we are told that Milton's snubs coming from outside the experience of the poem are necessary to jolt us from the self-love aroused by the poetry itself, whose demands, Milton believed (did he?), were illegitimate because they proceeded from and returned to the affections—as if we could be jolted by a mere assertion without imaginative force behind it. But of course the hidden assumption is that Milton and his audience were able to supply this force, so we ought to be able to do so. Fish adds, with a most peculiar candor, "There is only one true interpretation of *Paradise Lost*—the others expose the illogic of God's ways." So they do, and therefore only one reading of the poem is to be permitted! Surely the passionate overstatements of Romantic criticism are preferable to this cold rigidity.

Milton's God seals off all uncertainty, allows no loose ends. Nothing foreign to His own will, no chance, may exist. But at the same time His will is to be totally exempt from necessity. In many prose passages as well as in *Paradise Lost*, Milton declares with emphasis that God's design does not darken 99 human liberty with the least shadow of necessity. His design is to signify a perfect freedom, untainted by either necessity or chance:

> Boundless the Deep, because I am who fill
> Infinitude, nor vacuous the space
> Though I uncircumscrib'd myself retire,
> And put not forth my goodness, which is free
> To act or not, Necessity and Chance
> Approach not mee, and what I will is Fate. (VII,168–73)

But this and other passages describing the divine will are capable of a radical analysis which makes "boundless" and "uncircumscrib'd" seem the least appropriate words. Milton's God equals both law, the opposite of chance, and liberty, the opposite of necessity. Thus, all law is liberty, all liberty is law. In this design there is no conflict whatever, and a contradiction such as Raphael's statement, "Our voluntary service he requires" (V,529), can become a paradoxical truth. As theology this is traditional, but, in so explicitly arrogating everything to God, Milton hardly leaves room for the human freedom he values so highly. He repudiates Calvinism, but certain passages in his poem are quite Calvinistic in effect, for instance the narrator's appalling picture of the bridge built by Sin and Death:

> by which the Spirits perverse
> With easy intercourse pass to and fro
> To tempt or punish mortals, except whom
> God and good Angels guard by special grace. (II,1030–33)

A simpler way of expressing dissatisfaction with Milton's God—and a way that many critics accept but accept too casually—is to say that He is too anthropomorphic. A distinction made by Lawrence (apropos, as it happens, of W. E. Henley's "Invictus") brings this pat statement to life. Asserting one's freedom, he says, is admirable "in the face of men, and their institutions and prisons" but is a "slave's bravado" in "the face of the open heavens." We may say that Milton's God too seldom resembles Lawrence's open heavens, a truly boundless deep, and too often resembles the all-too-human tyranny of men and their institutions. The central principle of

His justice is the sickeningly familiar one of rewarding the obedient and punishing the disobedient. Referring expressly to *Paradise Lost*, Lawrence calls it "the clue to the bourgeois psychology: the reward business."

Milton's God strikes us as not only jealous of his privileges but also vengeful like Satan himself, indeed as unjust as Shelley's piercing description makes Him out to be: "one who in the cold security of undoubted triumph inflicts the most horrible revenge upon his enemy, not from any mistaken notion of inducing him to repent of a perseverance in enmity, but with the alleged design of exasperating him to deserve new torments." The evidence is easily adduced. Satan is permitted "his own dark designs" so that "he might / Heap on himself damnation" (I,213–15). Man is created specifically in order to spite the devils (VII,150–55). The stairs are let down to tempt "the Fiend by easy ascent, or aggravate / His sad exclusion from the doors of Bliss" (III,524–25). On hearing of Satan's plan to rebel, God does not feel dismay or regret—He "smiles" (V,718). And, when men built the tower of Babel, "great laughter was in Heav'n" (XII,59–60). To say that God is righteous hardly solves the problem, for His is a "brutal righteousness," in Erik Erikson's phrase. *Paradise Lost*, like the Old Testament, makes much of a distinction between the just and the wicked, but what is the basis of this distinction if the just are also envious and revengeful? Are we really shown that God is "worthiest, and excels / Them whom he governs" (VI,177–78)? This is not to question Milton's conscious sincerity or to doubt in the least that his conscious motives were the highest. Milton was no more a Satanist, as we customarily mean that term, than Hamlet was a parricide, a point that continues to be misunderstood even by sophisticated critics. Of course Milton did not approve the assassinations of the earl of Strafford and William Laud for Satanic reasons but for the most high-minded aim, to establish a commonwealth of saints. But high-mindedness and cruelty are not always incompatible.

The case against Milton's God can be easily summarized, though the summary would have seemed facilely dismissive without the preceding pages. Even all the intellectual resources of Milton and Augustine can make it nothing but nonsense to say that God made man but did not make the weakness in man that caused him to fall or to say that God knew exactly what was going to happen, pointedly permitting every event which contributed to the outcome, yet bore no responsibility for man's first disobedience. Since these arguments are not foreign to Christian doctrine, one could follow Shelley and Empson in applauding Milton for exposing the wickedness and absurdity of Christianity. But many Christian writers do not insist so literally on these points. Milton's age seems to have demanded an attempt at a grand rationalized synthesis, and Milton's individual temperament prompted him to answer the call.

I have tried to clear the ground for an approach to the areas of *Paradise Lost* that are richest and most valuable for us, its human centers. From my point of view its most pertinent theme concerns the attitudes toward authority, the authority mainly of conscience, although Milton is still comfortable enough with the old allegorical tradition to dramatize his argument with supernatural machinery. We had first to understand God, but our interest then turns to the fallen angels, who have disobeyed Him and can find no path to reconciliation; to Adam and Eve, who have disobeyed Him but do find such a path; and to Christ, the unfallen angels, and the few just men, who remain in complete harmony with His will.

Satan is of course the focus of Milton's probing interest in a conflict of attitudes toward authority. For Satan there are only two possible attitudes, defiance and submission. And his defiance is shown to be as false a freedom as his submission, its mere opposite, because it is accompanied by an immitigable sense of guilt. In neither posture is there escape from conflict, from "hateful contraries." Filial obedience, represented by Christ and by Adam and Eve before the Fall, is the means to true freedom and thereby "true authority in men" (IV,294). Milton is on sound psychological ground in distinguishing a false freedom of defiant licentiousness on the one hand and of submissive self-denial on the other from a true freedom consistent with the idea of obedience to a purposive will. We might note, however, that the word *submission* is not used with clear consistency in *Paradise Lost*. Sometimes it signifies a forced subjection, the willed suppression of guilt-laden defiance, and sometimes a fitting deference (IV,309;V,359; X,195–96,942;XII,597) and the ambiguity is surely related to Milton's difficulty elsewhere in keeping aligned his feelings and thoughts about authority. In the same spirit Lawrence wrote many years later, "Men are free only so long as they obey." Shaw also phrased for himself the same paradox: "Liberty means responsibility. That is why most men dread it."

Satan, locked into his conflict by stubborn pride, cannot find his way to a true—a spontaneous—obedience:

> is there no place
> Left for Repentance, none for Pardon left?
> None left but by submission; and that word
> Disdain forbids me. (IV,79–82)

Milton does not indicate how Satan might become capable of an obedience that is not mere submission, though by powerfully conveying Satan's anguish he raises the question. Defiance, after all, is not necessarily accompanied by guilt. Guilt is involved only when there remains a strong underlying love for, or dependence upon, the person defied. In justifying the assassination of King Charles, Milton himself apparently believed in the possibility of a guilt-free defiance of authority, but when it came to the authority of God he offered no such possibility. Satan is permitted no way out. Unlike Adam, he does not fall from an inward harmony into a state of conflict or recapture even a modified form of inward harmony after falling. He begins with and retains a feeling of exclusion from the love of God.

The poem emphasizes strongly Satan's exclusion from bliss—hence, the pathos of his role, which only Harold Bloom, among modern readers, has sufficiently stressed. This emphasis controls our view of him in the most dramatically charged books: I, II, IV, and IX. Of course his thirst for revenge is evident as well, but revenge is clearly shown to be a   103

reaction to a primary deprivation, a balm to suffering: "For
only in destroying I find ease to my relentless thoughts"
(IX,129–30). His pride is also shown to be not prior to but
dependent upon his sense of exclusion, a compensation for it.
"I who erst contended / With Gods to sit the highest"
(IX,163–64) is simultaneously a brag and a complaint, involving a fantasy of bigness and littleness. "None shall partake
with me" (II,466) indicates both arrogant contempt for fel-
lowship and submerged yearning for it. Milton flatly and
frequently asserts the evilness of Satan and, in an unambigu-
ous though purely symbolic way, indicates his degeneration.
But there is a discrepancy, which no demonstration of irony
eliminates, between this bald intention and the effect of very
considerable sympathy generated by Satan's suffering. I do
not want to undermine the important psychological truth implied in Milton's describing a mind that cannot find its own
way out of a state of conflict. Nor do I want to undermine the
important moral truth implied in his admirably unsentimen-
tal refusal to make suffering and social deprivation excuses,
however much they may be explanations, for vicious acts. But
I do want to say that the repudiation of Satan seems to be
prompted in part by the author's attempt to suppress a conflict
in his own mind. That is, Satan's evident conflict corresponds
to a similar conflict in the mind of the poet and also apparently in his culture, and the degradation of Satan—for it is
hard not to agree with Waldock that degradation is a more
accurate word than degeneration—is precisely the means by
which a full recognition of this felt association is denied.

We saw in Shakespeare that vicious impulses were given
considerable dramatic play before the moral screws were
gently applied. We find some of this flexibility in Spenser and
Milton too, but in them the polarizing influence of Puritan
moralism is clearly more apparent, either in the excessive
attractiveness of the temptation or in the excessive zealous-
ness of the repudiation. Surely, if Milton wants to teach that
vice is its own torment and virtue its own reward, that "to
obey [God] is happiness entire" (VI,741), the point is vitiated
by our discerning a vindictive motive in God's justice. The

transmogrification of Satan appears, in short, to be Milton's revenge.

I have no real argument with the ironic view of Satan as far as it goes. There obviously is a good deal of deliberate and effective irony in the presentation, *e.g.*, the brilliant playing off of "The mind is its own place, and in itself / Can make a Heav'n of Hell, a Hell of Heav'n" (I,254–55) against "within him Hell / He brings, and around about him, nor from Hell / One step no more than from himself can fly / By change of place" (IV,20–23). I doubt if one should call this kind of delayed irony a trap for the reader, who will be humbled by the belated recognition in himself of lawless temptation. After all, the reader is quite aware that the first passage, despite its seductiveness, is intended as a vain heroic boast, and he perceives the second as clinching this effect rather than shocking him into realizing it. But irony it certainly is.

Another modern critical position disturbs me more. I doubt that the sophisticated modern reader is being quite honest with himself in accepting without protest or skepticism Milton's intention to show Satan's misery as inevitable and deserved. The Romantics certainly resented this intention. They were offended by Milton's God and did not see why a defiance like Satan's should be tainted with unworthy motives. But they clearly saw that it was so tainted; they did not fall into any trap for Satanists. Shelley stated the case plainly: "The character of Satan engenders in the mind a pernicious casuistry, causing us to weigh his faults with his wrongs, and to excuse the former because the latter exceed all measure." The Romantic position, basically, is that freedom under that kind of God is no freedom at all and that Satan is worthy of more conscious sympathy than Milton gives him because he makes the most energetic effort to live by that belief. M. H. Abrams and others question the validity of the Romantic perception of a problematic Satan by observing that no earlier critic had noticed anything of the sort. This is not quite true. The Romantics had a different (a more "modern") way of putting the matter, but it seems to me that Dr. Johnson was getting at essentially the same idea when he wrote that Milton "felt not so much the love of liberty as repugnance to authority."

Without endorsing the Romantic position, Helen Gardner draws an analogy (not pursued as far as it should be) between Satan and the Elizabethan tragic hero. C. S. Lewis objects, implying that it makes the prince of darkness too sympathetic, too much like the prince of Denmark. In some ways, to be sure, Satan is more like the Elizabethan tragic villain than hero: his pride is not humbled but stubbornly maintained; he is tough and cynical as well as tormented and profoundly self-deceived. But Lewis sees him as an "ass," without even the dignity of a villain's role.

Now, some of his remarks do prompt us to ask how Satan could be so foolish, how Milton could expect us to fit such seeming naïveté with the other aspects of the devil's portrait. How can we reconcile such an asinine remark as "till then who knew / The force of those dire Arms" (I,93–94) with the depth of Satan's own torment or the subtlety of his malice? If it is a tactical remark to cheer up Beelzebub rather than a foolish one, Milton hasn't implied so. Milton moves him around too quickly from malice, "my dwelling haply may not please / Like this fair Paradise" (IV,378–79), to pathos, "What do mine eyes with grief behold . . . whom my thoughts pursue / With wonder, and could love" (IV,358–63), to self-deception, "And should I at your harmless innocence / Melt as I do, yet public reason just, / . . . compels me now / To do what else though damn'd I should abhor" (IV, 889–92).

My own inference is that Milton maintained two rather different objectives in the characterization of Satan: first, to present him subjectively or naturalistically in a framework of psychological realism and, second, to present him as a self-defining, exemplary figure derived from an allegorical tradition in which the psychology is, as it were, flattened or objectified so that no curiosity about causes is aroused. I see Satan, in other words, the way Bernard Spivack sees Iago—as a character partly explicable psychologically and partly opaque to any but a foreshortened, allegorical perspective.

The "subjective" Satan is my main concern, but the "objective" Satan (I am thinking of Lewis' memorable definition of allegory as "the subjectivity of an objective age") deserves a moment's attention. I think the frankly allegorical passages in *Paradise Lost*, chiefly those involving Sin and Death, are among the most effective in the whole poem. There is something very satisfying in the picture of Satan and Death confronting each other fiercely and fearlessly and unknowingly, stopped only by Sin's grotesque cry:

> O Father, what intends thy hand...
> Against thy only Son? What fury, O Son,
> Possesses thee to bend that mortal Dart
> Against thy Father's head? (II,727–30)

Even better are Sin's glad words to her father-husband on hearing his project:

> thou wilt bring me soon
> To that new world of light and bliss, among
> The Gods who live at ease, where I shall Reign
> At thy right hand voluptuous, as beseems
> Thy daughter and thy darling, without end. (II,866–70)

And her triumphal words upon his return are better still: "Thine now is all this World" (X,372).

These moments are rich and witty because they must be understood in two opposite but inseparable ways; they are at the same time straight and ironical, tender and horrible. The pervasive grand style of the poem, which in the more realistic passages runs the risk of inflating or falsely idealizing the action, here serves only to define it more vividly. That is true also of the noncomic allegorical passages. How richly concise is Zephon's not recognizing the "revolted Spirit" because his brightness has diminished (IV,35). How much is neatly conveyed in the mere phrase, "Tempter ere th' Accuser of mankind" (IV,10), a vivid way of describing the parties of psychological conflict that makes pale such analytic phrasings as impulse versus inhibition or instinct versus guilt.

Milton's exploration of the subjective, pathetic Satan is inevitably more problematic since it arouses questions about causation that recede finally behind the very bounds of the

poem's conception. But, his exploration is searching and
suggestive (actually the analogy between Satan and the Elizabethan tragic hero is justified much more by the abundant
pathos of his role than by the proud resolution of his early
speeches) and deserves more than the rather flat handling it
gets from the poet's unpsychological or antipsychological
commentators. I have said that the pathos of Satan's situation
is conveyed from the beginning; the narrator speaks of Satan's "lost happiness," describes Hell as "Regions of sorrow,
doleful shades, where peace / And rest can never dwell, hope
never comes / That comes to all," and exclaims, "O how unlike the place from whence they fell!" (I,54,65–67,75); and
Satan echoes the phrase, addressing Beelzebub, "If thou beest
hee; But O how fall'n! how chang'd / From him, who in the
happy Realms of Light" (I,84–85). But the broadest and
deepest explorations of the tragic Satan are found in the dramatically crucial Books IV and IX. He has two soliloquies in
the one and three in the other. Some extensive quotation is
needed here as a basis for what follows:

> Now conscience wakes despair
> That slumber'd, wakes the bitter memory
> Of what he was, what is, what must be
> Worse, of worse deeds worse suffering must ensue.
> Sometimes towards *Eden* which now in his view
> Lay pleasant, his griev'd look he fixes sad,
> Sometimes towards Heav'n and the full blazing Sun,
> Which now sat high in his Meridian Tow'r:
> Then much revolving, thus in sighs began.
>   O thou that with surpassing Glory crown'd,
> Lookst from thy sole Dominion like the God
> Of this new World; at whose sight all the Stars
> Hide thir diminisht heads; to thee I call,
> But with no friendly voice, and add thy name
> O Sun, to tell thee how I hate thy beams
> That bring to my remembrance from what state
> I fell, how glorious once above thy Sphere;
> Till Pride and worse Ambition threw me down
> Warring in Heav'n against Heav'n's matchless King:
> Ah wherefore! he deserv'd no such return
> From me, whom he created what I was
> In that bright eminence, and with his good

Upbraided none; nor was his service hard.
What could be less than to afford him praise,
The easiest recompense, and pay him thanks,
How due! yet all his good prov'd ill in me,
And wrought but malice; lifted up so high
I sdained subjection, and thought one step higher
Would set me highest, and in a moment quit
The debt immense of endless gratitude,
So burdensome, still paying, still to owe;
Forgetful what from him I still receiv'd,
And understood not that a grateful mind
By owing owes not, but still pays, at once
Indebted and discharg'd; what burden then?
O had his powerful Destiny ordain'd
Me some inferior Angel, I had stood
Then happy; no unbounded hope had rais'd
Ambition. Yet why not? some other Power
As great might have aspir'd, and me though mean
Drawn to his part; but other Powers as great
Fell not, but stand unshak'n, from within
Or from without, to all temptations arm'd.
Hadst thou the same free Will and Power to stand?
Thou hadst: whom hast thou then or what to accuse,
But Heav'n's free Love dealt equally to all?
Be then his Love accurst, since love or hate,
To me alike, it deals eternal woe.

. . . .

So farewell Hope, and with Hope farewell Fear,
Farewell Remorse: all Good to me is lost;
Evil be thou my Good; by thee at least
Divided Empire with Heav'n's King I hold
By thee, and more than half perhaps will reign;
As Man ere long, and this new World shall know. (IV, 23–113)

Like Hamlet and Macbeth, but unlike Iago and Edmund, Satan is tormented by conscience. Conscience wakes despair, and the felt cause of this despair is the frustration of his yearning for love. His address to the kingly Sun, "with surpassing Glory crown'd," and his thoughts about "Heav'n's matchless King" are suffused with awe and tenderness that are somehow twisted into hate. It is as if his love encountered some barrier or ban, changed into despair, and thence into active revenge. Though he can acknowledge his fault, he can

see no way of recovering God's precious love (nor can we,
since there is no indication that his basic nature is alterable),
so he curses that love and embraces evil. In confirming his
revenge again, and conclusively, in Book IX, he clearly indicates a prior frustration of sexual love and even throws a little
light on the substance of the inward ban by mentioning the
"terror" that inheres in "Love / And beauty":

> But the hot Hell that always in him burns,
> Though in mid Heav'n, soon ended his delight,
> And tortures him now more, the more he sees
> Of pleasure not for him ordain'd: then soon
> Fierce hate he recollects, and all his thoughts
> Of mischief, gratulating, thus excites.
> . . . .
> Shee fair, divinely fair, fit Love for Gods,
> Not terrible, though terror be in Love
> And beauty, not approacht by stronger hate,
> Hate stronger, under show of Love well feign'd,
> The way which to her ruin now I tend. (IX,467–93)

In Satan's later soliloquies, Milton tends to associate this
original impulse of love with envy, and he works out a basic
sequence of motivation from envy to despair to revenge:

> With what delight could I have walkt thee round,
> If I could joy in aught, sweet interchange
> Of Hill and Valley, Rivers, Woods and Plains,
> Now Land, now Sea, and Shores with Forest crown'd,
> Rocks, Dens, and Caves, but I in none of these
> Find place or refuge; and the more I see
> Pleasures about me, so much more I feel
> Torment within me, as from the hateful siege
> Of contraries; all good to me becomes
> Bane, and in Heav'n much worse would be my state.
> But neither here seek I, no nor in Heav'n
> To dwell, unless by maistring Heav'n's Supreme;
> Nor hope to be myself less miserable
> By what I seek, but others to make such
> As I, though thereby worse to me redound:
> For only in destroying I find ease
> To my relentless thoughts. (IX,114–30)

First is the envy, "With what delight could I have walkt thee
round," then the despair, "but I in none of these / Find place

or refuge," and finally the revenge, "only in destroying I find ease." The sequence is worked out twice in quick succession some lines farther on:

> O foul descent! that I who erst contended
> With Gods to sit the highest am now constrain'd
> Into a Beast, and mixt with bestial slime,
> This essence to incarnate and imbrute,
> That to the highth of deity aspir'd;
> But what will not Ambition and Revenge
> Descend to? who aspires must down as low
> As high he soar'd, obnoxious first or last
> To basest things. Revenge, at first though sweet,
> Bitter ere long back on itself recoils;
> Let it; I reck not, so it light well aim'd,
> Since higher I fall short, on him who next
> Provokes my envy, this new Favorite
> Of Heav'n, the Man of Clay, Son of despite
> Whom us the more to spite his Maker rais'd
> From dust: spite then with spite is best repaid. (IX,163–78)

First is envy, "I who erst contended / With Gods to sit the highest," then despair, "am now constrain'd / Into a Beast," and, finally, revenge, "what will not Ambition and Revenge / Descend to?" Again we have envy, "on him who next / Provokes my envy," despair, "[although revenge] Bitter ere long back on itself recoils," and revenge, "spite then with spite is best repaid." Farther on, Adam makes the sequence explicit:

> what malicious Foe
> Envying our happiness, and of his own
> Despairing, seeks to work us woe and shame. (IX,253–55)

Milton thus keeps raising the question of causes and origins. Although Satan's motives are traditionally given and unanalyzable, there is a new historical or genetic thrust in Milton's characterization, a psychological curiosity peeping through the theological dogmatism. Is Satan's will to rebel primal, or is it brought into being by the act of rebellion? Satan favors the former view, and one would think it correct from such evidence as Gabriel's scornful speech:

> And thou sly hypocrite, who now wouldst seem
> Patron of liberty, who more than thou

Once fawn'd, and cring'd, and servilely ador'd
Heav'n's awful Monarch? wherefore but in hope
To dispossess him, and thyself to reign? (IV,957–61)

But there is considerable hedging on the matter. Some passages, *e.g.*, Sin's account of her birth, imply that his will to rebel originated later, and certainly the primary motive of envy is closely linked with the specific event of God's announcement of the Messiah.

This linkage bears more investigation. We notice that two major factors provoke the devil's envy: the prelapsarian happiness of Adam and Eve and the elevation of Christ. A scrutiny of these will show that Milton's intuitive if not conceptual understanding of envy goes beyond the flat Augustinian definition that "envy is hatred of another's happiness and unites with pride as the mainspring of the devil's nature." Satan's envy of Adam and Eve, as we have seen already, clearly has a sexual basis:

> aside the Devil turn'd
> For envy, yet with jealous leer malign
> Ey'd them askance, and to himself thus plain'd.
>   Sight hateful, sight tormenting! thus these two
> Imparadis't in one another's arms
> The happier *Eden*, shall enjoy their fill
> Of bliss on bliss, while I to Hell am thrust,
> Where neither joy nor love, but fierce desire,
> Among our other torments not the least,
> Still unfulfill'd with pain of longing pines: (IV,502–11)

Adam makes the point even more explicitly: "Conjugal Love, than which perhaps no bliss / Enjoy'd by us excites his envy more" (IV,263–64). Satan's envy of Christ is more ambiguous. The chronological action of *Paradise Lost* begins with God's announcement of the elevation of Christ, and the announcement certainly sounds peremptory and threatening, as if God is provoking the rebellion that He must, in His omniscience, be expecting:

> him who disobeys
> Mee disobeys, breaks union, and that day
> Cast out from God and blessed vision, falls

112

Into utter darkness, deep ingulft, his place
Ordain'd without redemption, without end. (V,611–15)

This inference has irritated some readers, but the text does raise the disconcerting question, Why, if God needed a viceregent, did He not appoint His brightest angel? Not to do so and to give no reason certainly are arbitrary and provocative. The literary critic is obliged to analyze the figures of sacred tradition as he would any other fictional creations, and so there remains this question, which Milton would not answer or did not see. I think Waldock's statement is proper as well as correct: "Milton succeeded in suggesting a rather greater degree of provocation [for Satan's revolt], and therefore of reasonableness in it, than he ever intended."

In any case Satan is "fraught with envy":

he of the first,
If not the first Arch-Angel, great in Power,
In favor and preeminence, yet fraught
With envy against the Son of God, that day
Honor'd by his great Father, and proclaim'd
Messiah King anointed, could not bear
Through pride that sight, and thought himself impair'd.
(V,559–65)

Two pictures are presented here—as elsewhere in the poem —and the hedging opening of the passage is a measure of the inconsistency between them: (1) Satan, formerly unfallen, conceives envy and thereby revenge at this moment; and (2) Satan, tainted with pride from the beginning, succumbs easily to envy and the thirst for revenge. The second picture is closer to tradition, but it makes Satan less blameworthy. Milton encountered a problem and did not solve it. He encountered a somewhat similar problem in regard to the Ptolemaic versus Copernican cosmologies (VIII,70ff.). There he dramatizes one and allows the other to be entertained, without the equivocation mattering very much. But the problem is not so easily put aside when the motivation of a major character is in question.

The sexual envy which marks Satan's relation to Adam and Eve is not apparent in his relation to Christ and God. But envy is envy; despite the loftiness of Milton's subject, which

makes it seem indecorous to consider "low" motives too curiously, we might well wonder about the difference. We are of
course shown a picture of Satan in sexual relation to Sin and
Death, but this is not associated with his envy either in Eden
or in Heaven, and in fact the allegorical dimension of his
character is quite unrelated to the realistic one. I realize we are
now touching upon the limits of Milton's artistic conception,
so I will say only this much more. In *Hamlet* Shakespeare
maintains a strong intuitive grasp on the profound intimacy
between libidinal and murderous wishes. In *Paradise Lost* the
connection is explored in some depth but then becomes
obscure, as if a veil passed over the poet's vision. When Melville, 250 years later, came to create a villain on the model of
Milton's Satan, the sexual element comes insistently to the
fore. Melville also tries to retreat to an idea of causeless depravity, but he is forced, by a self-awareness he could not
escape, to "work in close" (as Hemingway might have put it),
and his story goes farther than Milton's in this particular
direction.

Adam and Eve are introduced to us midway through Book IV,
and their character and situation quickly gain definition in
contrast to Satan's. They have not yet become victims to
hateful contraries, and their prelapsarian freedom from
conflict is poignantly rendered. But very soon we run into a
problem. God must insist in this case too—even more strongly,
in fact, than in the case of Satan—that their fall is entirely
their own fault.

It is hard to see that they were created "sufficient to have
stood, though free to fall," for, as God predicts, they "easily
transgress" (III,98,80). Like Billy Budd, they can really be
happy only in happy circumstances, in a garden without a
tempter. Can they be responsible for the presence of Satan or
for his intentions? Another aesthetic problem here is that the
buildup of the temptation scene is weakly dramatized.
Raphael, whose coming down "fulfilled All Justice" (V,245),
instructs Adam at some length, but Adam puts up little resistance in the crucial action. Eve has been granted a dream so

closely previsioning the circumstances of her fall that her heedlessness of it at the critical moment must seem (by the standards of realism, which prevail here over those of allegory) exceedingly dim-witted. Adam even comments on her dream with admirable psychological and moral insight:

> Evil into the mind of God or Man
> May come and go, so unapprov'd, and leave
> No spot or blame behind: Which gives me hope
> That what in sleep thou didst abhor to dream,
> Waking thou never wilt consent to do. (V,117–21)

But then Milton musses over the insight by Eve's heedlessness.

Some of Milton's difficulty in dramatizing the temptation is doubtless inherent in the task of transforming a spare, primitive story into extended literary epic. The little story can hardly bear the moral and psychological weight put upon it. When Satan returns to Hell and jokes about having seduced our first parents with an apple, we are half inclined to laugh with him rather than at him, despite our knowledge of his imminent transmogrification. The idea of representing so momentous an event as man's first disobedience by the eating of an apple is not silly in Genesis because the story is so brief, so naïve, so frankly legendary. We accept this symbol of a divine test without finding it awkward. A modern poet might have mined the symbolism to expose, for example, what appears to be a universal association in the human mind between fruits or fruit trees and female bodies, particularly breasts. This could open the old legend to at least two significations capable of extended treatment: (1) a stern father's prohibition of a child's incestuous wishes, accompanied by the threat of withdrawing love; and (2) a kind father's encouragement to transfer sexual affection from those in the family to those outside. This tactic, with its implication of a psychosexually burdened childhood, was hardly available to a seventeenth-century poet (it makes the concept of a prelapsarian state, for one thing, virtually meaningless), but only in some such way, it seems to me, can the archaic biblical story escape silliness in an extended, rationalized form.

Whatever the difficulties in dramatizing Adam and Eve's state before the Fall, their state afterward, like Satan's, is admirably conveyed. Milton shows us something of the real effort men must make to incorporate a sense of guilt into their psychic economy, and he does so without lapsing into the sentimental attitude of absolving his sinners or the cynical attitude of treating their despair as unalterable. Eve's successive reactions after sinning are shrewdly imagined: she feels pleasure before she experiences guilt; she thinks that maybe no one else will know her act; she worries how she shall appear to Adam; she wonders if it might be better not to tell him in order to gain power over him; she worries that she might lose his love; she decides he must join her in sin. Adam's corresponding reactions are also well conceived. He says: how can I live without her; how could she do it; we can't undo it but surely God wouldn't destroy us since he troubled to create us; and, finally (the latent fear in the rationalization becoming manifest), to lose her would be to lose myself. And Eve's capping exclamation, "O Glorious trial of exceeding love" (IX,961), is ironic in that rich and witty way we observed in some of Sin's exclamations; it is both true and false, an intimation simultaneously of human strength and weakness.

The postlapsarian state is especially well dramatized in the second half of Book IX and in Book X. The last two books, many critics agree, show some slackening of invention and rhetorical force, though the plangency of the close is as fine as anything earlier. It may be significant in this connection that Satan is virtually absent from them, for Milton is characteristically stimulated by the opportunity to take arms against error. The explanation I want to focus on, however, concerns Milton's particular difficulty in identifying beyond a certain point with the character of Adam.

Even when Adam is fully instructed by Michael in the knowledge needed to sustain the trial of life, he falls short of heroism. Consider the passage in which he sums up the wisdom he has gained:

Henceforth I learn, that to obey is best,
And love with fear the only God, to walk

As in his presence, ever to observe
His providence, and on him sole depend,
Merciful over all his works, with good
Still overcoming evil, and by small
Accomplishing great things, by things deem'd weak
Subverting worldly strong, and worldly wise
By simply meek; that suffering for Truth's sake
Is fortitude to highest victory,
And to the faithful death the gate of life;
Taught thus by his example whom I now
Acknowledge my Redeemer ever blest. (XII,561–73)

These lines initially stress submissiveness (to obey, to love with fear, sole depend, by things deemed weak, by simply meek) but finally stress conquest (overcoming evil, accomplishing great things, subverting worldly strong, highest victory). And in the role of spiritual conqueror—the role of Christ in *Paradise Regained* and of Samson in *Samson Agonistes*—we do not see Adam. Adam is led to the recognition of ideals that Milton espouses but cannot, because of the exigencies of the plot, be led as far as "vertuous action," which Sir Philip Sidney, speaking for Renaissance or any other humanism, called "the ending end of all earthly learning."

The question of Adam's heroism is much complicated by the presence of Eve, for she is someone toward whom the poet has great difficulty in maintaining a consistent attitude. Misogynistic implications are present in the biblical story (see Theodore Reik's *The Creation of Eve*), but Milton both suppresses them in favor of a more idealized picture and seizes on them a little too readily. When he pities Eve—"hapless Eve," the "unsupported flower" (IX,404,431)—the effect is a little patronizing, for the immediate contextual fact is her willful resistance to Adam's sensible advice about working together. When Milton expresses admiration for her, he usually betrays quite other attitudes at the same time. For example, Adam's report to Raphael on first experiencing Eve's beauty begins as a tribute to "beauty's powerful glance," but as it goes on it seems to be less a tribute than an attack. Adam wonders first if "Nature failed in me," but then seems to say that Nature failed in *her:* Eve was given too much "Ornament" and is of "inward [beauty] less exact"; "All higher 117

knowledge in her presence falls / Degraded." The enjamb-
ment here underlines the already strong word "Degraded."
Raphael's summary advice about self-esteem—"weigh her
with thyself; / Then value: Oft-times nothing profits more /
Than self-esteem grounded on just and right."—puts the responsibility back on Adam. Yet the lines mean not merely
that the will of the woman is best subordinated to the man's
but that it is absolutely deficient in "just and right" (VIII,
531ff.).

The closing passage of Book IX provides a similar, perhaps
more telling example of such equivocation. It begins strongly
with Eve's, not Milton's, shaky self-defense. She says, first,
It might have happened to you. Then she asks, Was I to have
never been parted from your side? And finally, Why didn't
you command me absolutely not to go? Adam replies in kind:
Is this gratitude when I chose death with you? Anyway, if I
had used force it would have restrained your freedom of
choice. Then he adds words which, despite the indication of
irony, betray Milton's shakiness:

> . . . and perhaps
> I also err'd in overmuch admiring
> What seemed in thee so perfect, that I thought
> No evil durst attempt thee, but I rue
> That error now, which is become my crime,
> And thou th' accuser. Thus it shall befall
> Him who to worth in Woman overtrusting
> Lets her Will rule; restraint she will not brook,
> And left to herself, if evil thence ensue,
> Shee first his weak indulgence will accuse.
>   Thus they in mutual accusation spent
> The fruitless hours, but neither self-condemning,
> And of thir vain contest appeared no end. (IX,1177–89)

The phrase "neither self-condemning" seems to be directed at
Adam's attack on Eve as well as hers on him. But the irony
doesn't work very well. Adam *does* condemn himself. And his
touch of self-condemnation ("perhaps / I also err'd") is precisely what seems to clear the way for an unusually sweeping
and direct attack on woman. The homiletic generalization

might be defended on grounds that Adam represents mankind, but in this context it has an unpleasantly self-justifying effect, foreshadowing Adam's more blatant attack on woman (X,899–908) on grounds that are all too reminiscent of Milton's personal circumstances. Milton is reluctant to impugn Adam. We know that he dealt more harshly with him in an earlier draft. Unlike Eve, Adam is "not deceiv'd"; his fault is to be "fondly overcome with female charm" (IX,998–99). But that is the kind of fault that can also be read as a covert attack. In any case it is scarcely heroic.

Another cause, or perhaps effect, of Adam's imperfect heroism is the noticeably more resigned tone of the last two books. Adam is supposed to be learning to neither love nor hate his life, but the actual emphasis falls much more on submissive repentance than on moderation in self-loathing. It is hard to know how much of this emphasis is due to Milton's resistance to identifying with the Adamic role, how much to an inherent tendency in the traditional story, and how much to something negative that may have affected Milton's state of mind in the latter periods of composition. The negativism seems to be pervasive rather than specific. In the earlier books some effort is made to oppose the Puritan tendency to separate flesh and spirit and to intimate a higher synthesis of the two, but in these books the synthesis lapses into black and white antithesis. And the negativism does seem to persist beyond this work, for I agree with W. W. Robson: "It is, indeed, hard not to feel that an element of penitential exercise, of deliberate self-mortification, entered into Milton's conception of his purpose in *Paradise Regained*."

As Adam is not raised sufficiently above the all-too-human, so Christ, the second Adam, is not sufficiently lowered from the divine to become heroic. The Son is assigned a will but does not in effect possess one. His acts and words appear automatic, and it is hard to imagine how they might have appeared autonomous if Milton the poet stands by his assertion in *Christian Doctrine* that "the Son can do nothing but what he sees the Father do." Christ says:

Father Eternal, thine is to decree
Mine both in Heav'n and Earth to do thy will
Supreme, that thou in mee thy Son belov'd
May'st ever rest well pleas'd. (X,68–71)

That is certainly the spirit maintained throughout the poem. Christ performs some impressive acts—he defeats Satan in battle, creates the world, and volunteers to die for the redemption of man's sins—but none of these, not even the last which lies at the heart of the Christ story, is dramatized as a *spontaneous* action. And the unfallen angels who spontaneously applaud his volunteering are much like the devils whose applause for Satan's volunteering to undertake alone the expedition to Eden is only mock spontaneous.

Milton's picture of the Son's will as identical with the Father's is inherent in Christian theology, so our difficulty with this aspect of *Paradise Lost* can be traced to that source. But Christian writers also emphasize the Son's achieving oneness with God, which inevitably implies a temporary apartness, for, as Stephen Dedalus points out in *Ulysses*, "there can be no reconciliation unless there has first been a sundering." The last phrase of Christ's speech ("that thou in mee thy Son belov'd / May'st ever rest well pleas'd") faintly implies the possibility of sundering, but the implication is not developed in *Paradise Lost*.

The almost incredible success of the Christ story in Western civilization surely has much to do with the powerful feeling generated by the idea of atonement, of the Son's initial separation from the Father and eventual restoration of love achieved at the cost of renunciation. Milton does not release the potency of this idea in portraying Christ, or he does so only insofar as, in Michael's relation to Adam, he briefly links the figure of Christ with Enoch, Noah, and the few just men who are heroic martyrs to the cause of God's truth. In *Paradise Lost* it is of course Adam who seeks and attains reconciliation with God, and Christ's function is explicitly to assist him in this endeavor: "let him live / Before thee reconcil'd . . . / Made one with me as I with thee am one" (XI,38–44). But Christ's mediating function here is only 120 technical, not dramatic.

A curious unintended effect results from the combination of the Son's extreme dependency and the Father's extreme authoritarianism: Christ sometimes seems either silly or sly. When the Father derides Satan's rebellion, the Son says, "thou thy foes / Justly hast in derision" (V,735–36), which makes him sound either like a toady twitching in agreement or like a shrewd Prince Hal reassuring a doubtful Bolingbroke about his right to put down the rebels. When God declares man's complete freedom yet predicts man will easily transgress, the Son applauds His kindness (which sounds foolish), but then goes on, almost cleverly, to solicit concessions of graciousness:

>   should Man
> Thy creature late so lov'd, thy youngest Son
> Fall circumvented thus by fraud, though join'd
> With his own folly? that be from thee far,
> That far be from thee, Father, who art Judge
> Of all things made, and judgest only right. (III,150–55)

These awkwardnesses testify to Milton's difficulty in reconciling the dramatic need to show Christ and the angels as free with the doctrinal belief that they are wholly encompassed by God.

In working out attitudes toward authority in his epic poem, Milton identified himself most intensely with neither Adam nor Christ but with a few minor characters, with God, and (more than he knew) with Satan. The matter of unconscious identification with Satan might be pursued psycho-biographically, if one were so inclined, but in a broad historical context this identification makes sense. Satan embodies attitudes—individualism, atheism, naturalism—that evidently formed an upwelling undercurrent in seventeenth-century England, an undercurrent that Milton for the most part fought against. It is not really surprising, however, to discover that so strong a current (which, after a last-ditch resistance from the neoclassicists, did finally take over) should have engaged his feelings more than he knew.

A century or two after Milton, the most energetic literary talents in the heroic tradition found themselves in Satan's position, cut off from a moral order yet longing for connection with one, proudly but anxiously compelled to continual self-definition. (C. S. Lewis mocks just this compulsion in Satan to restate his position, but mockery is pointless if one believes with Ibsen that "there is no judge above us; therefore we must judge ourselves.") One of their basic strategies was to seize on the energy of defiance embodied in Satan and attempt to purify it not only of pettiness and perversity but also of underlying guilt. Another was to quiet the guilty will in gestures of renunciation, hoping thus to be graced with an influx of creative energy. The advance in self-consciousness (or, less sentimentally, in self-awareness) meant that guilt had to be dealt with at closer quarters. It increased the urgency of the need to override or circumvent inner constraints, especially when there persisted imaginatively a longing for heroic action. In trying to find forms that incorporated both their desire for victory and their guilt-prompted need for defeat, many writers from the Romantic period on have been drawn to the Christ story, which so powerfully and definitively combines the two. The keenest of them have been aware of the self-pity inherent in this attraction and have struggled against it in their art by dramatizing both the individual will and the forces opposed to it as toughly, as convincingly as possible. This in brief is the subject of the next three chapters.

THE QUEST FOR GUILTLESSNESS: **III**
MELVILLE'S *BILLY BUDD*

MELVILLE dramatizes unconscious conflict with profound insight in the opposite figures of Billy Budd and John Claggart. He assigns to the third major figure of the story, Captain Vere, the severest kind of conscious conflict and amplifies our understanding of it with rich and intricate parallels, but his picture of Vere wobbles about a good deal, apparently under the pressure of an unconscious conflict in his own mind. Yet, Melville seems to know that he cannot keep a steady balance between his contrary attitudes toward Vere. And as a result he shifts the focus of his story, he alters the intention—and not for the first time. If the artist had found a neater formal solution to the problem of accommodating his changing and conflicting feelings, the layerings of his intention unfolding during composition would have only psychological, not aesthetic, interest. As it is, those layerings, admirably discriminated in the genetic text worked out by Harrison Hayford and Merton Sealts,* bear directly on the critic's job of interpretation and evaluation.

What we get in this story, then, is not exactly a discrepancy between intentions and effects, though there are instances of

---

* Herman Melville, *Billy Budd, Sailor (An Inside Narrative)*, ed. from the manuscript, with intro. and notes, Harrison Hayford and Merton M. Sealts, Jr. (Chicago: University of Chicago Press, 1962). All citations, indicated by page numbers in parentheses, are to this definitive text, which traces the stages of composition of Melville's incompletely revised manuscript.

evasion. Rather, we get an unusual opportunity to observe an extraordinarily searching and imaginative intelligence building a story out of a sequence of intentions, each new one prompted by dissatisfaction with the last. If the result is not a beautiful coherence, it is not the opposite either, an unbeautiful incoherence. For one thing, each phase of meaning is so richly accreted. For another, the improvisatory aspect of the whole and the inner logic of the sequent intentions are qualities of the tale which the artist comprehends and brings under a kind of control.

Billy and Claggart

Good and evil are inexact labels for the antagonists of Melville's searching story, whether we consider their deeds or their motives. Melville clearly discourages us from basing a moral judgment on their deeds alone, on outward appearances rather than inward realities: "the apparent victim of the tragedy was he who had sought to victimize a man blameless; and the indisputable deed of the latter, navally regarded, constituted the most heinous of military crimes" (103). He emphasizes the inward truth, "the dark side popularly disclaimed" (96), and he does so with a special insistence, for he calls his story not fable or fiction but fact and truth: "The symmetry of form attainable in pure fiction cannot so readily be achieved in a narration having less to do with fable than with fact. Truth uncompromisingly told will always have its ragged edges" (128). His truth has ragged edges in contrast to the symmetry of pure (conventional or popular) fiction, because it is the truth of "an inside narrative," profound and elusive.

Nor do the terms good and evil describe very well the motives of Billy and Claggart. In their crucial actions they are shown to be in the grip of compulsions beyond their control. And their motives, as Melville leads us into the depths of their minds, come to seem so complex that we find ourselves discovering the clue to Billy's action in a profound fear of hatred and to Claggart's in a profound fear of love: hate is intolerable to Billy and Hamlet; love, to Claggart and Satan. An analysis of their characters had, therefore, best begin descriptively.

The distinguishing feature of Billy Budd is a physical beauty lit from within by a genial, trusting, and serene nature; it is epitomized in his "singularly musical" voice "expressive of the harmony within" (53). His basic quality is innocence. But the opposite of innocence is not evil, it is guilt. So we may describe Billy's innocence as a freedom from the awareness of guilt or, more simply, freedom from conflict. Claggart's being, we are told, is also "lit from within, though from a different source" (77). His pale complexion, penetrating eyes (versus Billy's dilated eyes), suddenly changing expression, and guarded, ironical manner point to the complexity and distrustful restlessness of his nature—*i.e.*, to guilt and conflict.

Melville to some extent discourages us from searching behind these phenomena for psychological and social causes. We are apparently to regard the natures of Billy and Claggart as given, absolute, causeless. Billy's benevolence is "instinctive"; his stutter, which hints at a darker will within him, is "organic," a word Melville habitually uses in the sense of incurable or constitutional; it is "the work of the envious marplot of Eden" (53). Correspondingly, Claggart's malevolence is a "depravity according to nature" (75); he has "no power to annul the elemental evil in him"; he is "like the scorpion for which the Creator alone is responsible" (78). Similes which connect Billy and Claggart with myth figures —Adam, Christ, Satan—work, of course, toward the same effect. But Melville does in fact provide grounds for some explanation in terms of natural cause.

Billy's stutter, as Melville himself presents it, can be interpreted in terms of unconscious motives. We note that it is aroused by particular circumstances and elicits particular responses. It is dramatized twice, and there are two other incidents which shed light on its psychological meaning.

The first dramatized occasion is when Billy is invited by Claggart's man Sneak to join a trumped-up mutiny plot and to take gold coins for his help: "But Billy broke in, and in his resentful eagerness to deliver himself his vocal infirmity somewhat intruded. 'D-d-damme, I don't know what you are

125

d-d-driving at, or what you mean, but you had better g-g-go where you belong!... If you d-don't start, I'll t-t-toss you back over the r-rail' "(82). The invitation to criminal disobedience and the suggestion of kinship with other impressed men who are prospective mutineers apparently arouse in Billy a powerful rage which has been held down unconsciously by an equally powerful fear; the stutter seems to indicate both the strength and incomplete success of this repression. After this first, dimly comprehended "encounter with evil," "Billy was like a young horse fresh from the pasture suddenly inhaling a vile whiff from some chemical factory, and by repeated snortings trying to get it out of his nostrils and lungs" (84). Billy has no experience of disobedience because the idea is intolerable to him and, conversely, it is intolerable partly because he has no experience of it. All he can do at this juncture is either to annul the externally exciting cause (he begins to do this by threatening Sneak) or to reeffect the repression like the young horse getting the vileness out of his system.

The second—and critical—occasion is in Vere's cabin just after Claggart has falsely accused him. The passage needs to be quoted at length:

> Not at first did Billy take it in. When he did the rose-tan of his cheek looked struck as by white leprosy. He stood like one impaled and gagged. Meanwhile the accuser's eyes, removing not as yet from the blue dilated ones, underwent a phenomenal change, their wonted rich violet color blurring into a muddy purple. Those lights of human intelligence, losing human expression, were gelidly protruding like the alien eyes of certain uncatalogued creatures of the deep. The first mesmeristic glance was one of serpent fascination; the last was as the paralyzing lurch of the torpedo fish.
>
> "Speak, man!" said Captain Vere to the transfixed one, struck by his aspect even more than by Claggart's. "Speak! Defend yourself!" Which appeal caused but a strange dumb gesturing and gurgling in Billy; amazement at such an accusation so suddenly sprung on inexperienced nonage; this, and, it may be, horror of the accuser's eyes, serving to bring out his lurking defect and in this instance for the time intensifying it into a convulsed tongue-tie; while the intent head and entire form straining forward in an agony of ineffectual eagerness to obey the injunction to speak and defend himself, gave an expression to the

face like that of a condemned vestal priestess in the moment of being buried alive, and in the first struggle against suffocation.

Though at the time Captain Vere was quite ignorant of Billy's liability to vocal impediment, he now immediately divined it, since Billy's aspect recalled to him that of a bright young schoolmate of his whom he had once seen struck by much the same startling impotence in the act of eagerly rising in the class to be foremost in response to a testing question put to it by the master. Going close to the young sailor, and laying a soothing hand on his shoulder, he said, "There is no hurry, my boy. Take your time, take your time." Contrary to the effect intended, these words so fatherly in tone, doubtless touching Billy's heart to the quick, prompted yet more violent efforts at utterance—efforts soon ending for the time in confirming his paralysis, and bringing to his face an expression which was as a crucifixion to behold. The next instant, quick as a flame from a discharged cannon at night, his right arm shot out, and Claggart dropped to the deck. (98–99)

Two factors are stressed here that make the situation in the highest degree intolerable for Billy: Claggart's accusation (accusing eye) and Vere's sympathy (sympathetic hand and voice). Billy ardently desires to obey and please his captain, as the comparison to Vere's schoolmate indicates, but to do so in this case he would have to criticize, even accuse, another authority figure; he would have to admit into a consciousness that has never learned to modify them through experience a primitive rage against a father and a consequent dread of losing his love. Billy has buried these inadmissible feelings, but the situation has roused them and they seek expression. The results are paralysis, the stutter, and an explosion of involuntary physical action. In the trial scene a little later, the partial stutter accompanying Billy's acknowledgment of Vere's good opinion—"God will bless you for that, your Honor"—indicates that the fresh repression has not quite been completed. But a few minutes later, at the moment of hanging, Billy's famous words, "God bless Captain Vere," are, we are told, "wholly unobstructed in the utterance" (123).

That Melville understands Claggart's attack and Billy's mute defense to have a sexual basis is shown by the strong imagery. Claggart's accusing expression—"The first mesmeristic glance was one of serpent fascination, the last was as the paralyzing lurch of the torpedo fish"—suggests a sexual assault that is both devouring and penetrating. The words describing Billy's reaction—impaled, gagged, suffocated, paralyzed—suggest a defense against such an assault, and the comparison of his blow to the discharge of a cannon is a kind of sexual retaliation. These images embody enough feeling-tone to make it unnecessary for the critic to employ the risky procedure of purely symbolic interpretation, which always implies that the author did not understand what he was saying. Even the connection between Billy's muteness and the missing finger of Jack Chase, the hero of *White-Jacket* and dedicatee of *Billy Budd*, does not seem to have been lost on Melville.

Claggart's attack, be it noted, is voluntary; Billy's is involuntary. Claggart above all fears sexually charged passivity; Billy, sexually charged activity. The fact that Billy's blow has such dire consequences, then, is partly due to the intensity of the emotional conflict that innervates his arm. But it is also partly due to chance, since a man felled even by such a blow does not usually die. This degree of implausibility points to some weighting of the scales by Melville; it gives us some sense that he is manipulating the tragedy and relishing the insoluble bind into which he has put Billy and, even more, Vere. I shall return later to this point.

Two earlier episodes—the scene with Red Whiskers aboard the *Rights of Man* and the gangway flogging on the *Bellipotent*—support the dynamic picture of Billy's mind. The episode with Red Whiskers is designed as an attenuated version of the critical scene in Vere's cabin. Captain Graveling is a less rigid captain facing a less extreme situation. Red Whiskers is like Claggart motivated by envy and antipathy, which he expresses in the same ironic phrase, "a sweet and pleasant fellow." But he offers slighter provocation (a poke in the ribs) and is better able to let his underlying love for Billy come to the surface after an exhibition of self-protective hostility. And Billy's reaction is a comparable but less intense version of his later one: he "forbore" longer, then gave his

man "a terrible drubbing" but (Melville cooperating) without
killing him. As for the flogging incident, Billy's reaction to
"the first formal gangway-punishment he had ever wit-
nessed" indicates both the strength of his wish to obey
authority and his correlative fear of disobedience. Normally
punctilious, he now goes about his duty with "heightened
alacrity," for "Billy was horrified. He resolved that never
through remissness would he make himself liable to such a
visitation or do or omit aught that might merit even verbal
reproof" (68). Melville's own attitude toward flogging sometimes wavers, but here the question of whether it is a necessary aspect of naval discipline or a barbarism is contained by
the truth of his characterization.

From the evidence, then, which Melville himself provides,
we can say that Billy has, out of fear, utterly banished his
aggressive impulses from consciousness, but that these impulses may be aroused by malevolence from without and that,
when they are, they can find expression only through stutter-
ing and blind rage. In short, it is Melville's powerful dramatized insight, despite some wavering in his theory or discursive commentary, that such extraordinary innocence as
Billy possesses is not given but achieved through an energetic,
though unconscious, effort.

The story also provides a social, or psychosocial, explanation of Billy's nature. His ancestry, Melville implies, is pure
Saxon and aristocratic, although he is a foundling. Further, in
a passage extending over two pages, we are shown that Claggart's is the opposite: foreign, from a submerged class,
vaguely criminal. We cannot regard these suggestions of social
advantage and disadvantage as simply rhetorical en-
hancements of ideas of purity and corruption. If Melville had
wanted to show that Billy's innocence is uncontingent and
God-given, he would persuade us more by not tacking on
social advantages. I think Melville is reaching for an insight
he is not quite willing to claim, although it sounds almost
commonplace nowadays—namely, that the capacity for trust
and distrust, exemplified in extreme forms by Billy and Claggart, has something to do with one's social experience of

acceptance or rejection, inclusion or exclusion. It is a question why Melville didn't pursue the implications of his characters' social backgrounds. Perhaps he sensed the inconsistency between relative (psychosocial) and absolute (metaphysical) views of character. Billy's pure Saxon lineage, in connection with the Handsome Sailor "of the unadulterate blood of Ham" in the story's opening paragraph, actually points toward both views at once. The connection suggests that the pure-blooded enjoy the advantage of being favored by their respective societies but also that personal charisma is a phenomenon that transcends social or racial distinctions, since it may be found in Africans as well as Saxons.

The flaw in Billy's character can thus be seen naturalistically. But Billy cannot be called a tragic hero (as one interpreter, having also discerned an unconscious conflict in him, would have it), however tragic his fate may be. A tragic hero experiences intense conflict, whatever the unconscious basis of that conflict. But Billy does not suffer, or does only for a few blinding moments. Whereas the tragic hero struggles to understand what is going on in his mind and to resolve his conflict by conscious effort, Billy struggles only to rebury his conflict by blindly destroying the external cause that excited it. There is agony on his face in the cabin scene, but it never really enters his consciousness. It is like a spasm, and passes; we are told that it does not survive the interview with Vere a little later when Billy is reassured of a father's love.

Claggart's nature is also amenable to some degree of interpretation in terms of psychological and social causes despite talk of "defective blood" (64) and of "a depravity according to nature" (75), for, though Melville is drawn to the idea of hatred without a cause, he is, like Aldous Huxley's Mr. Propter, also skeptical of this naïve view. Claggart's antipathy is *in relation to* something. It is of the kind "evoked in certain exceptional mortals by the mere aspect of some other mortal, if not called forth by this very harmlessness itself." Specifically, it was Billy's "significant personal beauty" that "had first moved" Claggart against him. Melville explicitly reduces this to a seeming paradox by appealing from logic to experience. He calls envy and antipathy "passions irreconcilable in reason [which] nevertheless in fact may spring conjoined" (77). To understand Claggart's mentality fully, we must add a third fundamental motive—despair—to envy and revenge. Melville writes of it in two moving passages:

> Claggart's envy struck deeper [than Saul's of David]. If askance he eyes the good looks, cheery health, and frank enjoyment of young life in Billy Budd, it was because these went along with a nature that, as Claggart magnetically felt, had in its simplicity never willed malice or experienced the reactionary [i.e., reactive, as of envy] bite of that serpent. . . . And the insight but intensified his passion, which assuming various secret forms within him, at times assumed that of cynic disdain of innocence—to be nothing more than innocent! Yet in an aesthetic way he saw the charm of it, the courageous free-and-easy temper of it, and fain would have shared it, but he despaired of it.
> . . . .
> When Claggart's unobserved glance happened to light on belted Billy rolling along the upper gun deck in the leisure of the second dogwatch, exchanging passing broadsides of fun with other young promenadoes in the crowd, that glance would follow the cheerful sea Hyperion with a settled meditative and melancholy expression, his eyes strangely suffused with incipient feverish tears. Then would Claggart look like the man of sorrows. Yes, and sometimes the melancholy expression would have in it a touch of soft yearning, as if Claggart could even have loved Billy, but for fate and ban. But this was an evanescence, and quickly repented of, as it were, by an immitigable look. (78,87–88)

With these passages as a base, we can construct a three-frame picture of how Claggart's feelings toward Billy typically function. First, he envies Billy for his beauty, popularity, and freedom from sad and vengeful thoughts. Envy is a primitive form of love, a desire not simply to be like but to be the envied person, to swallow or incorporate him. Claggart conceals but cannot surrender his envious wishes, and they return with consuming force in the presence of someone like Billy Budd, the loving and loved insider. But, second, he despairs of achieving this impossible goal. He cannot love Billy as the other sailors do because of "fate or ban"—that is to say, because of some inhibition born of fear—and he de-

velops a defensive "disdain of innocence." In the simpler
sailors, presumably, both impulse and inhibition are weaker,
and they have less need to develop a defensive disdain; in any
case they lack the intellectual energy to sustain one at such a
pitch. Pride or disdain is a defensive attitude maintained by
intellect; it is not so much the root of an emotional conflict as
a way of preventing some underlying fantasy from being
exposed to criticism. Billy with his simple intellect can altogether shut out from awareness his primitive wishes and
fears, but the sophisticated Claggart can at best only suppress
his. Billy is virtually free from awareness of conflict whereas
Claggart, like Satan, is torn by the hateful siege of contraries.
Active revenge, the third frame of our picture, is Claggart's
solution to this intolerable dilemma. W. H. Auden comments, in *The Enchafed Flood:* "Claggart wishes to annihilate
the difference [between Billy and himself] either by becoming
innocent himself or by acquiring an accomplice in guilt." Becoming innocent is for him out of the question. So, apparently, because of his pride, is the possible but difficult alternative
of modifying his conflict by becoming more aware of his
underlying fears; he must regard his nature as unchangeable,
as Ahab does, and indeed as Melville tends to do in both cases.
He is left with the choice of acquiring an accomplice in guilt.
Each of the two men, in fact, is compelled to destroy the other
lest he destroy himself. Guileless Billy can only destroy his
antagonist in unconscious fury; guileful Claggart does so, like
Satan, through cunning and fraud. Claggart and Satan choose
revenge, and revenge, says Melville in a strong phrase that
demonstrates a clearer analytic understanding of it than Milton had, "is always an inordinate usurer" (80).

In Claggart, if not in Satan, the homosexual aspect of this
psychology of evil is too evident to be ignored, although it
usually is ignored. The verdict of one critic, Geoffrey Stone,
who at least brings the question into the open, suggests
perhaps the major reason that silence has been the rule: if
"the metaphysical implications of Claggart's depravity . . . are
not [Melville's] chief concern with the matter, we are left with
the curious spectacle of a highly intelligent old man devoting

the last three years of his life to pondering a simple [*sic!*] case of thwarted pederasty." Such a comment quite fails to indicate how profoundly typical homosexuality is; despite overwhelming evidence to the contrary, the critic perceives it as a form of physical or moral degeneracy incompatible with a high and sensitive intelligence.

In this context Melville's comparison of Claggart to Christ, "the man of sorrows" (which no critic, so far as I know, has tried to account for), may be illuminated. It *is* puzzling, for Billy is at several points compared to Christ, so how can his opposite, his very un-Christ-like opposite, also be? Does Melville's love of multiple suggestion get out of hand here? I think not. Perhaps Claggart even has as good a claim to the comparison as Billy has. One can think of Christ as wholly free from sin, wholly loving, and wholly an innocent victim of political enemies. Thus He would resemble Billy (discounting, of course, the stutter and its implications, which include, by extension, the killing of Claggart). On a more sophisticated level, one can think of Christ as undergoing a mental struggle similar to Claggart's, but with this difference—that He uses His will and intellect to transform envy and revenge according to His highly developed ethical sense. Envy becomes a yearning for a complete union, even an atonement, with the Heavenly Father. Revenge becomes a noble anger directed at the Father's enemies and, more subtly, at the Father's law which the Son is going to replace. That all such transcendencies are doomed to be imperfect is indicated by the fact that, even in this exalted case, despair nevertheless breaks through from time to time.

Claggart comes somewhat nearer than Billy to being a tragic figure. He experiences conflict. In his moments of banned love for Billy, as in Satan's for Adam and Eve, he might even be called fully tragic. But, like Satan, he falls short of tragic stature because his will is perverted and ignoble. I do not wish to ennoble Claggart by comparisons to Ahab, Satan, and Christ; he lacks their heroic energy altogether, even though Melville wishes us to regard him as in some sense like Billy and Vere, an exceptional or phenomenal man. The point I wish to stress is that Melville, like Milton, has succeeded up to a point in humanizing evil. We do not forgive Satan or Claggart, for their actions are vicious no matter what the causes: to understand is not to forgive. But they themselves must have felt hurt in order to want to hurt.

We can now see more clearly the crucial difference between Billy and Claggart. The difference is the level of sophistication, the degree to which a sense of guilt has been admitted into consciousness. For Melville, it is a matter of how civilized they are, for the story has it that guilt is inseparable from civilization. There is an ambiguity inescapable in any comparative moral estimate of Claggart and Billy, as in any such estimate of Satan and Adam. That is, Satan and Claggart are both morally inferior and morally superior to prelapsarian Adam and to Billy—inferior because they have lost their freedom from guilt through disobedience or through awareness of the will to disobey; superior because one must become civilized or self-aware to attain a freedom that is not childlike and vulnerable. Whether a writer emphasizes one or the other depends, I should think, on what chance he believes there is of attaining freedom untainted by guilt. In *Paradise Lost* such freedom, under God, is possible for those humble enough to submit. In *Billy Budd* such freedom is doubtful because the Creator is as much responsible for Claggart as for Billy and hence for their mutual destruction.

It is through Captain Vere that Melville tries to reconcile experience and innocence, to absorb consciousness of guilt into a viable idea of freedom.

The main focus of the extensive critical commentary on *Billy Budd* during the past twenty-five years has been Melville's attitude toward Captain Vere. The central term of this discussion has been irony, and the central question has been with what degree of irony Vere's position is presented to us. Critics who take one view of the story (the "testament of acceptance" school, as they have come to be known) emphasize Melville's sympathy for an honorable man who, forced into a painful choice between the rigid law he is duty bound to serve and the natural justice his heart yearns for, chooses the law, suffers remorse, is forgiven by his victim, and dies serenely reconciled. Critics who take the opposite view (the "testament of resistance" school) emphasize Melville's ironic detachment from Vere, his indirect but angry criticism of a reactionary authoritarian who too abruptly condemns to death an appealing victim of an inhuman law. There have also been some compromise positions, which propose the idea of partial irony or question the very coherence of the story as we have it. My own position is a compromise. I question the aptness of the term irony itself in this context and claim for the story not neatness of form but what might be called an incremental coherence based on the supposition that Melville recognizes the insoluble contrariness of his attitude toward Vere and finds another climax of his story in a further phase of meaning.

Captain Vere is carefully introduced to us in two successive short passages:

> [He was] a bachelor of forty or thereabouts, a sailor of distinction even in a time prolific of renowned seamen. Though allied to the higher nobility, his advancement had not been altogether owing to influences connected with that circumstance. He had seen much service, been in various engagements, always acquitted himself as an officer mindful of the welfare of his men, but never tolerating an infraction of discipline; thoroughly versed in the science of his profession, and intrepid to the verge of temerity, though never injudiciously so. . . . [His] unobtrusiveness of demeanor may have proceeded from a certain unaffected modesty of manhood evinced at all times not calling for pronounced action, which shown in any rank of life suggests a virtue aristocratic in kind. As with some others engaged in various departments of the world's more heroic activities, Captain Vere though practical enough upon occasion would at times betray a certain dreaminess of mood. . . . [He had] sterling qualities without any brilliant ones.
> . . . .
> He had a marked leaning toward everything intellectual. . . . [H]is bias was toward those books to which every serious mind of superior order occupying any active post of authority in the world naturally inclines: books treating of actual men and events no matter of what era—history, biography, and unconventional writers like Montaigne, who, free from cant and convention,

honestly and in the spirit of common sense philosophize upon
realities. In this line of reading he found confirmation which he
had vainly sought in social converse, so that as touching most
fundamental topics, there had got to be established in him some
positive convictions which he forefelt would abide in him essentially unmodified so long as his intelligent part remained unim-
paired. In view of the troubled period in which his lot was cast,
this was well for him. His settled convictions were as a dike
against those invading waters of novel opinion, social, political,
and otherwise, which carried away as in a torrent no few minds in
those days, minds by nature not inferior to his own. While other
members of that aristocracy to which by birth he belonged were
incensed at the innovators mainly because their theories were
inimical to the privileged classes, Captain Vere disinterestedly
opposed them not alone because they seemed to him insusceptible
of embodiment in lasting institutions, but at war with the peace
of the world and the true welfare of mankind.

With minds less stored than his and less earnest, some officers
of his rank [found him] dry and bookish [with] a queer streak of
the pedantic running through him. (60–63)

I can detect no distance between the author and narrator in
these passages, no irony. More precisely, I can detect only a
kind of dramatic irony in that Melville is scrupulously defining the limits of Vere's virtues with an eye toward establishing the ensuing tragic dilemma. The passages present a
sympathetic picture of a sincere and superior but not quite
heroic man, a man who needs support from what he later calls
"measured forms," a man who is likely to prove somewhat
rigid and theoretic in a crisis.

But this judicious tone is not maintained, especially in light
of the genetic text. Editors Hayford and Sealts demonstrate
how Melville's revisions, particularly his late revision of the
surgeon's role, have the unmistakable effect of withdrawing
sympathy from Vere. Before, the surgeon's reaction to Vere's
dismay over the timing of Billy's blow was sympathetic and
indistinguishable from authorial commentary. "Then followed a chapter . . . erroneously printed in all previous editions of *Billy Budd* as the 'Preface' which in effect underwrote
Vere's view of the case" by linking the mutinies in the English
navy with the spirit of the French Revolution and by implying

that this revolutionary spirit must have seemed at the time, to someone in Vere's position, "inordinate" and "monstrous." But this preface was meant to be deleted, and for it Melville substituted a passage which emphasized Vere's "excited manner" and the fact that the surgeon was "profoundly discomposed" by it, even wondering whether the captain was "unhinged"; the revised surgeon is said to think that, instead of convening a drumhead court, Vere should "place Billy Budd in confinement and in a way dictated by usage, and postpone further action in so extraordinary a case, to such a time as they should rejoin the squadron, and then refer it to the Admiral"—an opinion with which the officers are said to agree.

This revision seems to show that Melville intended finally to treat Vere as an ironic figure. But other facts prevent so neat an interpretation. He left standing in the midst of this revision, as well as before and after it, passages that point the other way. The chapter in which Claggart accosts Vere and accuses Billy, a chapter that climaxes in Vere's crucial decision to handle the matter by closeting and confronting accuser and accused, tells us also that Claggart approaches Vere before the excitement of a just concluded sea chase had passed, that Vere knew Claggart only slightly and instinctively felt a "vaguely repellent distaste" for him but was "not excessively suspicious," and that his decision to closet the antagonists was based on the thought that it would be "not judicious . . . to keep the idea of lingering disaffection alive by undue forwardness in crediting an informer." Still more striking evidence of the inadequacy of a merely ironic view is the fact that Melville left unmodified, immediately after the surgeon's doubts of Vere's sanity, paragraphs which present Vere's position sympathetically. Also, as Hayford and Sealts point out, "Melville retained a quotation from 'a writer whom few know' (obviously Melville himself), the tenor of which is exculpatory, or at worst extenuative. The next chapter (Ch. 22), also retained after revision, reports Vere's closeted interview with Billy in a tone unmistakably favorable to the captain." Furthermore, "given the near-caricature of the surgeon embodied in Ch. 26 . . . which emphasizes his unimaginative obtuseness—in line with Melville's usual treatment of doctors and other 'men of science'—it is hardly justifiable to take his views of Vere as embodying Melville's own."

With this kind of contradictory evidence abundant in the best text of *Billy Budd* that can be put together, it is no wonder that opposite interpretations have been urged. To me the whole notion of irony in this particular context has become more confusing than helpful. It implies Melville's complete control of his material, which many critics feel duty bound to defend. It seems clear that Melville was trying to maintain complete control—his extreme judiciousness of tone in the passages about Vere indicates that—but it also seems clear that powerful feelings of impatience toward Vere and toward authority in general splinter the tight grain of his ambiguity. At the same time that a strong conscientiousness is working to coordinate his thoughts about Vere, a strong contrary force is driving them to opposite poles. Thus I seem to be agreeing that the story is incoherent. But, if Melville became aware of his difficulty in maintaining a consistent attitude toward Vere, he could incorporate that difficulty into the story's total pattern of meaning. And I believe this is the case. But before we can show how he surmounts the problem we must show just how acute it was.

Let us follow the emotional logic of Chapter 21, where tone and point of view are most complex and confused. It begins with two carefully noncommittal paragraphs, concluding: "Whether Captain Vere, as the surgeon professionally and privately surmised, was really the victim of any degree of aberration, every one must decide for himself by such light as this narrative affords." The next two paragraphs are plainly extenuative, stating that Billy's deed occurred at a time "very critical to naval authority," that "the martial code whereby it was formally to be judged" regarded it as "the most heinous of military crimes": "Yet more. The essential right and wrong involved in the matter, the clearer that might be, so much the worse for the responsibility of a loyal sea commander, in as much as he was not authorized to determine the matter on that primitive basis." The tone of the next paragraph, however, is hostile to Vere: "The maintenance of secrecy in the matter, the confining of all knowledge of it for a time to the place where the homicide occurred, the quarterdeck cabin; in these particulars lurked some resemblance to the policy adopted in those tragedies of the palace which have occurred more than once in the capital founded by Peter the Barbarian" (103). But the next three paragraphs are again extenuative, though less convincingly. There is a discernible air of rationalization about them, not on Vere's part but on Melville's:

> Feeling that unless quick action was taken on it, the deed of the foretopman, so soon as it should be known on the gun decks, would tend to awaken any slumbering embers of the Nore among the crew, a sense of the urgency of the case overruled in Captain Vere every other consideration. But though a conscientious disciplinarian, he was no lover of authority for mere authority's sake. Very far was he from embracing opportunities for monopolizing to himself the perils of moral responsibility, none at least that could properly be referred to an official superior or shared with him by his official equals or even subordinates. So thinking, he was glad it would not be at variance with usage to turn the matter over to a summary court of his own officers, reserving to himself as the one on whom the ultimate accountability would rest, the right of maintaining supervision of it, or informally interposing at need. Accordingly a drumhead court was summarily convened, he electing the individuals composing it: the first lieutenant, the captain of the marines, and the sailing master. (104)

The first three statements in this passage are not quite consistent with statements made elsewhere in the story, and Hayford and Sealts point out that Vere's idea of a drumhead court *was* at variance with usage (178), though Melville is usually meticulous about his naval facts. The following paragraph is still more equivocal, both in style and idea. Indeed, the excess of double negatives and the contextual inconsistencies make the passage sound almost like double-talk:

> In associating an officer of marines with the sea lieutenant and the sailing master in a case having to do with a sailor, the commander perhaps deviated from general custom. He was prompted thereto by the circumstance that he took that soldier to be a

judicious person, thoughtful, and not altogether incapable of grappling with a difficult case unprecedented in his prior experience. Yet even as to him he was not without some latent misgiving, for withal he was an extremely good-natured man, an enjoyer of his dinner, a sound sleeper, and inclined to obesity—a man who though he would always maintain his manhood in battle might not prove altogether reliable in a moral dilemma involving aught of the tragic. As to the first lieutenant and the sailing master, Captain Vere could not but be aware that though honest natures of approved gallantry upon occasion, their intelligence was mostly confined to the matter of active seamanship and the fighting demands of their profession. (104–105)

The logic here leaves much to be desired: Vere believes the officer of marines is capable of judging a tragic moral dilemma yet he doubts it; he is concerned here about the ability of these men to understand motives yet in the trial scene which follows immediately he will tell them to ignore motives; he picks them to judge yet he arrogates judgment to himself.

The trial scene itself is similarly troublesome. We can hardly agree with the ironists that, in it, Melville is trying to discredit Vere, but something clearly interferes with our response. There appears to have been in Melville himself an underlying revulsion against Vere's decision, which works against his deliberate effort to make the decision seem regrettably necessary. This is certainly the effect of the passage that describes the officers' acceptance of Vere's reasoning, where again an excess of double negatives suggests a conflict of intentions: "Loyal lieges, plain and practical, though at bottom they dissented from some points Captain Vere had put to them, they were without the faculty, hardly had the inclination, to gainsay one whom they felt to be an earnest man, one too not less their superior in mind than in naval rank. But it is not improbable that even such of his words as were not without influence over them, less came home to them than his closing appeal to their instinct as sea officers" (113). The whole Chapter 21, in fact, exemplifies a tension between a rational effort to measure exactly Vere's tragic predicament and an only half-suppressed predilection to protest the very necessity of that predicament. How strong and simple, by contrast, is Vere's voice in the momentary opportunities given him to speak from an impersonal, transcendent point of view: "Struck dead by an angel of God! Yet the angel must hang"; and, even more Olympian, "At the last assizes it shall acquit."

The problem is not at all specific to the figure of Vere. Melville's attitudes in this story toward various figures of authority are similar, which becomes readily evident when we focus on the story's political and theological implications. The central political theme is the competing claims of the individual and society, of nature and law, of Thomas Paine's ideas and Edmund Burke's. In view of our discussion so far, it is no surprise that some critics find the story to be a passionate endorsement of Paine's views and others find it to be an equally strong endorsement of Burke's. There is evidence for both interpretations, for picturing the French Revolution as a product of rational discontent or irrational combustion, but the story does not settle to the Left or to the Right—or even in the middle. In his presentation of Vere, Melville tries to locate a middle ground between anarchy and tyranny, to respect the captain's "measured forms" yet reject the sometimes excessively strict legal codes which regulate society. But at the same time Melville shows that Vere *is* something of a tyrant and that, on the other hand, the naval code he enforces has something of the status of necessity in a civilized society. We are told that good-natured Captain Graveling is "a staunch admirer of Thomas Paine [and his] rejoinder to Burke's arraignment of the French Revolution," but it is incorrect to regard Vere as Graveling's ideological opposite. Graveling flexibly combines the rights of man (nature) and the claims of law (civilization), whereas Vere, less flexible by temperament and more hard pressed by circumstance (for he is captain of a man-of-war, not a merchant ship), is forced to choose between them. The crucial difference between the two captains is not between Left and Right but between flexibility and absolutism.

Hayford and Sealts note that Melville's late revisions have the effect of making not only Vere but also his world problematic. Vere's world is civilization in a state of war—"this man-of-war world," to use the phrase recurrent in *White-Jacket*. The story presses beyond politics to raise still broader questions. What is the fate of love that cannot be separated from hate, of innocence that cannot be separated from guilt, of religion that cannot be separated from war? Perhaps the ultimate question is, Who made war? The changes of ship names which Melville made in late revision—*Indomitable* to *Bellipotent* and *Directory* to *Athée*—emphasize the war versus religion theme. For a writer as searching as Melville, the question could be rephrased as, Who made the emotional stuff of which wars are made? Which is to say, Did He who made Billy also make Claggart?

The story seems to answer yes: "With no power to annul the elemental evil in him . . . what recourse is left to [a nature like Claggart's] but to recoil upon itself and, like the scorpion for which the Creator alone is responsible, act out to the end the part alloted it" (73). Yet the story intimates at least once an ultimate order. Upon Billy's death the heavens offer a benediction: "The vapory fleece hanging low in the East was shot through with a soft glory as of the fleece of the Lamb of God seen in mystical vision" (124). It is hardly possible to have tragedy in a traditional sense without the intimation of an order beyond the limits of human consciousness, for otherwise the operative fate or necessity is likely to seem manipulated; therefore some critics of modernism (*e.g.*, Frank Kermode in *The Sense of an Ending*) have argued that existential fictions have replaced tragic ones in modern literature. Melville, I think, finds himself somewhere between a tragic and an existential view in *Billy Budd*. He approaches tragedy insofar as he manages to convince us that Vere or what Vere represents is something more than an arbitrary human will, but, insofar as he does not, he seems to be exacting some obscure revenge against the god who failed. It is noteworthy that Vere himself finally bows out as a victim much as Billy does. After achieving an inward peace beyond remorse or fear, he is killed by a musket ball from the *Athée*, a symbolic fate as blind and meaningless as Billy's.

The diffusion through the narrative of Melville's conflicted attitude to authority can best be indicated by comparing and contrasting the story's five chief authority figures: Graveling, Admiral Nelson, Claggart, the Dansker, and Vere. All are linked by having the words *prudent* or *circumspect* applied to them, a fact which should puzzle critics more than it does since these figures compose a broad spectrum of types. "Humanely intelligent" Captain Graveling was usually peaceful of spirit, but he "had much prudence, much conscientiousness, and there were occasions when these virtues were the cause of overmuch disquietude in him" (45). Nelson's "ornate publication of his person in battle" may have "savored of foolhardiness and vanity," but "certainly in foresight as to the larger issues of an encounter and anxious preparations for it . . . few commanders have been so painstakingly circumspect as this same reckless declarer of his person in fight" (57). Claggart's "uncommon prudence is habitual with the subtler depravity, for it has everything to hide" (80). As for the Dansker, with his Delphic replies to Billy's naïve questions, "long experience had very likely brought this old man to that bitter prudence which never interferes in aught and never gives advice" (86). And Vere's prudence is mentioned several times: he is "intrepid to the point of temerity, but never injudiciously so" (60); he combines, as the times demanded, "prudence and rigor"; "though in general a man of rapid decision," he feels in the case of Billy and Claggart "that circumspectness not less than promptitude was necessary" (103).

How shall we interpret these curious links? Clearly Graveling and Nelson approximate ideal figures, and Claggart, the Dansker, and Vere are at best problematic ones. On reflection it is also clear that the first two can combine prudence and sympathy, head and heart, as the last three cannot. Graveling combines the two qualities harmoniously as a rule, though with occasional disquietude: he approximates the civilized or humane ideal. Nelson unites radical forms of duty to self and duty to others, of self-assertion and self-sacrifice, in one transcendent act: he exemplifies the heroic ideal. In Claggart, prudence merely masks hatred and guile: he is a demonic figure. In the Dansker, prudence is a check on love: he is an ironic figure. And in Vere a rigidified prudence is forced into painful opposition to spontaneous love: he approximates a tragic figure.

How does all this bear on Melville's complex attitude toward Vere and the civilization he represents? Graveling, a more flexible version of Vere, makes the civilized ideal attractive. His musical voice, "the veritable unobstructed outcome of the innermost man" (45), reminds us even of Billy, the graceful barbarian. But Graveling's nature and circumstances had no great hold on Melville's imagination in this story; a more radical problem was at issue, and a more radical solution was called for.

The relation of Nelson to Vere and civilization is more interesting. Nelson resembles Vere not only in being a captain but also in his bravery in battle and in the manner of his death. But the differences are more striking. Nelson is demonstrative and reckless; Vere, "the most undemonstrative of men" (60). Nelson's death was glorious and crowned a triumphant career, whereas Vere's truncated a career that "never attained to fullness of fame." In some important respects Nelson resembles Billy: both are pointedly called sailors; both are heroic personalities; both have the ability to evoke spontaneous homage; and both die as a result of a radical act of self-assertion (in Billy's case, of course, involuntary self-assertion). What is curious about the case of Nelson, however, is that, through him, Melville really glorifies war, the manifestation of what is centrally corrupt in civilization:

> Personal prudence, even when dictated by quite other than selfish considerations, surely is no special virtue in a military man; while an excessive love of glory, impassioning a less burning impulse, the honest sense of duty, is the first. . . . If under the presentiment of the most magnificent of all victories to be crowned by his own glorious death, a sort of priestly motive led him to dress his person in the jeweled vouchers of his own shining deeds; if thus to have adorned himself for the altar and the sacrifice were indeed vainglory, then affectation and fustian is each more heroic in the great epics and dramas, since in such lines

the past but embodies in verse those exaltations of sentiment that a nature like Nelson, the opportunity being given, vitalizes into acts. (58)

I think Melville sensed something questionable, if only in the context of his story, about this evocation of glorious war, but was not quite willing to surrender the heroic ideal. Despite the justification given, he removed the Nelson passages, then inserted them again but riddled with more justification and with those betraying double negatives:

> Nevertheless, to anybody who can hold the Present at its worth without being inappreciative of the Past, it may be forgiven, if to such an one the solitary old hulk at Portsmouth, Nelson's *Victory*, seems to float there, not alone as the decaying monument of a fame incorruptible, but also as a poetic reproach, softened by picturesqueness, to the *Monitors* and yet mightier hulls of the European ironclads. . . .
>
> There are some, perhaps, who while not altogether inaccessible to that poetic reproach just alluded to, may yet on behalf of the new order be disposed to parry it; and this to the extent of iconoclasm, if need be. For example, prompted by the sight of the star inserted in the *Victory's* quarter-deck designating the spot where the Great Sailor fell, these martial utilitarians may suggest considerations implying that Nelson's ornate publication of his person in battle was not only unnecessary, but not military, nay, savored of foolhardiness and vanity. (57)

The likeness of the Dansker and Claggart to Vere may seem remote at first but is significant. All belong to the civilized, sophisticated world of the *Bellipotent*, and all are thrown into conflict by the presence of Billy: Claggart and Dansker by the mere sight of him; Vere only after Billy's act of killing. All in some sense betray Billy and prove mock fathers. Vere at first, like his lieutenant who impressed Billy from the *Rights of Man*, feels rational admiration, a mature version of the sailors' "spontaneous homage." Later he comes to resemble Claggart and the Dansker in his attitude toward Billy, though of course with more dignity. They are provoked to ironic words and malicious deeds by Billy; he is thrown into an anguishing dilemma. Vere's eventual reconciliation with Billy, after his tragic decision, is, one may say, the furthest

**Literary Art
and the
Unconscious**

*The Quest
for
Guiltlessness*

phase of Melville's meaning. But it is not the last. The story takes one more important step—backwards.

In working out their genetic text, Hayford and Sealts show that the story passed through three major phases of composition, in which the emphasis shifts in turn from Billy to Claggart to Vere. The first phase, the germ of the story, is a ballad and short prose sketch constituting a sailor's reverie as he faces death, in the manner of the *John Marr* poems. Here Billy is an older man and captain of the gun crew and is apparently guilty of fomenting mutiny. But his guilt is ignored, and his beauty, geniality, and noble lineage are stressed, as are themes of sailor versus landsman and religion versus war. In the second phase Claggart is introduced, which results in a major shift of focus. Billy is now a model sailor who reacts to a false charge of mutiny by striking and killing his accuser. Here the story ends with a garbled news account, demonstrating the ironic discrepancy between the "outside" and "inside" views of the incident. In the third phase the development is greatly extended, especially between the killing and the final ballad, and another major shift of focus occurs with the careful delineation of Captain Vere, who previously had been only the commander in whose presence Billy strikes Claggart.

All three men are regarded as exceptional, presumably in the sense that, for each, spiritual gratification is far more important than sensual gratification or than self-preservation narrowly defined. In the light of the genetic text we can see the story as representing Melville's successive attempts to identify with each of them. And we can discover a fourth phase of identification, not indicated by Hayford and Sealts, for Vere is not the final focus of the story's interest. His reconciliation with Billy ought to be the climax of the story, but is not. As some critics note, the reconciliation scene takes place offstage and is peculiarly muted. In fact, as an emphasis, it is superseded by a renewed identification with Billy, but in a different key. To examine successively these four phases of emotional layering is to obtain the fullest understanding of Melville's intention in *Billy Budd*.

The core of the story, then, is an aesthetically and morally seductive image that haunted Melville's imagination from the beginning of his career: a man of beauty, geniality, and nobility as unafraid of death as an animal or young child. He is bisexual, combining masculine strength and feminine beauty, Hercules and the Graces. But significantly this bisexuality indicates a prelapsarian wholeness rather than a postlapsarian sexual conflict. It is a wholeness imagined in Plato's *Symposium*, elegized in Lawrence's "Tortoise" and in Melville's own powerful lyric, "After the Pleasure Party":

For, Nature in no shallow surge
Against thee either sex may urge,
Why hast thou made us but in halves—
Co-relatives? This makes us slaves.
If these co-relatives never meet
Self-hood itself seems incomplete.
And such the dicing of blind fate
Few matching halves here meet and mate.
What Cosmic jest or Anarch blunder
The human integral clove asunder
And shied the fractions through life's gate.

Billy in the first phase of composition is reminiscent of the story's dedicatee, Jack Chase, a father figure to the young Melville of *White-Jacket*. This is one solution to the problem of incompleteness, for, if we are willing to say that the feeling of incompleteness reflects an archaic experience of separation from a father, we can imagine it relieved by an identification with a father. Thus Billy, though a foundling, does not need a father because he is completely at home in the world. It becomes clear in subsequent phases, however, that his world is a world of *many* fathers whom he has never learned to disobey. Now, proliferated images of a desired object usually indicate an underlying fear of possessing even one, so we are not quite surprised to see emerge a certain resentment, as in the poem, against some presence imagined as the depriver. In the story, attitudes of impotence and resentment become manifest in the second phase of composition, where Billy is made the victim of a malevolent man named Claggart. The critic cannot help wondering, if only parenthetically, about the influence of certain well-known shocks in Melville's life: his father's early

death, his son's suicide, and his uncle's condemnation of a
mutinous sailor in what came to be known as the Somers
incident. The last fact does enter the text at a late stage of
composition but so faintly as to deny the literary critic enough
basis for a nontrivial interpretation. Yet it is strikingly in line
with the major motif of a father forced to sacrifice his son,
and we may surmise that Melville's loyalty to his uncle made
it impossible for him to deal with the Somers material as
honestly, as complexly, as he would want to.

By introducing Claggart to the plot and humanizing him to
a degree, Melville, in the twilight of his career, is making one
last effort to actualize and expel the guilt that taints our freedom. Satanic figures had haunted his imagination for many
years. Bland in *White-Jacket*, Jackson in *Redburn*, and Radney in the Town-Ho episode of *Moby-Dick* are often spoken
of as predecessors for Claggart (Jackson and Radney are even
malevolent in relation to a handsome sailor), but the heroically Satanic Ahab is also a predecessor. It is important to see
that Melville is to some degree identifying himself with—and
soliciting our identification with—the man who could love
Billy but for fate and ban, who despairs of ever being what
Billy is, and who vengefully exults in corrupting innocence.
True, Melville hardly dramatizes the struggle in Claggart's
soul, preferring to remain analytic. But he has not de-
humanized the Satan of this story. We are shown despair and
frustrated love as well as stark pride and perverted will. Claggart is, after all, as helpless as Billy in the grip of a compulsion
he himself hates but cannot change. And we may even discern
a touch of Melville's own vengefulness in the extreme means
he chooses to contrive his tragic bind: Billy is not only tainted
with that fatal stutter but transported from a peaceful,
homeward-bound vessel under a Graveling to an outward-
bound man-of-war under a Vere during a time of war. Of
course, this is how Melville makes his tragedy, but, unless
Billy were flawed inwardly and hard pressed by circumstances, he would not be brought down. Innocence is rarely so very
vulnerable. Billy and Claggart are such extreme cases that the
desired effect of inevitability is a little marred by an effect of

manipulation.

Because they are virtually deprived of the freedom to struggle, neither Billy nor Claggart can be thought of as a genuine tragic figure. Only Vere has such freedom, and he is tragic insofar as he holds antinomies in some sort of balance. But we have seen that beyond a certain point Melville himself loses faith in the balance and lets it fall into fragments.

Tragedy failing in the third phase of composition, Christianity is tentatively called upon to solder the fragments into a meta-tragic significance. But such repair requires that either Vere or Billy be accepted as the representation of a more than human will. Some critics indeed speak of Vere as a divine figure. His sacrifice of Billy is compared to Abraham's of Isaac, itself a traditional analogy with Jehovah's of Christ. But the analogy breaks down as soon as we realize that the necessity Vere symbolizes is wholly circumscribed by civilization. Other critics, emphasizing the imagery that identifies Billy with Christ as well as with Adam, try to make the Handsome Sailor into a divine figure. But this too, for more complicated reasons, doesn't work, as Auden in *The Enchafed Flood* skillfully explains:

> If the story were to be simply the story of the Fall, i.e. the story of how the Devil (Claggart) tempted Adam (Budd) into the knowledge of good and evil, [the combination in Billy Budd of sinfulness and beauty] would not matter, but Melville wants Budd also to be the Second Adam, the sinless victim who suffers voluntarily for the sins of the whole world. But in order to be that he must know what sin is, or else his suffering is not redemptive, but only one more sin on our part. Further, as long as Billy Budd is only the Prelapsarian Adam, our nostalgic image of what we would still be if we had not fallen, his beauty is a perfectly adequate symbol but the moment he becomes the Second Adam, the saving example whom we all should follow, this beauty becomes an illegitimate aesthetic advantage. The flaw of the stammer will not quite do [for this is unconscious] not a deliberate abandonment of advantages.... We can never look like that, any more than, once we have become conscious, we can go back to unconsciousness, so how can we imitate his example? He becomes an aesthetic hero to admire from a distance. Melville seems to have been aware that something must happen to Billy to change him from the unconscious Adam into the conscious Christ, but in terms of his fable, he cannot make this explicit and the decisive

149

transition has to take place off-stage in the final interview between Billy and Captain Vere.

Five chapters follow this interview. And in them the hanging man whom the sailors adore is not the redeeming Son of God but the man who represents most excellently their own naïve selves. They give him the same reverence shown by sailors in general to the archetypal Handsome Sailor of the opening chapter: "spontaneous homage to some superior member of their own class" (43). It is the first, not the second, Adam they pay homage to, not Christ who died for their sins but Adam who died before sin was. Billy's death is finally not a reunion with God but a guarantee that he will never be separated from Him, will never fall into disobedience, into the consciousness of sin, into the sense of guilt. This Handsome Sailor is now removed from all possible conflict by death. His fellow sailors, whose lives are based on blind obedience to authority and need never suffer the task of rivalry and reconciliation with the Father, worship their apotheosized image. And Melville does through them.

The story thus circles back to where it began. The symmetry is strikingly brought out by two late changes in the composition: the omission of the supposed preface about the political background, which makes the story now begin with an account of the Handsome Sailor; and the reversal of the last two chapters, which places the ironical news account next to last and the chapter describing the sailors' reverence for Billy, including their ballad in his honor, at the very end. But now the story can go no farther. It tells us that, since guilt consciousness is intolerable, the only possible freedom is in regression.

The words of the ballad are not Billy's own, but words ascribed to Billy by another sailor, the composer. This sailor is a little less innocent (he shows himself capable of puns and refers to a romance with a Bristol Molly, which we have no reason to think is a literal recollection of Billy's history) but innocent enough to offer spontaneous homage without the ambiguous smile of the Dansker or of Claggart. The tone of
150   the ballad is grimly accepting, melancholy, fatalistic. The se-

renity which Melville is said to have achieved at the end of
Billy Budd is present only in the sense that the ballad is
beyond conflict and argument, but the serenity is not the kind
that bespeaks a creative *resolution* of conflict:

> ... So I'll shake a friendly hand ere I sink.
> But—no! It is dead then I'll be, come to think.
> I remember Taff the Welshman when he sank.
> And his cheek it was like the budding pink.
> But me they'll lash in hammock, drop me deep.
> Fathoms down, fathoms down, how I'll dream fast asleep.
> I feel it stealing now. Sentry, are you there?
> Just ease these darbies at the wrist,
> And roll me over fair!
> I am sleepy, and the oozy weeds about me twist.

It is the serenity of a man in the shadow of death who accepts
grudgingly, because he must, certain renunciations of ambition and thus feels his spirit eased even as it is saddened.

Billy Budd was not put into final, publishable form by
Melville before he died. But I find it difficult to believe he
could have done any more with it, aside from clearing up a
few technical inconsistencies. The phases of development the
story goes through compactly recapitulate the conflicts he
wrestled with during a long, literary career—which is one
reason the story seems so central an expression of his sensibil-
ity. The Adamic mentality vulnerable to the encroachments
of civilization is the central theme of his early South Sea
novels. The psychology or theology of Satanism is adum-
brated in *Redburn* and *White-Jacket* and fully explored in
Moby-Dick. The task of reconciling this man-of-war world
with Christianity is the burden of *Clarel*, the representative
work of what might be called the third phase of Melville's
career. And the poems in *Timoleon* and *John Marr*, which
just preceded *Billy Budd*, evoke nostalgically a retreat to innocence under the aspect of death.

The density of implications in *Billy Budd* expresses Melville's devotion to the complexity of experience, to "truth," a
devotion so faithful that it is indistinguishable from a restless
dissatisfaction with the pleasing coherence of artistry, of "fable": "The symmetry of form attainable in pure fiction cannot

be so readily achieved in a narration having less to do with
fable than with fact. Truth uncompromisingly told will always have its ragged edges" (128). There is in the story a
constant tension between a centrifugal imaginative activity
which keeps adding to the design other levels of meaning,
other points of view, a greater variety of words, and a centripetal activity which keeps coordinating contraries, ad-
judicating differences, attempting to resolve conflicts. Hawthorne's often quoted statement captures an essential truth
about Melville: "He can neither believe, nor be comfortable in
his unbelief, and he is too honest and courageous not to try to
do one or the other." As far as art is concerned, this means
that he is too restless emotionally to give us that easy, flexible
interplay of contrary implications that we find in Shakespeare
and too energetic intellectually to be guilty of the repeated
and unconvincing manipulation of effects that we find in
Hemingway.

A profound similarity exists, it seems to me, despite the
lack of overt skepticism in Milton, between *Paradise Lost* and
Billy Budd, a profound sense in which the later fiction repays
consideration as a post-Romantic version of the earlier one.
Both works attempt with formidable but inevitably imperfect
success to coordinate a psychological or naturalistic with a
theological or metaphysical view of experience, and both
works pass through the same sequence of phases in a kind of
progressive quest. Milton's work, to be sure, seems more
rounded, more classic, more assured of its final goal. Much of
what I mean by calling *Billy Budd* a post-Romantic version of
Paradise Lost is that the former gives us the sense of being
truly exploratory, of letting its quest take its own course and
incorporating even failure into the total design. In this rather
special sense there is irony in the design of *Billy Budd*. The
goal at last is not what it seemed at first. The story attempts to
dissolve even the contours of fabulation in order to come
nearer to what, in the face of his devout skepticism, Melville
is able to think of as truth.

TWO ANTIPURITAN PURITANS: **IV**
BERNARD SHAW AND
D. H. LAWRENCE

By the mere energy of his expanding spirit, [the Puritan] remakes, not only his own character and habits and way of life, but family and church, industry and city, political institutions and social order. . . .

It is will—will organized and disciplined and inspired, will quiescent in rapt adoration or straining in violent energy, but always will—which is the essence of Puritanism.

                   R. H. Tawney, *Religion and the Rise of Capitalism*

THE TWO extraordinary writers whom I link here were themselves so keenly analytic, and even so systematic in their own unsystematic ways, that one of the best ways to evaluate their achievements is to confront their analytic and imaginative writings as a total structure. It is not difficult to discover problematic effects in their individual works, to show how some motives are not convincingly assigned and how images of great vividness and truth seem nevertheless to be manipulated.* But the troublesome implications in their fictions (notably, fear of weakness, of domination by women, of domesticity and marriage) are not simply evaded but reaffirmed at a higher, heroic level. What you may call homosexuality, Lawrence seems to say, I call blood brotherhood. What you may call fear of parenthood, Shaw seems to say, I call a deep striving to create a higher kind of human being.

Many pages of Shaw and Lawrence thus generate a high

---

* As I have done in "*Women in Love* and the Lawrencean Aesthetic," in Stephen J. Miko (ed.), "*Women in Love*": *Twentieth-Century Views* (Englewood Cliffs: Prentice-Hall, 1969).

excitement but, at the same time, because the rhetoric is
coercive in its intensity, the uneasy suspicion that the excitement is unnaturally elevated, that one will sooner or later
suffocate in that rarefied atmosphere. Judicious attempts to
separate their strengths and weaknesses, their triumphs and
failures, therefore work less well than with most writers. Such
attempts do not seem to get to the heart of the matter. A more
paradoxical approach recommends itself, and an effective way
of establishing one is to find a pivotal term. R. H. Tawney's
highly suggestive remarks lead me to believe that the term
"puritanism" will serve the purpose very well.

Puritanism generally signifies self-denial, more specifically
the equation of the instincts with "vice" and "sin" and of their
suppression with "virtue" and "righteousness." According to
this sense of the word, Shaw and Lawrence were vehemently
antipuritan, and they combined their vehemence with keen
psychological understanding. The crux of this mentality,
wrote Lawrence, "is fear and hate of the instincts. . . .But of
course this fear and hate had to take on a righteous appearance, so it became moral, said that the instincts were evil, and
promised a *reward* for their suppression." He understood
well, as did Shaw, that moral attitudes, under the pressure of
unconscious fears, tend to become polarized into ideas of good
and evil. Indeed, their awareness of the role of fear in the
formation of certain oppressive social ideals is one of the most
emphatic as well as valuable insights in their work.

The ideals they particularly had in mind—what Lawrence
often scorned as the love ideal, what Shaw called the deadly
sins of conventional virtue, filial affection, modesty, sentiment,
devotion to woman, and romance—suggest a target wider
than historical puritanism, although they often trace these
ideals to that source. They were really contending with the
dominant ethic of their day, with puritanism as it merged into
Victorianism and popular Christianity in general. Idealism,
which they defined theoretically as the determination of instincts in *any* direction but practically as the glorification of
purity, meekness, etc., was their *bête noire:* it choked vital
energy and permitted us to revenge ourselves on others—to
154 shame, punish, deprive, vivisect, wage war—in the name of

love, justice, truth, or peace. This unconscious hypocrisy they loathed, for it precluded self-knowledge and thus the possibility of change; conscious hypocrisy however, like Ann Whitefield's in *Man and Superman*, was even admirable, for it provided a means of getting what one wanted within an oppressive society.

But they were as opposed to libertinism and materialism as they were to purity and idealism. The glorification of one and the glorification of the other were, in fact, faces of the same coin. They detected this conjunction in much popular art, which titillated its audiences with sin while carefully rewarding virtue; Lawrence found it also in many modern classics, for example in Dostoevski, who both wallowed in sin and adored purity, not realizing that "Sodom and Madonna-ism are two halves of the same movement, the mere tick-tack of lust and asceticism, pietism and pornography." And they cleverly dramatized the idea in their own art. Shaw's Devil in *Man and Superman* and his Sergius in *Arms and the Man* are, at the same time, libertines and sentimental idealists. Lawrence's Loerke in *Women in Love* and his New England couple in "Things" worship both machinery and the religion of art. The real alternative, then, is to smash the whole complex and to establish a new moral center beyond good and evil.

The new center in this transvaluation of values is vital energy itself, whatever possesses it or promotes its flow. Evil is redefined as whatever lacks vital energy or obstructs its flow: mechanism, fear, boredom, obsolete ideals and institutions. Vital energy, of course, may be destructive as well as constructive, and so, from the nonvitalist's point of view, the Shavian or Lawrencian vitalist may well appear the diabolist. But he is justified in his own eyes because "pure passionate constructive activity and pure passionate destructive activity are the same, religiously" (Lawrence), and because "destruction clears [the way] and gives us breathing space and liberty" (Shaw). He is not a nihilist, however, because he believes that the instincts, freed of hindrance, are profoundly moral and purposive.

As this begins to suggest, the instincts, although meant to

be simply liberated, are actually subjected by Lawrence and
Shaw to an intense process of purification in parallel opposition to the process they deplored. The common happiness of
man in work, love, and recreation, the pleasure he takes in
contiguity with self, others, and things, what is commonly
meant by the words *personality, neighborliness, enjoyment*
—all of this is passionately repudiated as vulgar and degrad-
ing. And in its place looms an impersonal, metaphysical world
of value that is, first and foremost, morally superior to the
world it scorns. Both men seem to have been engaged in a
strenuous, almost ceaseless effort to get below or rise above
fear and inhibition (the metaphors of ascent and descent
coalesce, for transcendence is located in the purified unconscious) and to identify themselves, through their tremendous
creative energy and tremendous will, with a better world
below or above or beyond. The instincts we call aggression
and sexuality are transfigured into "mastery" and "life force,"
"nobility" and "splendor," "power" and "glory." The motives
of envy and revenge, which they penetratingly detect in other
work, become in their own work heroic yearning for a better
world and noble anger directed at those who are dragging us
down or holding us back. So successful are they in thus lifting
themselves by their bootstraps, in identifying themselves
with their visions, that some critics call them natural or
secular saints.

Renunciation combined with compensation at a higher level
makes up the basic plot of their fictions. Almost every tale or
play begins with the assumption that, in Shaw's words, "to
want to retain our present sinful individuality is to want Hell"
and works toward a transformation of self and society. Lawrence does struggle, especially in his essays, to embrace the
normal and reject the higher plane, though just as often his
essays are busy transforming concrete human conflict into
transcendental contraries or into some ultimate unity. His art
is usually visionary. Its basic patterns are these: the man and
woman shed their personal selves and attain some more inef-
fable mode of relationship (Ursula and Birkin in *Women in
Love*); the man or woman stands in awe before an exotic hero

156

from another world (Cipriano before Ramón, Kate before Cipriano, in *The Plumed Serpent*); the woman waits in proud isolation for her exceptional lover to come to her from the unknown (Ursula in *The Rainbow*, Lou in *St. Mawr*). The tragic or semitragic plot of his most well-known novel *Sons and Lovers* is not typical of the mature Lawrence, though even this story finally moves in the direction of casting off female will and touch for the sake of a higher or at least more indefinite connection.

Shaw sometimes condenses this plot by making the renunciation virtually identical with the heroic compensation. Thus Ellie in *Heartbreak House* says, "I feel as if there is nothing I could not do, because I want nothing," to which Shotover replies, "That's the only strength. That's genius." But, insofar as he works in terms of relationship, his stories display the same patterns as Lawrence's. Marchbanks, Lady Cicely, Cleopatra, and John Tanner renounce happiness for something higher, called greatness; Cleopatra and Rufio stand in awe before Caesar; Epifania in *The Millionairess*, quite like Ursula or Lou, says, "I will live in utter loneliness and keep myself sacred until I find the man who can stand with me on the utmost heights and not lose his head—the mate created for me in heaven. He must be somewhere."

The renunciation of the ordinary world is presented, in their work, with too much intensity to be sufficiently explained by the real plight of man in modern society or even by the real plight of genius. Their intensity surely points to some unadmitted guilt connected with the usual social roles of a man, to the blocking of normal gratification which leads to the compensatory creation of a higher plane. How else can we explain both the proud, insistent repudiation of society and the poignant longing for fuller connection with it that breaks through again and again? In lesser men beset by a similar conflict, this renunciation is likely to be expressed in the form of envy and self-pity, this compensating moral superiority as spite and vanity. In mentally energetic men these motives may be transfigured, to a remarkable degree if not completely, into martyrdom and apotheosis, crucifixion and resurrection. The natural and consuming wish of such a person is to resolve the conflict between what he really feels and what, ideally, he wants to feel. If he cannot get at and reduce the obstructing guilt and so bring his wishes and his moral will into better harmony by modifying them, he may turn to more extreme modes of resolution, such as apotheosis and martyrdom: by assuming all or renouncing all, the tension between desire and its internal critic is relieved.

Shaw and Lawrence, so keen in detecting the unconscious polarization of moral attitudes in the puritan mind, do not seem to have been altogether aware of the polarization of their own moral attitudes, and this blindness does, I think, help to explain the peculiar inextricability of the humanistic and antihumanistic components of their thought.

Martyrdom they rejected as violently as the puritan rejects sin. Finding "a victim the most depressing thing in nature" (Shaw), they tended to hold him entirely responsible for his misfortune: Birkin tries to take a complex view of his friend Gerald but indicates nevertheless that any victim must want to be victimized, as if he would endorse Nietzsche's memorable remark, "There is something dreadful about people to whom dreadful things happen."

Martyrdom was probably a constant underlying temptation which their moral will could not approve, but the tendency toward it is evident throughout their work. Their heroes are proudly but sadly cut off from their societies, superior to them but frustrated and embittered by lack of social support. In Shaw, the martyr and the conqueror are often twin heroes, though the balance between them tends to fall one way or the other—Dudgeon and Anderson in *The Devil's Disciple*, Marchbanks and Morrell in *Candida*, Keegan and Broadbent in *John Bull's Other Island*—and they are condensed into one in Saint Joan and Caesar. Caesar says that the man who can rise above vengeance "will have either to conquer the world as I have, or be crucified by it." In the play he is the conqueror, but the alternative is implied: he is a dreamer as well as a doer, and he envisions his forthcoming assassination acceptingly. Lawrence often requires of his heroes a painful

158

crucifixion if they are to actualize or at least potentialize a
triumphant resurrection, as in the popular and typical tale,
"The Horse Dealer's Daughter." The definitions of real happiness which Lawrence and Shaw offer are curious and similar in the mixture of pain and pleasure, defeat and triumph. According to Lawrence, "real happiness lies in being used by life, hurt by life, driven and goaded by life, replenished and overjoyed with life. . . . A large part of it is pain." To Shaw, "this is the true joy in life, the being used for a purpose recognized by yourself as a mighty one; the being thoroughly worn out before you are thrown on the scrapheap."

Both men seek a supreme resolution of the intolerable conflict of flesh and spirit either by casting out flesh—Shaw's way—or by transforming flesh into spirit—Lawrence's way. (Shaw's revulsion from sexual pleasure is more consistent than Lawrence's, less counterposed by a drive toward it, but it is too easy to speak of Shaw as temperamentally, let alone constitutionally, averse to passion. The strength of his revulsion makes much more sense as a measure of the strength of his underlying desire and of its inhibition. Furthermore, Lawrence and Shaw both, despite their antagonism to female will, are highly empathetic feminine psychologists.) Shaw the prophet of brain and Lawrence the prophet of blood move finally toward the same point or vortex: pure act, pure energy. When they carry out the logic of their quest to its end, we realize that the Life they worship is identifiable not with people at all but with a disembodied, purely creative will. In *Back to Methuselah* Shaw prophesies, "The day will come when there will be no more people, only thought. And that will be life eternal. Press on to the goal of redemption from the flesh, to the vortex freed of matter, to the whirlpool in pure intelligence. Life set free from Matter. Of life only there is no end." A parallel to this in Lawrence is a passage in *Women in Love* where Birkin says, "Let mankind pass away—time it did. The creative utterances will not cease, they will only be there. Humanity doesn't embody the utterance of the incomprehensible any more. . . . There will be a new embodiment in a new way."

Their effort to deny their attraction to martyrdom is indicated by their sweeping and punitive search for evidence of such attraction in Western tragic literature from the story of Christ to that of Anna Karenina. Profoundly and, it seems, inevitably drawn to the story of Christ, both endeavored mightily to winnow the self-transcender from the self-denier, the soldier from the saint, the victor from the victim. Both asserted that the meek and mild Jesus was a sniveling modern invention and that the real Jesus was a natural aristocrat, above fear, sin, and the need for propitiation. To Shaw, "Jesus with his healthy conscience on his higher plane was free from the terrors of sin and death," unlike Paul the debaser, who won a victory over sin and death at the cost of all moral responsibility by introducing the pernicious doctrine of atonement and absolution. "Forgiving," Shaw knows, can only be achieved by an unstable conversion of affect, and therefore "forgetting" is the profounder moral goal. To Lawrence, the corrupter often was John of Patmos, whose other-worldliness was motivated by envy and spite toward the privileged of this world. Both at times criticized Jesus for rejecting worldly temptations. But, when Lawrence in *The Man Who Died* exposes his Jesus to sex, the account is highly formal and ritualized, carefully distanced from the vulgar sexuality of the common slaves. And Shaw in his preface to *Androcles and the Lion* is inclined to believe that Christ knew what he was doing in choosing the cross rather than the sword: perhaps the world needs one exemplary martyrdom.

They consistently challenge literary tragedy for picturing not only heroic resistance but also a measure of consent to defeat. Shakespeare, they concede, is free of self-pity—"Now who can think of Shakespeare," says Shaw, "as a man with a grievance"—and, though they are sometimes irritated by the weaknesses of his heroes, they also admire the fact that these heroes are at war more with nature than with society, in contrast to the weaker heroes of nineteenth-century tragedy, who are defeated more by social pressure. Modern tragedy seems to them all too often a rationalization of the artist's lack of will. The pity it evokes, Lawrence asserts, is "merely self-

pity reflected onto some obvious surface"; it shows "man in
love with himself in a defeated role." To Shaw, "Compassion
is the fellow feeling of the unsound"; it is a form of idealism
by which we cover over with sentiment the burdens of our
"half-satisfied passions." Lawrence concedes that Tess of the
D'Urbervilles and Anna Karenina are great characters because
their authors project real physical sympathy for them and are
true to them in showing how defeat follows from their natures; but why, he asks, do Hardy and Tolstoi have to assign
to Tess and Anna a meek adherence to the social idea of good
and evil, a lack of the strength needed to fight society on equal
terms?

To Shaw and Lawrence, every evil but mortality itself,
which they characteristically belittle as "mere mortality," can
be overcome by will. In their intolerance toward the rigidity
of emotions and institutions they are impatient to the point of
absurdity. "Why have money and machines?" cries Lawrence. "They degrade us." Preaches Undershaft to Major Barbara, "Come, come, my daughter! Don't make too much of
your little tinpot tragedy. What do we do here when we spend
years of work... on a new gun or an aerial battleship that
turns out just a hairsbreadth wrong after all? Scrap it....
Well, you have made for yourself something that you call a
morality or a religion or what not. It doesn't fit the facts.
Well, scrap it.... If your old religion broke down yesterday,
get a newer and better one for tomorrow." Mechanism and
will are such perfect opposites in Shaw and Lawrence that, as
here, the two forces sometimes resemble one another; some
of their will-honoring schemes and heroes, as critics have
noticed, are surprisingly mechanical in their effect. It was
they as much as Christ who would not compromise with the
world, the flesh, the devil.

It often seems to be will and will alone which keeps the
Shavian or Lawrencian hero from lapsing into despair. Will or
courage is, at any rate, "the virtue of virtues" (Shaw, via
Bunyan), "the only thing worth having, anyhow" (Lawrence). They do not attack us for our lack of natural abilities
but for our lack of courage and sincerity; we too could see 161

what they see if only we *would,* or we *do* see it but won't
admit that we do. "England could be a paradise in a few
years," declares Shaw. "The difficulty is not the way but the
will. . . . [But] if there is no will, we are lost." Lawrence often
distinguishes a pernicious mental will that bullies spontaneous emotion from a true, prereflective will that directs it, but
the latter tends to be within his control and scarcely distinguishable from the former. Both Shaw and Lawrence insist
that, although the Holy Ghost is within, it is not merely
equal to the self but is "a will of which I am a part" or "some
greater inhuman will" with which the self is in touch, yet
both speak for it with great assurance.

Both believe passionately in freedom, but neither can see
freedom apart from purpose or acknowledge any purpose
that does not conform to this greater will. And so, what
begins as liberal and humane often passes into something
reactionary and oppressive. Both, for example, denounce the
forcing of children's minds in education and passionately ad-
vocate laissez-faire, but soon laissez-faire becomes more re-
pugnant than any orthodoxy. Shaw acknowledges as much,
saying that unlike orthodoxy "laissez-faire doesn't even let us
learn from our mistakes." When they present their own edu-
cational schemes (Shaw in his preface to *Misalliance,* Lawrence in "Education of the People" and *Fantasia of the Unconscious*), it becomes clear that children are to be more severely
disciplined than they had been under the system being im-
proved upon. Their antipuritan attacks tend to boomerang,
and their idea of freedom after a while resembles an idea of
revenge. Shaw writes, "Self-sacrifice enables us to sacrifice
other people to ourselves without blushing." A palpable hit,
but what *he* shows us is that a man who sacrifices himself to
some higher idea of self—admittedly a noble one but perhaps
not to everyone's taste—can also, in the name of that ideal,
sacrifice others without blushing. No principle is more sacred
to both men than the indefensibility of murder. But in the
throes of prophetic righteousness they almost condone it.
Lawrence virtually does so in "The Fox," "The Woman Who
Rode Away," and *The Plumed Serpent.* Shaw in dozens of

places, more in earnest than in jest, declares that people whose slothful or criminal conduct cannot be altered by better social organization should be "painlessly killed" or "executed in a kindly manner."

Both abominate democracy because it promotes mediocrity at the expense of excellence, but their ideal of excellence takes the double form (already evident in Milton, the founder of the modern heroic tradition) of libertarian resistance to tyrannic authority and endorsement of a leader who adopts the Cromwellian principle, "not what they want but what is good for them." Not surprisingly, the authoritarian attitude is recessive at first and acquires strength over the other as the writers grow older. Shavian socialism before 1900 is primarily individualistic in emphasis, then becomes more and more preoccupied with efficiency, social control, and the elimination of the unfit. After 1916, Lawrence's fascination with sexual freedom yields ground to a fascination with sexual obedience. Supporting all their opinions, even the most seemingly impulsive and eccentric ones, are definite theories of mind, which are liberal in intention but which, driven by the need for total solutions, are strangely oppressive at the same time.

Both believe that man is fundamentally good, that he possesses or could achieve a pure unconscious, and that all seeming impurities of the unconscious mind could be traced to social ideals as they have been introjected by the fearful individual mind. The root of all evil is the fear of society and the fear of death. And fear can be expelled by will and purpose. As a theory of mind it has a Romantic heritage, deriving equally from Rousseau and Blake.

The theory supports a cogent attack on democracies, which declare that man is born free yet punish nonconformity harshly. But their ideal of freedom is two-edged. It not only implies greater social toleration but also greater psychological purity, in fact exhorts us to virtuous wishes as well as virtuous deeds. Shaw speaks for both in his striking epigram: "Virtue consists not in abstaining from vice, but in not desiring it. Self-denial is not a virtue." He illustrates this idea most

vividly in the character of Caesar, a man who, because he does
not even desire vice, has no need of goodness and can be
utterly selfish and selfless at the same time. For him, "ought"
and "is" are identical. For him, as for John Tanner, "moral
passion is the only real passion." They reject beliefs in the
necessary conflict of ought and is, conscience and passion, for
such beliefs only lock the self into conflict instead of granting
it a way out. Their ideal of unified being, although opposed by
the prevailing ideals of their society, retain a subsisting actuality, which is why they liked to call themselves realists rather
than idealists, truth seekers or even scientists rather than
imaginative writers.

Just as society should not and need not impede the will by
means of false ideals that the individual introjects, so it should
not and need not impede the will by means of circumstantial
frustrations. Like good puritans, they believe that character is
all and circumstance nothing. This seems to be contradicted
by Shaw's socialistic emphasis on the importance of circumstance in determining behavior, but it isn't really.

Shaw's socialism consists essentially of two principles.
First, there are no absolute scoundrels, only a few impractic-
able people; immoral behavior therefore can almost always be
traced to circumstances, not character; so if we simply change
the circumstances we shall dispel all wickedness (the few im-
practicable people having been painlessly killed). Second, circumstances hinder man from his true business, which is to
stand naked before his Maker; laws are stronger than indi-
viduals and so must be changed first, but they must be
changed in order to leave the self untrammeled.

Lawrence is much more sketchy and impatient on the subject of economics but his is generally the Shavian view. "It is
time we made haste to settle the bread question," he writes
impudently, "which is after all only the ABC of social economics, and proceeded to devote our attention to more profound questions," for "the proper study of mankind is man's
relation to the deity." In short, both confront money values
only in the hope of dispelling them. When Shakespeare wants

to show us a true alternative to the Shylockian confusion of

life values and money values, he shows us, in the Bassanio-
Portia relationship, the two combined without conflict, but
Shaw and Lawrence absolutely oppose a compromise, hoping
to bring all men to God by burning out their attachment to
money.

Shaw and Lawrence are nothing if not earnest, Shaw's lev-
ity notwithstanding, and the last thing they intend to assert is
a merely personal superiority over other men. The whole
rationale for their extreme Protestant individualism is that
their truth should become universal, catholic. Tawney writes:
"The moral self-sufficiency of the Puritan nerved his will, but
it corroded his sense of social solidarity." This applies to Shaw
and Lawrence, but I must add that they were trying as writers
to create an ideal, complete society—though, to be sure, a
society governed by "geniuses" and "great souls" like themselves, with the lower orders obeying a proper leader.

Self-divided, they were driven to seek unity not only in
mind but also in history. If they couldn't overcome their
painful sense of exclusion by adapting themselves to the
world, they would adapt the world to themselves. They
turned to history again and again to discover, if they could, a
unity compatible with their own deep purpose. Shakespeare
could tolerate heterogeneity in the world around him; Shaw
and Lawrence could not. Nor could they tolerate Shakespeare's toleration. They had to make him either a prophetic
writer like themselves or a coward. Lawrence gives us the
prophetic Shakespeare: "He was working to disintegrate the
old social conception—in Hamlet by suggesting conflicting
duties toward it; in Lear by resolving it back into its con-
stituent element, paternity; in Henry IV and V by making
Prince Henry real and a man when with Falstaff and unreal
when a king. Because the artist works inevitably toward a
more perfect social conception—of fraternity, as opposed to
paternity, and now of complete fraternity upon this earth."
Shaw gives us the cowardly Shakespeare: "I read Dickens and
Shakespear without shame or stint; but their pregnant observations and demonstrations of life are not coordinated into
any philosophy or religion.... They are concerned with the

diversities of the world instead of with its unities.... They
have no constructive ideas; they regard those who have them
as dangerous fanatics: in all their fictions there is no leading
thought or inspiration for which any man could conceivably
risk spoiling his hat in a shower, much less his life."

This overriding need to maintain control over all experience, lest their own disunity be mirrored before them, I think
explains their more peculiar prejudices. The professions "are
conspiracies against the laity" because they ask a man to surrender his judgment to someone else, though of course Shaw
is right to suggest that our trust in the professions often has
an irrational component. Evolution cannot be true because "I
don't feel it" (Lawrence), because "it banishes Mind from the
universe" (Shaw, via Samuel Butler). In their extreme moments (*Fantasia of the Unconscious, Back to Methuselah*),
they even say, with a literalness more insistent than that of
Yeats or Blake, that the individual mind created life and death.
Machines, which threaten our sense of human importance,
exasperated Lawrence and were somehow reduced to toys by
Shaw. Shaw was dead wrong in predicting that, with contraception easily available, the world would soon suffer from
underpopulation. He evidently believed that most people
shared his aversion to parenthood. And the point, though
unimportant in itself, helps to suggest why prophetic writers
are often poor prophets: they believe that their own experience is representative.

I have been tracing the complex and energetic response of
these extraordinary writers to the challenge of an inferred
unconscious conflict, following their arguments to the limits,
as they themselves do, for they are utterly sincere and unin-
hibited in expression. But it would be wrong to explain everything in their work in such terms, because unconscious
conflict, though basic and far-reaching, is never the sum of
any human mentality.

An area of Lawrence's work that seems free of it, for example, is his writing about birds, beasts, and flowers. Auden
observes perceptively that Lawrence "loves creatures neither

as numinous symbols nor as aesthetic objects but as neighbors." That sense of contiguity (relaxed, friendly, loving, sane), which is usually missing when he deals with people, emerges here. Then, too, Lawrence stuggles with his conflict as often as he rationalizes it. When his ideas are put forward in his fiction, they are subjected by the very nature of fiction to some question, but it must be admitted that the questioning is sometimes dismissed rather than allowed to stand as a form of genuine self-confrontation. His criticism is richly descriptive of the modes of feeling that his emotional-imaginative self had difficulty embracing, and he brilliantly analyzes overreaching and unconscious prejudices in other writers. One can easily quote Lawrence against himself, *e.g.*, "The greatest blasphemy of all against the phallic reality is this lifting it to a higher plane." The question is, How often does he show this?

Shaw more often compromises with rather than contradicts his heroic ambition. The very structure of comedy compromises with the prophetic-heroic mode in an important way by distributing the responsibility for change between the individual and society, whereas Lawrence's fiction, for all its terminal tentativeness, tends to place full responsibility on the individual. The element of self-criticism in Shavian drama, though it hardly attains a Shakespearean complementariness, is nevertheless more honored than its counterpart in Lawrence. Shaw's visionaries, one may say, are graciously part fools; Lawrence's, grudgingly so. Sometimes indeed Shaw's knack for seeing the other side is so developed that the enemy seems to bear off the palm. The Devil in Act III of *Man and Superman* almost too easily damages the magnificent polemic constructed by Don Juan when he says, "Beware of the pursuit of the Superhuman. It leads to an indiscriminate contempt for the Human." And the line is spoken just after Don Juan has left the stage, as if Shaw does not want his hero to answer it. In Shaw's nondramatic writings, moreover, the radical positions are likely to receive just enough qualification to let them fit within a generously conceived liberal tradition: "Let us privilege heresy to the last bearable degree since all saints are self-selected. All we can hope for at any point is as much toleration as possible. The degree of toleration at any point depends on the strain society is under to maintain its cohesion."

The habitual recourse to fiction itself, I have implied, is a way to compromise with moral absolutism. What is so interesting in Lawrence and Shaw is how strong their inclinations are both to dramatize and to assert. No sooner do they assert than they feel compelled to test their ideas as dramatic actions, for "art speech is the only truth" (Lawrence) and "fine art is the only teacher" (Shaw). Yet no sooner do they dramatize than they feel compelled to escape the hypothetical nature of art and return to discourse. Both have securely in mind the sophisticated knowledge that no verbal construction can be more than a symbolic approximation of the truth (the knowledge that structuralists have seized upon as if they discovered it), yet in their earnestness they seem to resent the limitations of language and to attempt to take the citadel of truth by storm.

The consistent exuberance of their style points to a similar ambiguity. On the one hand this spirit surely reflects the great pleasure they very naturally took in practicing the skills of expression and representation in which they were so expert. On the other hand, there is something reckless and half-mad about their wit and buoyancy, as if they are wrestling with God and hardly care who kills who.

Shaw and Lawrence are intensely intellectual writers in that they see everything in the light of a fierce, dominating idea. Reading them, I sometimes have the sensation of confronting a trunkless, talking head. They are compulsive talkers even when, as they now and then admit, they have nothing to say. "I must preach even with nothing to say" is the poignant admission of one of Shaw's later spokesmen. "Allons, there is no road before us," cries Lawrence in a gay despair. Such a compulsion suggests that more than an imaginative impulse is at work. Shaw comments revealingly, "An author of my sort must keep in training like an athlete. How else could he wrestle with God as Jacob did with the angel." The implication is that writing is both a means and an end, that imaginative will and moral will are one and the same. That is why it is so difficult to separate the artistic and ideological aspects of their work. Our delight in the one inevitably involves us, beyond the consent of our judgment, in the other. Yet the Eden we are beckoned to is uninhabitable. It is held aloft by their own powerful will and their "glittering-eye" rhetoric, and it lives for us only insofar as our own will can respond.

I have focused on similarities between Shaw and Lawrence. There are, of course, obvious differences, which ought to be at least briefly noted. Lawrence is a less consistent and controlled writer, partly I think because of his more determined, abrasive effort to break down, not merely transcend, his inner division. Shaw is always lucid, genial, elegant. Lawrence is sometimes turgid, irascible, messy. But Lawrence has far more range in the lyrical mode. Shaw's sprightly and invigorating art, though its language is usually concrete and individually expressive, is stylistically modeled on oratory and discursive argument. Its rhetorical virtues are clarity, ease, force, vivacity, and wit. Lawrence also has force, vivacity, and at times an angry wit, and what he lacks in clarity and ease, he more than compensates for in his greater talent for symbolic suggestiveness and for rendering the immediacy of experience. One might say that Shavian rhetoric more often resembles the style of jokes and Lawrencian rhetoric the style of dreams, remembering that both jokes and dreams are forms of mental action that reach into the depths. A simple way of stating the contrast is to say that both writers remind us equally of Blake; that Shaw sometimes, but Lawrence seldom, reminds us of Swift; that Lawrence sometimes, but Shaw seldom, reminds us of Wordsworth.

It is doubtful, but unprovable, that either man would have been a better writer had he been a more balanced one. In any case they are too valuable as they are for us really to wish them different. Although they wrote with the urgency of reformers, Shaw and Lawrence both realized that their urgency had more importance aesthetically than politically,

that their conclusions were too fundamental and too colored
by temperament to be practically implemented. Their goal
was not action in the strict sense but expression or revelation.
And, toward this end, the truth of feeling was what mattered.
Because they brought so much mental energy to that kind of
self-knowing which is a self-making, they earned the right,
more than most artists, to say, in Shaw's words, "Each man
who records his illusions is providing data for the genuinely
scientific psychology which the world still waits for."

THE SON AND THE FATHER:
RESPONSES TO CONFLICT IN
HEMINGWAY'S FICTION

ERNEST HEMINGWAY'S fiction has attracted psychological
critics for two reasons. One is its extraordinary concreteness.
The other is its overriding concern with psychomachy, or
inner battle. There will be little dispute on the first point but
the second may seem to need strong qualification. It doesn't.
Although Hemingway characteristically concentrates on the
outer, objective fact and event, these are almost always either
ways of talking about inner conflicts or ways of not talking
about inner conflicts. His hero's typical remark, "Let's not
think about it," invariably calls attention to what he is not to
think about.

But psychological critics should be wary of their opportunity in this case. The insights they are led to are sometimes
ones that Hemingway himself is not in full possession of and
hence has not presented with much verbal or dramatic energy. Freud's comment on the connection between the fear of
death and the intimate forms of loss which go back to the
small child's fear of castration is nowhere given more abundant literary documentation than in the pages of Hemingway,
but it is hard to say what sort of credit this is, since the artist
lacked the awareness to make the insight quite his own.

Hemingway is an unusually "sincere" writer. That is, he
always writes about what deeply engages his feelings; he returns persistently to the substance of his fears. But too often
the intended effects of his work are undermined by other,

presumably unintended, effects. He is often unconsciously insincere. He often lies, not to us but to himself, or so we infer from perceiving that what must have been tragic or satiric intentions often issue forth as sentimental and cynical effects. Needless to say, not all critics perceive alike. So it is a question, at some point, of what we are willing to take at face value.*

Critical commentary on Hemingway emphasizes the two most apparent themes in his work: courage in the face of death, mutilation, and loss, summed up in the memorable phrase "grace under pressure"; and fear in the face of war's traumas and the "nada" of modern life. Hemingway would have us believe that his hero is a courageous victim of war, society, fate, parents, and women. But what we often sense beneath the protestations and denials is a strong current of self-pity, the moral pleasure which his hero seems to get from his victimized state (implied, for example, by his contempt for those who do not share it). The fear of the Hemingway hero is also difficult to accept at face value. The stories, viewed synoptically, trace it to a war wound sustained at the beginning of manhood, but they also suggest that the hero's fear originates in childhood and concerns his psychosexual relationship with his mother and especially his father. The "traumatic neurosis" hypothesis, proposed by Philip Young and widely respected, does not explain very well the fact that sexual fears always accompany the wound or the fact that they do not subside after a time. (The psychoanalyst Henry Lowenfeld contrasts the repetition compulsion of the artist with the "genuine traumatic neurosis": the latter originates externally, remains a solitary experience rather than being reexperienced, and usually subsides after a time.) If the hero were

---

* In the thirties and forties some of the more penetrating critics, notably Edmund Wilson, W. M. Frohock, and the early Maxwell Geismar (see their essays in *Ernest Hemingway: The Man and His Work*), observed the discrepancies between intentions and effects in Hemingway's fiction. Psychological implications of these discrepancies have been explored in recent years by Philip Young, Richard Hovey, Richard Drinnon, and John Thompson. But that these discrepancies exist at all is by no means the commonplace it ought to be. Carlos Baker dismisses the idea, and many other critics ignore them, including two who take a more or less Jungian view, Earl Rovit and Joseph DeFalco.

an actual person, we might hypothesize that he is indirectly prevented by a sense of guilt from direct gratification through a belief in the moral superiority conferred by his suffering. This is obviously a risky hypothesis, aesthetically speaking, since it is urged not only from the text but also against it. Pursuing it leads to repeated questioning of the author's intentions. But we can hardly avoid it if we want to confront Hemingway's work frankly.

Consider the memorable final exchange in his best long fiction:

> "Oh, Jake," Brett said, "we could have had such a damned good time together. . . ."
> "Yes," I said, "Isn't it pretty to think so?"

It is stylish certainly, and we would like to accept it unreservedly. But there is too much smirking beneath Jake's stoicism, indicating not merely a superior sophistication, a more highly developed acceptance of fate, but also a sneaking satisfaction as of relief from importunities. The denial of self-pity is too obvious. Or consider the structure of the in some ways admirable fable *The Old Man and the Sea*. Determined to find his big fish which "must be somewhere," Santiago understandably seeks him in the depth, "beyond all people in the world." That is well and good, but then genuine romance declines into sentimentality. How can we grant Santiago the special sympathy he asks for when he says, "I went out too far" and "the sharks make everything wrong," since his big ambition requires the depths and entails the risk of sharks? Throughout Hemingway's work, the joy of bloodlust, what Homer calls "wrath sweeter than honey on the tongue," is not sufficiently admitted by his characters. Evidently for Hemingway war was as exciting as it was for General George Patton. (Charles Fenton in *The Apprenticeship of Ernest Hemingway* informs us that young Hemingway in 1917— quite unlike Nick Adams—was eager to go to war, that he was disappointed not to have met any German submarines on the trip across the Atlantic, and that he was proud of his wounds, which he described in detail, with diagrams, in letters home. Hemingway's positive interest in World War II is

well known.) He might, of course, have created *characters*
who are convincingly repelled by war, but he does not do so.
The horrors of war always sound like the horrors of something else in his work. He is more honest when he approximates the satisfying candor of Patton's "God forgive me, I
love it so much," as he does in Santiago's "Fish . . . I love you
and respect you very much. But I will kill you before this day
ends."

But there is also real imaginative energy in Hemingway.
Some of his tales *in toto* and parts of many others dispel any
temptation to refer to psycho-biography. And these tales illuminate two themes of broader interest which I have been
developing in the preceding pages: the son-father relationship, particularly as it attaches itself to the story of the Crucifixion; and the heroic tradition, particularly as it attempts to
absorb an increasing burden of guilt. I will look at Hemingway's major books as successive responses to inner conflict.
Even some of the slighter and weaker works will thus gain
seriousness as part of one inclusive, honorable effort, though
I do not want to undermine at any point the importance of
aesthetic evaluation.

In Our Time (1925) solidly establishes the son-father relationship and even sketches the types of response to conflict that
are found in the later work. The first two stories, "Indian
Camp" and "The Doctor and the Doctor's Wife," describe a
boy's admiration for his father and corresponding contempt
for his mother, with a few faint hints of potential complica-
tions. These become more prominent when Nick Adams
moves into the more active role of adolescence. In "The End
of Something" Nick rejects his girlfriend in favor of Bill and
fishing because "love isn't fun anymore." In "The Three Day
Blow" he enjoys Bill's companionship in a shelter against the
storm and admires a book for a rather odd reason: "That's a
real book. That's where his father is after him all the time."
The intervening war sketches bring up the subject of a military barricade called "the perfect obstacle." Hemingway may
have consciously intended this image to symbolize a severe

conscience (or something of the sort); in any case it does suggest this, as the tales begin to feature a wound in the spine, sexual rejection, and venereal disease. Some of them also become distinctly spiteful and self-pitying. In "Mr. and Mrs. Elliot" a pseudoliterary Harvard man can't even beget a baby. In "Out of Season" a young husband renounces a desired fishing trip because he does not want to be caught out of season—and because his wife is not interested. And in "My Old Man" a boy witnesses a loved father's death and then discovers that his father was dishonest, saying, "Seems like when they get started they don't leave a guy nothing."

When Hemingway does not require moral choices or stances of his heroes but focuses instead on a mood or a process, letting their fears remain shadowy, his art is surer. In this way "Cross Country Snow" improves on "Out of Season"; the pregnancy of Nick's wife palls the skiing pleasures of Nick and George, but, instead of choosing between his wife and his friend, Nick feels only the distant impingement of the responsible world of love on the innocent world of friendship. And in this way "Big Two-Hearted River: Part Two" improves on both; Nick, fishing with careful control in familiar waters, does not disguise his unconquered fears but puts them to the side—the troubling swamp downstream—to be faced another day.

The Sun Also Rises (1926) is Hemingway's most poised and exuberant novel. It is buoyed throughout by wit and charm as no later novel is: imagine the words of Count Mippipopolous—"This wine is too good for toast-drinking, my dear. You don't want to mix emotions up with a wine like that"—spoken, as they might well have been, by Colonel Cantwell! There seems so little spontaneity, so much brittleness, in the later Hemingway, as if too much energy has been drained off in personal conflict. Whereas the emotions of the later heroes are often merely reported, those of the earlier ones are dramatized.

Certainly *The Sun Also Rises* dramatizes nicely the perilous gaiety of a band of American and English expatriates in Paris who follow, unevenly, an unspoken pact according to

which particular matters, notably those pertaining to personal
ambition and sexual competition, are out of bounds. And the
most dangerous members of the group, the ones nearest to
being outsiders (Cohn, who doesn't understand the rules, and
Brett, who is compelled to break them), are carefully and
complexly conceived. Cohn strikes attitudes plausible enough
for Jake to be truly witty at his expense; like Jake himself he is
oppressed by female will; and his boxing skills earn Jake's
grudging but honest admiration. Brett is both feared and
loved: a symbolic castrator (she takes the bull's ear as a private trophy, puts it in a drawer, and forgets about it) but an
affectionate and charming friend, a demonic presence when
gripped by sexual compulsion (she pleads with Jake to pimp
for her and thus to disgrace himself in the eyes of Montoya)
but a forlorn spirit longing to be relieved of cruelty and lust.

The aesthetically problematic element in the novel centers
upon the wounded Jake. Can we take at face value the idea
that Jake's impotence is due to "that dirty war" and that he is
cheerful and manly *despite* his appalling circumstances?
Surely we also sense a hidden and contrary intention working
against this evident one in the idea that his impotence *contributes* to his cheerfulness by granting him freedom from
sexual rivalry and thus a moral pleasure comparable to the
sensual pleasure he gets from his "conflict-free" activities:
drinking, fishing, and watching bullfights. The admired victim seems to have more power and pleasure than the author
admits to; Jake Barnes takes his pleasure with considerable
gusto and manly savoir faire, although supposedly devastated
by injury, as if impotence is serving the unacknowledged
purpose of protecting some power in reserve. Don't we
sense that Cohn's inferiority to Jake is based not only on his
deficiency in stoicism but also on his proficiency in sexual
aggression? And looking beyond characterization itself, we
might say that what is problematic in Jake is paralleled by a
discrepancy between the tone and theme of the whole book, as
Philip Young observes in a passage from his first book on
Hemingway, which he saw fit to omit and even contradict in
his reconsideration. "There is a gaping cleavage," Young
176 writes, "between manner and message, between joy in life

and a pronouncement of life's futility.... the book now seems really the long *Fiesta* it was called in the English edition, and one's net impression today is of all the fun there is to be had in getting good and lost." Haven't a good many readers accordingly, after clucking over the lost generation, been charmed enough by the life-style to imitate it?

If we sense that Hemingway has "purified" Jake, we must perceive Cohn, Brett, and even Romero as scapegoats. Cohn, the outsider Jew, derives somewhat from stereotype; self-consciousness, querulousness, unworldliness, sobriety, and a taste for suffering might qualify as "Jewish" characteristics. But how shall we explain Cohn as boxer and lover, except on the assumption that he has also become (somewhat sneakily on his creator's part) the bearer of those aggressive and sexual wishes not wanted by Jake? If these were real people, we might say that Jake projects those wishes onto Cohn and then scorns Cohn for having them. It is noteworthy that Hemingway also invests Cohn with a characteristic reflecting a favorite idiosyncratic prejudice, an Ivy League background, though this is hardly part of a traditional scapegoat's role and hardly a Jewish characteristic; there was in fact only one Jew in the Princeton class of 1911, the year in which Cohn, aged thirty-four in about 1925, may be presumed to have graduated. Romero, the exemplar of the code, is apparently Cohn's polar opposite, but from our by now skeptical point of view he is not so different. He is admired because he fights and copulates according to the rules, whereas Cohn is degraded because he does not; but they are both embodiments of the same impulses unwanted by Jake. And Brett, though she shares in Jake's innocence insofar as she follows the rules, is also the tormenting outsider when she violates them.

But these characters are objectified and seem to have lives of their own; and so the important point to make about their scapegoat role is that they are not simply cast out as in primitive rituals and fairy tales. They haunt and nag the Hemingway hero. They are more disturbing forms of the troubling swamp downstream that Nick Adams, in the last story of *In Our Time*, knows he will someday have to wade into.

The oppressiveness of sexuality, of marriage, of women is a

dominating concern of the ambiguously titled volume of
stories, *Men Without Women* (1927). The hero's taste for
sexual action is sharper, and the "obstacle" is correspondingly
more imposing. The Major of "In Another Country," with
whom Hemingway identifies, is bereaved by the death of his
wife and advises the narrator not to marry ("A man . . .
should find things he cannot lose"). But, since the fact that
everyone must die is hardly a convincing reason for not mar-
rying, his apparent stoicism seems more like self-pity—*i.e.*,
the wife's death seems manipulated by the perverse will of the
author, perhaps a presumptuous way of saying that it is
an inadequate symbol in this context. In "Ten Indians"
Hemingway gives the lost-women idea a more directly Oedipal slant; Nick's father tonelessly informs the boy that he saw
the latter's Indian girlfriend making love to another boy. But
the story closes with an authentic little jab of irony: "In the
morning there was a big wind blowing and the waves were
running high up on the beach and he was awake a long time
before he remembered that his heart was broken." There are
also stories about a young husband who tries to persuade his
wife to have an abortion ("Hills Like White Elephants");
about a crazed peasant who nonchalantly hangs a lantern
from his wife's dead lips ("An Alpine Idyll"); about a marital
separation for which the author carefully refuses to suggest
any explanation ("A Canary for One"); about an innocent
traveler distracted from the simple pleasures of eating, friendship, and touring by a sexually aggressive waitress, a Fascist
hitchhiker, and a policeman ("Che Ti Dice La Patria"); and
about Nick again ("Now I Lay Me," the final story), who is
burdened by childhood memories, particularly a memory of
his mother burning his father's axes, knives, and arrowheads,
and who ("therefore" is *not* clearly implied) cannot take his
orderly's advice and cure insomnia by getting married.

The men quite without women in the volume are, significantly, martyrs. "The Killers" is the best story of this kind
because it does not justify or accuse but only concentrates on
the mood of expectant horror. The matador Maera in "Banal
Story" approximates a martyr in being unfairly ignored by

pompous journalists. And in "Today Is Friday" the Crucifixion itself (waiting in the wings, as it were) makes a first,
dramatic appearance. Hemingway's Christ, we notice, resembles a matador ("He looked pretty good in there" is a Roman
soldier's admiring and repeated comment). And his matador
resembles a crucified Christ. An intimate connection between
assertion and death (one is tempted to say between self-
assertion and self-destruction) is thus established. Two other
stories in this volume ("The Undefeated" and "Fifty Grand")
present this connection with a slight variation. In the first, the
aging matador, once he is seriously wounded, makes a supremely daring final thrust; in the other, the boxer who has
bet against himself, once he is fouled and tortured with pain,
is roused to the brilliant action of first averting the referee's
call of foul and then drawing the same call against himself.
Since I am judging Hemingway throughout by a very high
standard, I take an opportunity to adjust the perspective by
observing that the theme of the double double-cross is handled in this story with considerably more inwardness than it is
on scores of television dramas.

Frederic Henry in *A Farewell to Arms* (1929) both fights
and loves, but he deserts from the fight, having been
wounded first and then forced to retreat, and he pays for his
love with bereavement. Again it is difficult to accept the story
on the artist's terms. War can be hell, of course, and love can
cause anguish, but this war does not seem unpleasant
(Hemingway's writing is most vivacious in the scenes describing the mechanics of war and the bantering of warrior-
comrades), and this love affair seems undone more by the
author's will than by any tragic inevitability in character and
situation or by any absurd indifference in the universe. Who
are "they" who never let you get away with anything, who
must kill or break those who bring courage and innocence into
the world? The often quoted parable of the ants on the burning log destroyed by Henry himself gives the answer: it is the
god in the novelistic machine, the artist, who stacks the cards
against his characters.

On the hypothesis that Henry and Catherine must be pun-

ished for their "innocent" sexual pleasure, several puzzling
aspects of their romance become subversively meaningful.
Illness of a more or less sexual nature is their matchmaker.
Their relationship begins in a hospital where Henry is recovering from a leg wound and where he is soon to suffer from
jaundice, which is like a "kick in the scrotum." Later, just
after Catherine tells him that the birth may be dangerous
because of her narrow hips, he thinks of the gonorrhea he
once had and of his friend's syphilis; the forthcoming catas-
trophe is again linked to syphilis a few pages later: "The first
time they [sic!] caught you off base they killed you.... Or
gave you syphilis like Rinaldi." Finally, Catherine dies
agonizingly in an unwanted childbirth, leaving one wondering why there has been no mention of contraception and why
there has been mention of a Cesarean (she knew beforehand
there was risk) only when it is too late. In short, I suggest that
mutilation and disease are felt by Hemingway, though not
consciously perceived, as a punishment for erotic assertion.
There is, further, a hint in the novel that the Hemingway
hero, whose father (like Hemingway's) is usually a physician,
thinks of the punishment as coming from the father. Henry
says, "Doctors did things to you and then it wasn't your own
body any more." (Strikingly parallel, in *To Have and Have
Not*, is Harry Morgan's explanation of what happened to his
arm: "'I didn't like the look of it so I cut it off.' 'You and
who else cut it off?' 'Me and a doctor cut if off.'")

Even this much punishment seems not to be enough.
Henry must be absolved of having in any way invited the
romance. He is quite passive in the early stages of the relationship, having no desire to fall in love and only telling
Catherine he loves her when she orders him to. Actually,
Rinaldi courts Catherine and turns her over to Henry, whereupon she draws Henry into a relationship against his will!
Then Catherine, who has been aggressive enough so far, becomes wholly subservient: "There isn't any me. I'm you." It
is rather hard on poor Catherine to be made to do not only so
much of his dirty work but also to call our attention to his
180 bravery. She asks, "Won't they arrest you if they catch you

out of uniform?" And he replies, "They'll probably shoot
me. . . . Let's not think about it." One hardly fails to sense
here the pleasure the author seems to take in his hero's par-
lous state.

A Farewell to Arms is Hemingway's first fiction to directly
associate the hero with Christ:

[PRIEST:]	It is in defeat that we become Christian. . . . I don't mean technically Christian. I mean like Our Lord. . . .
[HENRY:]	I don't [believe in victory any more]. But I don't believe in defeat. Though it may be better.
[PRIEST:]	What do you believe?
[HENRY:]	In sleep.

Like the First Soldier of "Today Is Friday," Henry is attracted
to the image of the Crucifixion, though like the second and
third soldiers he is also a little repelled. Sleep certainly
suggests a retreat from heroic martyrdom but it is perhaps not
as much a retreat as it sounds, since for the Hemingway hero
the dragon to be slain is often the horror of insomnia.

The paradox of the title *Winner Take Nothing* (1933) requires explaining, for the statement does not correspond to
our usual experience of things. An explanation is provided, in
neat and consciously symbolic form, by the opening story
"After the Storm." This is a dreamlike fable of a driver who,
killing a man in self-defense, discovers a sunken vessel containing booty and a naked woman with floating hair, but who
(a) hasn't a strong enough tool to break the porthole window
("I couldn't get into her") and reach the woman, dead anyway, and (b) loses the booty he is entitled to as first discoverer
because some Greeks get to it before he does ("Even the birds
got more out of her than I did"). What the book title does not
imply clearly enough is that there is satisfaction in losing
when winning would cause too much guilt.

Other stories in the volume make it clear that even the
severest forms of loss—castration and death—are not altogether unwished for. In "God Rest You Merry, Gentlemen," Hemingway identifies with a sixteen-year-old boy,
who on Christmas Day asks to be castrated because he cannot

rid himself of his impure desires and who castrates himself
when the surgeon refuses. A certain amount of betraying
self-pity and spite is conveyed through the Jewish surgeon
who, although technically refusing the request, is the knife-
wielding punisher of Christian folklore, for he is a former
abortionist who ridicules both his less clever non-Jewish col-
league for taking seriously the coincidence of Christmas Day
and the boy himself. Another story, "A Day's Wait," shows
in an interesting way (*i.e.*, its insight, ironically rendered, is
Hemingway's own) that death itself may take on a positive
meaning. The boy-hero's unrealistic expectation of death for-
tifies him against the emotional weakness that overtakes him
when he learns the truth.

A certain desperation seems to creep into this volume, forcing the imagery to extremes. The war stories, "A Way You'll
Never Be" and "A Natural History of the Dead," are attempts
by Hemingway to convey radical shock, though the tales are
somewhat undermined by an all too evident contempt for
those less affected. It is significant that the theme of repulsive
homosexuality, merely touched on in each earlier book, appears in several stories here: "A Sea Change," "Mother of a
Queen," "The Light of the World." And it is significant that
the hero's father, who has been lying low since *In Our Time*,
should be elaborately and directly discussed in the final story
of the volume, "Fathers and Sons."

Before we look at this story, however, I must mention the
father's curious appearance in that curious story "The Light of
the World," in which Hemingway seems to have become
self-aware enough to criticize his own sentimentality but only
in order finally to yield to it again. Nick admires one whore
who punctures another whore's sentimental idealization of a
boxer whose "own father shot and killed him," but this only
seems to clear the way for the first whore to idealize the boxer
and for Nick and us to do so through his admiration of her.
The much admired "Snows of Kilimanjaro" is similar. The
writer-hero makes a stumbling effort to criticize his spiteful-
ness toward women, but ends up blaming his wife and justifying himself all the more.

"Fathers and Sons" lacks the economy and poise found in the best of Hemingway, but it is worth quoting from at length so that we may appreciate the nature of the artistic problem that the older, more experienced writer, committed to making his art out of the quarrel with self, had to face. Our purpose here is not wholly destructive because we will be clearing the way for "The Short Happy Life of Francis Macomber," written soon afterward, which shows us a very satisfactory solution.

A writer and now a father himself, Nick thinks of his own late father (who shot and killed himself as Hemingway's own father had done in 1928), pities him for his sentimentality, is grateful for his instruction in hunting and shooting, but repudiates his "unsound" instruction in sex:

> His father had summed up the whole matter by stating that masturbation produced blindness, insanity and death, while a man who went with prostitutes would contract hideous venereal diseases and that the thing to do was to keep your hands off people. On the other hand his father had the finest eyes he had ever seen and Nick loved him very much and for a long time. . . . If he wrote it he could get rid of it. He had gotten rid of many things by writing them. But it was still too early for that.
>
> . . . .
>
> Now . . . Nick was all through thinking about his father. . . . The towns he lived in were not the towns his father knew. After he was fifteen he had shared nothing with him. Nick loved his father but hated the smell of him and once when he had to wear a suit of his father's underwear that had gotten too small for his father, it made him feel sick and he took it off and put it under two stones in the creek and said he had lost it. [After being whipped for lying] he had sat inside the woodshed with his door open, his shotgun loaded and cocked, looking across at his father sitting on the screen porch reading the paper, and thought, "I can blow him to hell. I can kill him." Finally he felt his anger go out of him and felt a little sick about it being the gun that his father had given him.

This is not an impressive effort, dramatically or analytically. It staggers between deference and arrogance, pity and contempt, love and hate. Hemingway does not even seem to recognize as striking this sequence: Nick feeling sick at the   183

smell of his father's underwear, having to wear it but then
taking it off and hiding it, saying he lost it and being whipped
for lying, sitting with a gun and thinking he could kill his
father, feeling sick at the thought that his father had given
him the gun. Two phrases are poignant but not quite inten-
tionally so. "If he wrote it he could get rid of it": the statement moves us because the earnest hope will prove such an
illusion. "After he was fifteen he had shared nothing with
him": this one moves us, though Hemingway doesn't seem to
be controlling the effect, because it is profoundly untrue on
any but a literal level. How satisfyingly poignant by comparison are Santiago's words: " 'Fish,' he said softly, aloud, 'I'll
stay with you until I am dead.' "

"Macomber" handles with wonderful economy and in
purely dramatic terms the ongoing Hemingway needs: a
hero who admires a man, scorns a woman, achieves a heroic
action, and atones for it just before and/or just after (in this
case both, for Macomber pays with shame before the victorious moment when he has conquered his fears and pays with
his life afterward). The guide is an idealized figure, and the
wife is a bitch, but both seem fully objectified. Both have a
wit, a style, a spring of their own. We believe in Margot,
whose stylish cruelty is frustrated when she is barred from
the higher communion of male alliance and who then shoots
her spiritually escaped husband; and we believe in Wilson,
who has made sex and hunting into sciences, who gets what
he wants without internal complication and as far as external
reality permits. And so one thinks of the story no longer in its
relation to the man Hemingway but in its relation to other
stories. One is not stretching very far to see the martyr-hero
Macomber as the Son who, having said, "Woman, what have
I to do with thee," is accepted by the Father and exalted in
death.

To Have and Have Not (1937) is casual in construction but
otherwise intense to the point of crudity. Harry Morgan, the
most aggressive and potent of Hemingway's heroes, hurls
himself against the world. But the coarse strategy betrays
itself. The more lawless Harry becomes, the more he must be

shown as the "innocent" victim of economic circumstances, trying simply to feed his wife and kids ("What choice have I got. They don't give you any choice now") and the more he must be punished with mutilation, isolation, and death. Harry himself understands the loss of his arm as a symbolic castration: "The hell with my arm. You lose an arm you lose an arm. There's worse things than lose an arm. You've got two arms and you've got two of something else. And a man's still a man with one arm or with one of those. . . . I got those other two still." But Harry's anxiety about his *cojones* persists throughout the book. His sexual heroics do not conceal his fears, nor do his losses diminish his heroics. Even his death does not, for it is followed by a long picture of Harry's forlorn wife eulogizing his extraordinary *cojones*.

The representation of contemptible outsiders in this novel is facile and diffuse. There is the busybody lawyer and the Chinese who hires Harry's boat; both are described as "poisonous" though neither seems nearly as poisonous as Harry himself, who gratuitously insults the one and kills the other. There is the complaining Negro companion of the first adventure, who is not as badly wounded as the uncomplaining Harry. There are the pompous, misguided government officials who confiscate his boat, the excitable Latins who take his arm and later his life, the rummies who can't outface pain as Harry can. We are shown a variety of rich, idle tourists on yachts and in bars—Harvard men, male and female homosexuals, masturbators, bitches, pseudoadventurers who never risk themselves sexually or socially. And there is, conspicuously, the pseudowriter Richard Gordon, responsive merely to the winds of fashion, guilty of "dirty" love with his wife, impotent in one of his contemptible adulterous adventures, and utterly unaware of Marie Morgan's real satisfaction with Harry, although she is able to sense and pity Gordon's real distress. In fitful moments Hemingway sympathizes with a few of these (the rummies, Richard Gordon, the Cuban boy at the wheel of the boat in Harry's last adventure), but the sympathy is in no way integrated with the antipathy. The novel contains a certain energy of invention—it is not underimagined like *Across the River*—but the invention is crude.

To Have and Have Not is a "depression" novel in a psychological as well as historical sense. The Hemingway hero seems unable either to subdue his lust for enormous power or to avoid the penalty that guilt extracts from him, and the book is finally only hollow heroics culminating in an empty martyrdom.

Harry Morgan's dying utterance, "One man alone ain't got . . . no bloody . . . chance," is said by some to mark a turning point in Hemingway's career from a personal to a social ideal of human action. And indeed *For Whom the Bell Tolls* (1940) does attempt to present a hero who finds fulfillment by acting in concert with his fellows. But Robert Jordan's social awareness is actually slight. Hemingway is still fundamentally concerned with individual courage and fear, and in his last two novels the pretense of a social theme is quietly dropped.

Jordan is a much gentler protagonist than Harry Morgan. *Cojones* in this novel are significantly associated with restraint—contained semen equals bravery; spent semen equals death—rather than with daring as in *To Have and Have Not*. Hemingway is trying to solve the problem another way. Instead of a hero whose aggressiveness and eroticism are frustrated by circumstances, he creates a hero who purifies killing and copulating by raising them to the level of sacraments.

Jordan does not like to kill but permits himself to do so for a holy cause. The Spanish background helped Hemingway to justify killing as ritual. The Spaniards' lust to kill (compared to "a mare's lust in heat") is called their "extra sacrament," antedating Christianity. They can kill without being corrupted, as an act of faith. The theme of battle as religious purification is explicit throughout the book and is supported by the liturgical though flaccid language:

> You did the thing there was to do and knew that you were right. You learned the dry-mouthed fear-purged purging ecstasy of battle and fought that summer and that fall for all the poor in the world, against all tyranny, for all the things that you believed, and for the new world that you had been educated into. . . . It was

in those days, he thought, you had a deep and sound and selfless pride. . . . You were in a sort of state of grace. . . . Those were the days they all shared when everything looked lost and each man retained now, better than any citation or decoration, the knowledge of just how he would act when everything looked lost.

This is from the man who ten years earlier had written, "I was embarrassed by the words 'sacred' and 'glorious' and by the expression 'in vain'"!

The social perspective has gradually become individual; the hero's quest is basically for self-purification through commitment to a cause; what cause hardly matters: "Who else kept that first chastity of mind about their work that young doctors, young priests, and young soldiers usually started with? The priests certainly kept it, or got out. I suppose the Nazis keep it [*sic!*] and the Communists who had severe enough self-discipline." It has been remarked that Hemingway seems more sympathetic toward the Fascists (*e.g.*, Lieutenant Berrendo, whom Jordan shoots) than to the Loyalists, whose cruelty toward the Fascists is vividly described in a long digression. Colonel Cantwell, in Hemingway's next published novel, makes the point explicitly; speaking of his admiration for Rommel, he says, "I love my enemies, sometimes more than my friends." Like General Patton, the later Hemingway hero is most exhilarated by the presence of a worthy male opponent. But unlike Patton, or unlike the popularized image of Patton, he must pay for his excitement. The figure of romance must become the tragic figure, who degenerates into the pathetic figure since his death is a foregone conclusion. Or, since this transformation seems to answer a temperamental more than an artistic need, one feels entitled to say that the pleasure of martyrdom must take precedence over the pleasure of simple conquest.

Eros as well as Ares is transfigured in this novel. The rapturous scenes between Jordan and Maria are highly idealized, sacramentalized. The wise Mother Pilar bestows Maria on Jordan, and he addresses her in exalted, operatic accents: "I love thee as I love liberty, dignity and the rights of all men to work and not be hungry." Furthermore, Maria is exotic enough to blank out any resemblance to a familiar woman and so pliant to his will that she can be loved as an extension of himself rather than as a separate person. And, if that isn't enough to keep guilt at bay, their three-day hymn to the Eternal Now is carefully framed between doom and death: Jordan knows from the beginning that he is destined to die. It is difficult to credit Hemingway's picture of death as the ironic antagonist, striking just at the moment when his victim has learned so much so fast, for in both love and war it is the certainty of death that purifies and exalts the hero.

In none of the other later novels does the shadow of a father's suicide so darken the hero's consciousness. Nor has it here any formal relation to the narrative. It is rather a subject of private debate and indicates the private nature of the battle Jordan is fighting. The motives that emerge most clearly from his reflections on his father are: (a) denial of the father's spiritual paternity and concomitant identification with the grandfather; (b) displacement of competitiveness with the father to competitiveness with the grandfather; and (c) re-emergence of the suppressed identification with the father in the form of fear on Jordan's part that he will die in the same way. Two passages will illustrate:

> He realized that if there was any such thing as ever meeting [his progenitors, in an afterlife], both he and his grandfather would be acutely embarrassed by the presence of his father. Any one has a right to do it, he thought. But it isn't a good thing to do. I understand it, but I do not approve of it. *Lache* was the word. But you *do* understand it? Sure, I understand it, but. Yes, but. You have to be awfully preoccupied with yourself to do a thing like that. Aw hell, I wish grandfather were here. Maybe he sent me what little I have through that other one that misused the gun. . . .
> . . . I don't want to be a soldier . . . I just want to win this war.

And when Jordan is dying, hoping death will hold off long enough for him to shoot at the approaching enemy and protect his friends, he reflects: "You've had as good a life as grandfather's though not as long . . . I'll bet grandfather never had to do a show like this one . . . I don't want to do that business my father did, though I will if I must."

188 We get a picture of Jordan in these passages different from

the one we get in the narrative itself. There he is the competent, resourceful, and restrained leader of men; here he is a frightened and lonely man, struggling with his fears and his past. One is led to conclude that the struggle for an altruistic philosophy, implied by the title and dutifully expressed from time to time, screens a more personal struggle, that the confession, "I just want to win this war," following an intimate mediation, is a personal rather than a political declaration.

The posthumously published *Islands in the Stream*, written during the forties, is in most ways a lamentable book. Its three long Caribbean episodes—a visit by the hero's three sons, ending in the deaths of two of them; scenes of barroom and bedroom conversation, featuring news of the death of the third; and an adventurous chase of a Nazi submarine, climaxing in the hero's own dying—are saturated in vanity and self-pity. Thomas Hudson (the narrator always uses this full proper name but an abbreviated name for every other character) is invariably the idealized chieftain of his little society; others, though they may be temporarily front and center, are his myrmidons. He is apparently incapable of fellow feeling except for his cat and for sufficiently victimized human beings. Nevertheless, there is something moving in his desperate effort to survive, to cope with the rending loss of his first wife and of his youth in Paris. (An earlier title for the manuscript was "The Garden of Eden.") If we can empathize with a life felt as a choice between blank despair and marginal survival, we may be able to see as not quite silly the plight of a man who has lost his last Seconal tablet, who wonders whether he should order whiskey to get him through shaving, who believes that his sons' visit will undermine the vital prop of his work routine. One feels that the characteristic Hemingway attitudes, which lost all their dignity in *Across the River and into the Trees*, are here at the end of a thin rope: "There is no way for you to get what you need and you will never have what you want again. But there are various palliative measures you should take," and "There are no terms to be made with sorrow . . . if it is cured by anything less than death, the chances are that it was not true sorrow." So he locks himself into his pain. It is telling that the deaths of the sons, which supposedly crush Thomas Hudson's spirit, do not seem nearly so difficult for him to bear as daily life. It is as if the real opposition of fate is welcomed because it takes him out of himself, whereas the "remorse" of obscure origins which he is otherwise left with is too intimate to be dealt with. The style reflects an end-of-the-tether sincerity. Hemingway frequently uses, for example, a sentence with two nonparallel subordinate clauses introduced by the same conjunction: "The water of the Stream was usually a dark blue when you looked out at it when there was no wind." This is sloppy writing by usual standards, but it is as if the writer is suggesting that a perfect parallelism would seem too neat and self-possessed, that it would not register so well the rhythms of a broken spirit.

Finally, however, Thomas Hudson's suffering seems inauthentic. I cannot think of any writer who sets up and then refuses so many opportunities for insight as does Hemingway. His pages beg for psychological probing but crumble under it. He refuses to see what is near enough to be seen. The hero too clearly gets pleasure from his suffering for us to regard him merely as a victim. He also seems a fool.

In *Across the River and into the Trees* (1950), Hemingway cannot find a dramatic form to contain both the hero's aspiration to an ideal self-image and his rejection of the self's unwanted components, and the book sags badly as Hemingway shuffles about on his verbal feet. Cantwell's self-justifications and self-accusations pour forth in disorderly excess. He wants very much to think well of himself as nice, virile though aging, capable of wrath and agony, and needing confidence; but he comes across as cranky, boozy, childish, frightened, self-congratulatory, and almost limitlessly spiteful and self-pitying.

"Jerk," carefully defined as "a man who has never worked at his trade truly, and is presumptuous in some annoying way," is his favorite epithet, and he pastes it freely on just about any outsider who impinges on his consciousness: on his
orderly who, as far as one can see, is obedient, efficient, and

uncomplaining; on D'Annunzio, "the great, lovely writer . . . and jerk"; on a pockmarked writer at a nearby table, who is never introduced and whose greatest fault, aside from his complexion, is the likelihood that he will outlive Cantwell; on homosexuals, who hate him instinctively; on the military brass, who try not to get killed or wounded—and so forth, *ad nauseam*.

Dramatization of the insiders is equally petty and flaccid. Cantwell belongs to a secret order of retired soldiers so inane that it would have embarrassed Tom Sawyer. Its leader is a man of fifty known as the Cherry Buster, and its supreme secret, according to Cantwell, is that "love is love and fun is fun." The hero's return to the site of his first wounding is marked by a ritual defecation and the words, "a poor effort . . . but my own." And his "last and true and only love," the incomparable Renata, is merely an idolatrous auditor for his puerile lucubrations and a companion at his interminable meals, for the pleasures of the table are really the *summum bonum*. Love, on second thought, is too complicated (even Renata is accused of wishing to dominate), and the secret of his order is privately rephrased, "I'd rather not love any one, I'd rather have fun." Fun seems to mean not thinking about anything more complicated than the ordering and consuming of food, with perhaps a little duck hunting thrown in to work up an appetite.

In short, Hemingway-Cantwell does not make a serious effort to confront real courage and fear, much less to bring them into any meaningful relation; they are unwittingly parodied or shunted off into febrile digressions. There is only a bare glimmer of something more serious in Cantwell's passing thought about replacing a philosophy of soldiering. "You going to run as a Christian?" he muses. "You might give it an honest try." The simple renunciation of aggression did not ignite Hemingway's imagination, but his imagination did respond to the inverted aggression of the Crucifixion. Renata worships Cantwell's wounded hand because she "dreamed it was the hand of Our Lord," as Catherine and Lieutenant Henry compare Christ's wounds to Henry's blistered hands. 191

The likeness to Christ appears once more—and somewhat more feelingly—in his last tale and will best bear comment in connection with it.

The Old Man and the Sea (1952) in some ways marks a recovery of Hemingway's art. Woozy introspection is tightened into pithy and dramatically motivated meditations. Facile spite is mostly pruned away, for the contemptible outsiders in this story are mainly the swift and silent sharks, which are appropriate to the fable. The plot is the presentation of a physical process which Hemingway usually does well. And the theme is his truest later one, the hero's conjoined love and hate for an image of supreme male power.

There is some regrettable spite, however, in the final scene of the insensitive tourists who mistake the skeleton of the marlin for that of a shark. And there is some self-pity, not only in the idea of going out too far, but also in the role of the boy. Santiago wants, for the sake of greater glory, to make the adventure alone, so it is only sentimental for him to pity himself, as he often does, because the boy is not present to help. In fact, the boy's only function in the story is to augment a facile pathos. "How much did you suffer?" he asks. "Plenty," the old man says.

But what is most interesting in this tale is Hemingway's deepened intuition of the inseparability of protagonist and antagonist. I do not wish to make too much of this, because the intuition is not pursued with great dramatic or verbal energy, but in several places it achieves the intensity of poetry:

> Fish, he said softly, aloud, I'll stay with you until I am dead.
> . . . .
> Fish, he said, I love you and respect you very much. But I will kill you before this day ends.
> . . . .
> You are killing me, fish, the old man thought. But you have a right to. Never have I seen a greater, or more beautiful, or a calmer and more noble thing than you, brother. Come on and kill me. I do not care who kills who.
> . . . .
> Is he bringing me in or am I bringing him in?
> . . . .

If you love him, it is not a sin to kill him. Or is it more?

In the context of the Hemingway oeuvre these are moving
utterances. Never before have the profoundly opposite feelings of the hero been so carefully balanced. Never before has
Hemingway come so close to realizing that it is much the
same whether the son destroys the father-in-the-son or the
father-in-the-son destroys the son; whether killing a loved
object is victory or defeat, purity or sin. When Santiago in-
tones inspirationally, "A man can be destroyed but not defeated," he lapses from this realization. And indeed the fable
would be more perfect if Hemingway had caused the fisherman and fish to destroy one another rather than saving his
fisherman and introducing sharks to "make everything
wrong"; in this respect, I think, Hemingway failed to realize
the full implication of his story.

Santiago's martyrdom is clearly meant to resemble
Christ's. When the fisherman sees the sharks for the first
time, he makes "a noise such as a man might make, involun-
tarily, feeling the nail go through his hands and into the
wood"; and at the story's end he shoulders the mast and
stumbles as he climbs the hill to his shack. In Santiago's case
and perhaps in Christ's, depending on how we interpret the
Gospels, the real drama is the relation between the individual
and his chosen god, the technical crucifiers (sharks or Ro-
mans) being a side issue. In Christ's case, aggression is represented only invertedly, as a consent to martyrdom, whereas
in Santiago's case direct and inverted aggression are bound together. But the psychological meaning of both cases is similar.

The Crucifixion, psychologically considered, is one of the
supreme representations in Western mythology of the
conflict residual in us from childhood between the son's need
to retain his father's love and his need to overthrow and
replace him. I follow Freud (*Moses and Monotheism*) in this
provocative view of it, hoping that the foregoing discussion
enforces its cogency: "The way in which [Christianity] came
to terms with the ancient ambivalency in the father-son relationship is noteworthy. Its main doctrine, to be sure, was
reconciliation with God the Father, the expiation of the crime
committed against him; but the other side of the relationship
manifested itself in the Son, who had taken the guilt on his

shoulders, becoming God himself beside the Father and in truth in place of the Father." To this I would add only that Hemingway's interest in the Crucifixion is characteristically tentative, perhaps because his imagination was so oriented to action that the image of what seemed mere endurance a little repelled him, perhaps because he was so much the literary "realist" that the transcendental aspects held him off, perhaps even because he was humble enough to be shy of identifying the nonredemptive martyrdoms of his heroes with a martyrdom that so emphasized the redemption of mankind. But there is no doubt of his growing interest in the image itself.

Hemingway's work testifies genuinely to the charms and perils of romantic heroism. I began by claiming a discrepancy between his emotional honesty and intellectual dishonesty, and it might be well to conclude by conceding that this discrepancy is by no means absolute, that sustained emotional honesty in fiction—sticking with the material that moves one the most—is already a form of self-testing. The tales are marred by a form of cowardice, but they show at least a form of the courage that this writer so highly prized.

AFTERWORD

UNQUESTIONABLY the martyr-hero of Hemingway's fiction is a product of cultural as well as individual determinants. A few years ago the critic John Thompson, surveying Hemingway's career (*New York Review of Books*, April 28, 1966), doubted if it was possible for a modern writer to imagine heroes who don't prefer to damage themselves, and he added elegiacally, "It is a long way from Homer to Hemingway, a long way down perhaps, but the course is run." To dispute this view of the modern heroic tradition would be difficult. Demotic incarnations of the heroic are of course perennial, but the few examples from sophisticated literature that come to mind, notably certain novels by Saul Bellow and Norman Mailer, are too willed and theoretic to give one the sense of a living, contemporary genre.

One can seldom easily say why a certain artistic form declines. Thompson accounts for it by an increasing sense of guilt or an increasing internalization of judgment during the modern centuries. Surely this is pertinent, as I have been suggesting all along. Other reasons may be given also. One is that the rather sudden increases in population and advances in technology have diminished the opportunities for individual heroic action. Another is that the possibilities of the genre itself may have come to seem used up. Or perhaps the encroachments of psychological science, including its noisy popularizations, have turned writers away from characterization rooted in social and psychological detail toward more abstract or foreshortened modes of human representation.

But, even if writers are less interested in it as a psychological problem, one cannot say that the sense of guilt itself (or, let us say, that irrational anxiety itself, because the sense of guilt is really unconscious) has receded. Perhaps the most one can say is that any contemporary writer who seems indisputably an artist, *e.g.*, Samuel Beckett, is still detached enough from his images of reduced man to "play" with them and convey a sense of the imagination's freedom.

If art must give pleasure, as I believe it must, then many contemporary fictions have merely artistic pretensions. Sometimes their authors are too worried or earnest, and they sacrifice art to the claims of social criticism. To worry whether art is promoting a socially beneficial or harmful idea is especially common when and where there is much diffuse anxiety about the cohesion of a society. But there is no clear evidence that imaginative art corrupts its readers or, alas, that it civilizes them. It certainly stirs our thoughts and feelings, but the only clear result of that is to make us want to read more.

There are opposite ways of failing to give pleasure. One particularly common in contemporary American fiction is to make art out of mere display and parody. And I suspect that both of these attitudes—the too frivolous as well as the too earnest, the prancing as well as the preaching—are partly motivated by an underlying guilt associated with imaginative license.

If so, the problem is deep and will not be resolved by trotting out as a practical injunction the old Horatian formula of to please and to instruct. If heeded, this would probably lead to either entertainment or propaganda or to a combination of the two. But fine art is more than a utilitarian craft. Although its creation entails craftsmanlike calculations of effect, the artist writes because he must as well as because he can. Every work of fine art conveys in this respect a dual impression: that the artist above all has wanted to make something clear to himself whatever others may think and

that he has taken special pains to make his conception clear to others—perhaps, as Collingwood ingeniously suggests, because he cannot know for certain whether he has attained his objective of a truthful consciousness and craves the reassurance provided by the approval of others.

Exhortation is, in any case, decidedly uncalled for. If the temper of the time makes it virtually impossible to create the strongest kind of literary art because the imagination of writers is bound by a compulsion to either submit to anxiety or defy it, then that fact must be accepted. We don't, it is true, have much faith in our collective future, but we also do not know whether it is really too late to create heroic art. And as long as we are not sure, we may be helped by realizing that the pleasure inherent in art needs no justification—not because art is above considerations of moral value but on the contrary because moral value is, like pleasure, inherent in it. To render experience truthfully is not easy, especially if one is obliged to give pleasure. Doing so is not altogether in one's power. Therefore we are disposed to honor both the artist and the gods when a work of art succeeds.

INDEX

Index

Expressionism: in relation to formalism, ix, xvii, 8–11, 15–16, 42–44, 46; Langer's theory of, xxv, 13–14. *See also* Affective literary theory; Feeling; Self-expression

Faulkner, William, xxix, 47
Feeling: and language, ix, 20–28; and thought, xv, xxi, 40. *See also* Affective literary theory; Expressionism; Imagination
Fiedler, Leslie, xxiv
Fish, Stanley, 6n, 47–48, 99
Fitzgerald, F. Scott, 20, 35–36
Fleming, Ian, 47
Formalism: and expressionism, ix, xvii, 8–11, 15–16, 42–44, 46; and characterization, 12–13
Freud, Sigmund, xii, xxv, xxviii–xxix, 3, 25–28, 30n, 31–32, 34, 41, 42, 50, 55–56, 58, 64–65, 68, 71, 80–81, 171, 193. *See also* Psychoanalysis
Freudian revisionists, ix, xxiv–xxvi, 25–28. *See also* Structuralism
Frohock, W. M., 172n
Frost, Robert, 17
Frye, Northrop, xxvi, 12, 14–15, 18, 19, 46

Gardner, Helen, 106
Geismar, Maxwell, 172n
Genre: as a critical problem, 14
Glover, Edward, xxii
Goddard, Harold, 70
Goethe, Johann Wolfgang, 62, 63–64, 67
Gombrich, E. H., xxv–xxvi, 11–12, 14, 22n, 34, 43

Hamlet, xiv–xv, xxvii–xxviii, 6, 8, 15, 20, 36, 93–94, 114; Freud-Jones view of, 55–59; antipsychological criticism of, 55–59; neurosis as term in discussing, 56, 80, 88–89; and the heroic tradition, 57–58, 87; sources of, 59, 69, 76; in philosophical perspective, 61–62, 78–81; in political perspective, 62, 76–78; Ghost as problem in, 62–63; likeness of hero and villain in, 65–68, 75–76; Oedipal aspects of, 68–73; attitudes toward revenge in, 73–75, 77; Christian and non-Christian views of, 79–80, 85–87; as tragedy, 81–89 *passim. See also* Shakespeare, William

Hardy, Thomas, xvii–xviii
Hartman, Geoffrey, xxv–xxvi, 8, 27
Hawthorne, Nathaniel, xixn, 6, 37, 152
Hayford, Harrison, xxviii, 123, 136, 137, 141
Hegel, G. F. W., xxvi, 19, 33–34, 39
Hemingway, Ernest, xxviii, xxix, 7–8, 44, 81; concreteness of, 171; psychological themes in, 171–72; sincerity of, 171–72, 194; and unconscious insincerity, 171–74; sentimentality of, 173; Crucifixion imagery in, 174, 179, 181, 191–94; and the heroic tradition, 174, 194; works by, discussed in chronological order, 174–94
Heroic tradition. *See* Modern heroic tradition
Hirsch, E. D., xiii
Holland, Norman, xxii, 5–6
Homer, 92, 195
Hovey, Richard, 7–8, 172n
Hughes, Merritt, 99
Hume, David, 30, 40
Huxley, Aldous, 30, 130

Ibsen, Henrik, 122
Imagination: errors of, ix, xvi, xx–xxi, 3–4, 41–42, 48–50; theory of, ix, 29–33, 40–42, 48, 49; and intellect, xiii, xxi, 30–31, 47, 49–50
Intention: and the unconscious, xiii–xv, xvi, xix, 38, 39, 45; Romantic meaning of, 39; legitimate meaning of, for interpretation, 45–46. *See also* Imagination
Intentional Fallacy, 10–11, 18, 37n. *See also* New Critics
Irony: as critical problem, 17, 44, 105, 134–41

James, Henry, 18, 63
Johnson, Dr. Samuel, 20–21, 105
Jones, Ernest, xxvii, 55–57, 58, 63, 64, 71
Joyce, James, 120
Jung, C. G., xxii

Kant, Immanuel, 30, 33
Keats, John, 98
Kermode, Frank, 75, 142
Knight, G. Wilson, 46–51
Kris, Ernst, xxiii

Lacan, Jacques, 26–27
Langer, Susanne, xxv, 10, 13–14, 18